Cut to the Monkey

Cut to the Monkey

A Hollywood Editor's Behind-the-Scenes Secrets to Making Hit Comedies

Roger Nygard

APPLAUSE
THEATRE & CINEMA BOOKS

Guilford, Connecticut

APPLAUSE
THEATRE & CINEMA BOOKS

An imprint of Globe Pequot, the trade division of
The Rowman & Littlefield Publishing Group, Inc.
4501 Forbes Blvd., Ste. 200
Lanham, MD 20706
www.rowman.com

Distributed by NATIONAL BOOK NETWORK

www.CuttotheMonkey.com

Image on page 15: Photo by Suzie Hanover / Photo courtesy of Judd Apatow.

British Library Cataloguing in Publication Information available

Library of Congress Cataloging-in-Publication Data

Names: Nygard, Roger, 1962– author.
Title: Cut to the monkey : a Hollywood editor's behind-the-scenes secrets
   to making hit comedies / Roger Nygard.
Description: Lanham : Applause Theatre & Cinema Books, [2021] | Includes
   bibliographical references and index. | Summary: "Cut to the Monkey is
   the story of a filmmaker's journey through Hollywood-revealing the
   secrets behind how the experts find the funny in any project-by a
   filmmaker who has worked with some of the funniest people in the
   business and has edited Emmy-nominated episodes from series such as Curb
   Your Enthusiasm, Veep, and Who Is America?"— Provided by publisher.
Identifiers: LCCN 2021020943 (print) | LCCN 2021020944 (ebook) | ISBN
   9781493061235 (paperback) | ISBN 9781493061242 (epub)
Subjects: LCSH: Motion pictures—Editing.
Classification: LCC TR889 .N94 2021 (print) | LCC TR889 (ebook) | DDC
   778.5/35—dc23
LC record available at https://lccn.loc.gov/2021020943
LC ebook record available at https://lccn.loc.gov/2021020944

∞™ The paper used in this publication meets the minimum requirements of
American National Standard for Information Sciences—Permanence of Paper for
Printed Library Materials, ANSI/NISO Z39.48-1992

Halfway through every edit I always wished I'd written down some rules I could just give to editors on the first day, and then go, "What do you think of these?" Because about a month in, I always say, "Of course, you can't reveal the joke twice." And whoever's reading this, this is being written by one of the great comedy editors of all time.

—Sacha Baron Cohen

Contents

Foreword

W hen Roger Nygard asked me to write a foreword to his book, I was filled with that most human of emotions: annoyance. Then I read the book and realized Roger has interviewed a baker's dozen of comedy greats, all of whom will pick up the book to see how they came across. And then I was filled with my other driving emotion: fear. So, it is with fear and annoyance that I write this foreword.

I have had the pleasure of staring at the back of Roger's head for more than a decade while we worked on *The League, Curb Your Enthusiasm, Crashing*, and *Dave*. It's a good back of a head. Symmetrical, well groomed. But I guess we should also talk about what's inside that head: a treasure trove of knowledge about editing.

If you want to know how some of your favorite shows have gotten made, don't waste your time on the set. Hang around an editor in a small room with the windows blacked out. Yes, it looks like you've been kidnapped, but oddly everyone is there of their own volition. Because that's where the show *really* gets written. Filming is all about gathering as many choices as you can. But in the edit bay, you finally have to make *the* choice.

If you want to know why funny shows are funny; if you want to know why one take is *objectively* funnier than another; if you want to know what an editor thinks when the producers behind him are clearly watching ESPN or YouTube on their phones, then this is the book for you.

I've learned a lot from reading Roger's book. For starters, I learned it gets way better after the foreword—which I am well aware is too long. But Roger will edit it. He's the best.

—Jeff Schaffer

Introduction

A common thread in my work is a desire to find the humor in humanity. We are naturally ridiculous. Life is absurd. That is a message the universe is sending out every day. People who laugh live longer. And better. If you want to cheat death, laugh. A study in Norway found that cancer patients who laughed were 35 percent more likely to be alive several years later. Their explanation: "Humor works like a shock absorber in a car, you appreciate a good shock absorber when you go over big bumps in life."[1]

Why I edit or write or direct my projects the way I do is rooted in who I am. For me, creativity started as far back as I can remember. I partially credit my desire for creative expression to my mother. When I came home from kindergarten, my mother always praised my artwork. "Wow! You are so creative!" No matter what I drew or painted, it was celebrated. Was my art anything special? Hardly. But because my mother praised my creativity, she reinforced a way of thinking in my nascent brain. Today, when somebody critiques a project or dislikes my interior-design choice or writes a bad review, my first thought is not, "I'm not good enough." Instead, I think, "They don't get it." And sometimes simultaneously, "They're idiots." I *know* I'm creative. That's what my mother told me as my cerebral foundation was developing and hardening. And because that neural pathway is set, apparently for life, I have self-confidence in my creative endeavors. This (delusional?) belief is one reason I continue. I persist despite myriad failures.

Children want to please their parents. That is one reason it's important to pay attention, praise their efforts, and support their

Early artwork by Roger Nygard: acrylic on paper.

desire to express themselves. Children have amazing, natural creativity. But around age seven, the maturing prefrontal cortex starts to put the brakes on some behaviors. Kids begin to realize they could be doing things wrong. A brushstroke here or an idea expressed there could generate criticism. The creative impulse begins to shut down, a defensive maneuver against negative attention.

I grew up on the outskirts of Minneapolis, where the nearest house was a quarter mile away. The bus picked me up at the end of a long road. Initially, we didn't even have a house number, simply Rural Route Box 443F, Long Lake, Minnesota. On the bus to third grade at Orono Elementary School, I became enchanted with a girl with a sunny smile and spirited, mischievous laughter. One day I asked if we could play after school. When she agreed, after the bus dropped me off, I raced back on my bicycle, two and a half miles to her house. We played all afternoon, full tilt, enjoying squirt gun fights, screaming and laughing. I can't remember ever existing in such a blissful expression of pure happiness as that afternoon. Eventually her older sisters came home and put a stop to our fun, like older folks feel they must. As I biked home, my heart was so full of joy, I expressed myself, singing loudly to the trees, "I'm happy! I'm happy!" My overflowing emotions found expression in song. Suddenly I heard other voices. Two kids ran out of the woods, mocking my singing, laughing at me. I looked back, mortified. How did I not consider that other kids might hear me?! I turned forward and pedaled as fast as I could, away from ridicule, a painful lesson on the road to suppressing the expression of emotions.

Two of many competing motivations have been set in my framework since childhood: the desire to be boldly creative and the fear of criticism due to expressing myself. Luckily the need to create mostly wins out. There is no such thing as a bad lyric, a wrong brushstroke, or a weak line of poetry if it comes from the expression of a feeling. Any work of art is brilliant if it expresses an emotional perspective.

One reality I faced was that singing and music weren't my strengths. All I had to do was pick up a trumpet when I was nine years old to realize I was not good at making it sound pleasant. But when I started messing around with photography, it was different. My father was an amateur photo buff. He had a Yashica 120mm, twin-lens reflex camera. To him, cameras were for family photos: wearing our Sunday best for church, or birthday parties, holiday gatherings, waterskiing, or proudly displaying a northern pike caught off the dock.

One winter day, when I was seven years old, my father drove to work in Minneapolis, where he was a grain buyer for General Mills, purchasing trainloads of oats or corn or wheat at the Minneapolis Grain Exchange. He left the Yashica sitting out, with several unused shots. If something was unattended in the morning, I would have it disassembled before lunch. I constantly got in trouble for antics like blowing out the pilot light inside the furnace—I was curious to see how the mechanism would restart itself. Pro tip: It won't. When

Photo by Roger Nygard, Sr.

Nygard children dressed up for church: Jay, Steven, Theresa, and Roger.

Minnesota temperatures plummet in December, you notice quickly when the heat stops. I confessed. My action was not malicious. I was curious.

The day I borrowed my father's camera, I walked down to the lake, where waves had crashed and sprayed upward, coating shoreline vegetation. I thought the ice formations looked pretty, like something out of a painting on a holiday card. I photographed these frozen stalactites, clicking and winding, until the roll ended.

I put the camera back and forgot about it. A few weeks later, when a package arrived from the photo finishers, I heard my father yell, "Who wasted all this film on ice?!" I was in trouble again. But my mother intervened. She thought the photos were creative. And

Early photography by Roger Nygard: Ice formations coating a winter shoreline.

because she did, so did I. She put the shots in the family album, a place of honor. I have been shooting film ever since. My mother produced a creative monster.

A few years ago, my brother discovered a box of old color slides. I was amazed at how my father had expressed himself artistically, photographing with moody lighting. My dad died when I was thirteen years old; I never thought to ask him about his own impulse for creative expression. While making my documentary *The Nature of Existence* (2010), I interviewed Irvin Kershner, director of *Star Wars: Episode V—The Empire Strikes Back* (1980). When I asked about his

Photo by Roger Nygard, Sr.

Genevieve Nygard, photographed with moody framing and lighting.

thoughts on life after death, he said, "The afterlife is what remains in the memory of the people you have known—in the work you have left behind." My father's photos are part of what he left, part of how I know who he was.

I remember discovering my love of movies, lying on the carpet in front of the television, watching films with my parents. My mom enjoyed such Alfred Hitchcock thrillers as *Lifeboat* (1944), *The Man Who Knew Too Much* (1956), and *The Birds* (1963). I remember whirling clouds of birds and lots of bloody fingers.

My dad enjoyed sci-fi and action. We watched *When Worlds Collide* (1951), *Journey to the Center of the Earth* (1959), and *Where Eagles Dare* (1968), a movie so suspenseful that decades later I can still feel how my feet were tingling during the climax. The pacing builds to an incredible sprint. Richard Burton was matchless. The double and triple crosses were intense. And with Clint Eastwood wielding dual machine guns, how could anybody top that?

James Bond came close. It didn't matter what I was doing, everything had to wait if there was a Bond film on television. I came to prefer the Roger Moore era, because I liked the emphasis on comedy. Many have criticized the comedic turn the Bond films took, but as an eleven-year-old, I ate it up with two spoons. And the stunts reached a spectacular zenith with *Live and Let Die* (1973). The speedboat chase has no peer, with boats skidding across lawns, past priceless reactions of distraught wedding guests. And to cap it off, they added the funny, southern Sheriff John W. Pepper (Clifton James), who narrowly dodges Bond's speedboat as it jumps over him. And then another boat jumps and crashes into Pepper's squad car.

Two Louisiana State Police troopers drive up to the aftermath, enjoying Pepper's failure: "Does that look like a boat stuck in the sheriff's car there, Eddy?"

Trooper Eddy responds, "Boy, where you been all your life? That there is one of them new car-boats."

Jerry Lewis was my favorite comedian (with diversions to Abbott and Costello, Laurel and Hardy, and The Little Rascals). I would pass up a trip to the zoo anytime it was Jerry Lewis versus a ladder. Later I

Author's collection.

Sheriff Pepper is not happy that a boat dropped into his car. From *Live and Let Die*.

discovered Lewis's predecessors, Buster Keaton, Charlie Chaplin, and Harold Lloyd, but Jerry was my first.

I was also hooked on Minneapolis station KSTP's locally produced creature-feature show, *Horror, Incorporated*. There was no host, only a corpse struggling to get out of a coffin and a disembodied voice introducing movies. I would set my alarm for midnight on Saturday to wake and watch *Tarantula* (1955), *The Incredible Shrinking Man* (1957), or *The Monolith Monsters* (1957), and of course the myriad wolfmen, Frankensteins, and Draculas. Afterward it was a long, scary, shadow-filled walk back to my bedroom.

On Saturday afternoons, my dad used to take me and my siblings to the matinee at the Wayzata Theater, where they would replay recent hits. Our imaginations were expanded by *In Search of the Castaways* (1962), *Fantastic Voyage* (1966), and *The Computer Wore Tennis Shoes* (1969). One afternoon, I went to the Heights Theater in Columbia Heights with my cousin Tony to see a G-rated matinee of *Snoopy Come Home* (1972). Afterward, we decided to wait for the next film. As a ten-year-old, I was amazed by *Big Jake* (1971). It was an R-rated film (now downgraded to PG-13 by modern standards) starring John Wayne. For the first time, I became aware of all the groovy stuff I was missing in the edited-for-television frauds. For months afterward, I recounted every detail of the plot to my friends. *Big Jake* is a Western with motorcycle stunts, machete fights, and shoot-outs, and the topper was Jake McCandle's dog, named "Dog." If somebody got the drop on Jake, he yelled "Dog!" and his black collie would rip the guy apart. That was pretty cool to a ten-year-old.

My motion picture endeavors started when I got my hands on my father's 8mm Bell & Howell camera—a 1962 model similar to the one used by Abraham Zapruder when he filmed the Kennedy assassination; 8mm film was actually 16mm film, which you had to turn over in the camera halfway through, fumbling about in complete darkness. When you mailed the roll to a distant processing plant, they would split it down the middle and send it back for projection as one, spliced, 8mm roll.

My very first filmic project was to imitate the pixilation process of the Gumby cartoons I watched on *Clancy and Carmen*, a pair of Minneapolis children's morning shows. I animated the adventures of my Charlie Brown and Linus dolls as they tightrope walked and fell off the couch. Most of my shorts were pursuit films, a chase being the easiest story to tell without sound. Early silent films emphasized chases, such as Edwin S. Porter's *The Great Train Robbery* (1903), with a posse chasing bandits, Charlie Chaplain's *The Adventurer* (1917), which opens with a jailbird on the run, or anything featuring the Keystone Cops (1912–1917).

In high school my ambitions grew more sophisticated (though not much) as I upgraded to Super-8mm film, which added a magnetic sound stripe. I conscripted siblings and friends as actors and built stories around props and locations. My favorite prop was a semi-realistic dummy I built to prank-shock passersby. My friends and I thought it was hilarious when a suicidal dummy leaped off an overpass, causing panic. One school-bus driver didn't appreciate our effort to provide him with a funny story to tell his wife. He swore nonstop as he drove off with our dummy. This was a brief setback.

Around that time, I discovered a British television series that changed my life. I was captivated. It was like nothing else available on American television. I watched episodes of *Monty Python's Flying Circus* (1969–1974) religiously. "Sam Peckinpah's 'Salad Days'" was the funniest sketch I had ever seen, a parody of director Sam Peckinpah's penchant for violent, bloody movies such as *Major Dundee* (1965), *The Wild Bunch* (1969), and *Straw Dogs* (1971). It was over the top, sick, insane, and wonderful. It opened my eyes to possibilities I never knew existed in comedy.

In college I switched to the newest technology, a twenty-five-pound, portable three-quarter-inch videotape recorder, and

A still frame from Nygard's early 8mm film.

non-linear, tape-to-tape editing. There was no such thing as "undo." You had to get it right the first time. As film gave way to video, and video to digital, I never stopped playing with images—and comedic ideas. One of my early shorts, *Poltercube*, was a spoof of *Poltergeist* (1982). My film was about an unsuspecting chap who solves a Rubik's cube while plagued by apparitions. Parody is a great place to get comedic filmmaking experience because the formula is simple: Copy an existing movie trope and exaggerate it wildly. Voila, you have comedy.

After collecting a Bachelor of Arts in speech-communication (now called communication studies) from the University of Minnesota, I drove to Los Angeles in 1985 to apply to graduate school and look for a job. I didn't know anybody in the film business. I found a tiny apartment and spent a week stuffing envelopes, sending out nearly one thousand résumés. This led to nine replies, three job interviews, and two job offers—a one-out-of-one-hundred response rate. I accepted my first job at a production-management

Roger Nygard editing with three-quarter-inch videotape in 1983.

company called Rollins, Joffe, Morra and Brezner. They managed such comedians as Woody Allen, David Letterman, Robin Williams, Martin Short, and Billy Crystal. I got the call because my résumé arrived the day their production assistant put in his notice to quit. Timing is everything. Larry Brezner interviewed me and thought I would work harder than the prior candidate, Jerry Lewis's son. I had been in competition for the job with the son of the comedian I had most idolized growing up!

Rollins, Joffe, Morra and Brezner produced movies such as *Arthur* (1981), *Good Morning, Vietnam* (1987), and *Throw Momma from the Train* (1987). I started at the bottom as a messenger, but I endeavored to be the best they ever had. It's hard to shine when you are delivering packages and fetching lunches. But the job led to unusual opportunities. On one errand, as I walked through the production office of the Billy Crystal HBO special *Don't Get Me Started* (1986), I heard somebody yell, "Hey you, go stand next to Billy!" They were looking for a photo double, so Billy Crystal could play multiple characters as he acted with himself. It tuned out Billy and I were about the same height and build. I was a closer match than the other candidates. They put the character makeup and wardrobe on me, and I became Billy Crystal from behind. To this day, when I run into Billy Crystal, he still affectionately calls me "Back of My Head."

Occasionally the assistants would call in sick or go on vacation, and I was the nearest warm body who could sit in and handle the phones. Buddy Morra noticed how organized I was and promoted me. I hadn't intended to get Buddy's assistant fired; I only had tried to do my best. Part of my expanded duties as assistant to a talent manager was to scout for new comedy talent. I loved hanging out in The Comedy Store sound booth with my pal Scott Nimerfro, who worked there for six months. Scott was the first of my University of Minnesota college buddies to follow me out to Los Angeles. Our favorite comic was Sam Kinison, who caused vein-popping, stroke-inducing reactions from the audience. Scott would tell me what time Kinison was scheduled so I could rush over, and we would laugh ourselves sick.

Another comic I saw at The Comedy Store was Steve Oedekerk. He was primarily a prop comic falling somewhere between The Amazing Jonathan and Joel Hodgson. One of his best bits was "The Psychic Severed Head," which he would pull out of a bag and lay on the table. Then the head would tell him what items he was holding or what he was thinking. It was absurd, sick, and hilarious.

Steve Oedekerk was always writing scripts, and in 1989 he wrote *Pissed* (later titled *High Strung*) with Robert Kuhn. Steve had failed to raise the money to shoot the film himself. I asked Steve to let me try, with the understanding I would direct and Steve would star. I don't think Steve expected me to pull it off, but hey, you never know.

While working for Buddy Morra, I made a short film called *Warped* (1990), which lead to my first paid directing job, on an episode of a syndicated television series called *Monsters* (1988–1990). My episode was called "Small Blessing" and starred Julie Brown, Kevin Nealon, and David Spade. Because of my comedy connections, I brought in comedians to read for parts.

At the same time, I sent Steve Oedekerk's screenplay to everybody but got no bites. And then the composer I had hired for *Warped* read it and loved it. He knew a first-time movie investor from New York by way of Ukraine named Sergei Zholobetsky. Incredibly, Sergei's checks didn't bounce, and we started preproduction in the fall of 1990 on a $350,000 budget. (Years later, in 1996, Sergei Zholobetsky was indicted for defrauding New York hospitals out of millions of dollars for wheelchairs that he never delivered. He fled the United States and was finally apprehended in 2005 while hiding out in a Greek monastery. When you are a filmmaker, you are thrilled to have a budget. You don't think to ask your investor if the money is legitimate.[2])

We renamed the film *High Strung* (1991) because newspapers wouldn't print *Pissed* or *Pissed Off*. The word piss is one of the taboo four-letter words you aren't supposed to say on television or something terrible will happen.

Steve Oedekerk played the lead he had written for himself. Also cast were Thomas F. Wilson, Fred Willard, an unbilled Jim Carrey, Jani Lane (the lead singer from the rock band Warrant), and my future *Trekkies* (1997) partner Denise Crosby.

In the spring of 1991, I hired an editor named Tom Siiter. Apparently, *High Strung* was the first feature-length film to experiment with a digital, PC-based, non-linear editing-system called an EMC2, running on a 286 processor. The media was stored on optical discs and had a resolution so grainy that squinting actually helped. We had a total of 650 megabytes of footage—an absurdly low amount of data for an entire feature film by today's standards.

We had only six weeks to cut the film, which meant long days and nights. After five weeks of looking over Tom Siiter's shoulder,

Roger Nygard, Jim Carrey, and Steve Oedekerk on the set of *High Strung* in 1991.

I absorbed the process. By week six I was editing the film myself when Tom collapsed or went home to sleep. I was anxious to step in because it felt like the time it took me to explain what I wanted for the next edit could have been used to try three new variations if I was pushing the buttons. After that experience, I learned to use a D/ Vision Pro, Avid Media Composer, and Final Cut Pro. I found very little significant difference between editing technologies; they are all manipulators of image and sound. Does it matter whether you drive to Santa Monica in a Toyota or a Lexus? Does it matter whether you use Word or Pages to create a document? The end result is you arrive at the same place. The most important variable is the driver, or the writer, or the creativity of the person at the keyboard. Although I admit I quickly get used to the add-on comforts of a luxury model.

As a testament to how important early connections are, many of my most trusted friends are people I met the first year I arrived in

Los Angeles. At the same time that I landed my messenger job, Luis Estrada was a clerk in the Paramount Pictures Motion Picture Production Finance Department. We had a lot in common and became fast friends. We worked to try to raise funds to get our projects off the ground. We came close, but never succeeded. While I was pursuing my directing ambitions, Luis Estrada rose through the ranks to vice president of Creative Services at TNT–Latin America.

After finishing *High Strung*, I discovered how difficult it is to make a second film. After two years of pitching scripts, I was broke, with $30,000 in credit-card debt. I was about ten minutes from getting a job as a taxi driver or a telemarketer. Then Luis Estrada called and asked if by chance I wanted to try writing and editing promos for TNT–Latin America. I cannot point to one job or project as being the most pivotal in my career, but this would be near the top. My philosophy is to say yes to opportunity, because each is a rare gift. Actors are often told, "Work generates work." You do not know where a project will lead, but doing nothing leads nowhere. Saying yes to doing promos for Luis led to a two-year stint writing and editing advertisements for classic movie marathons. This experience was crucial to improving my editing skills because it taught me how to remove every inessential frame in a fifteen-second message. It was like practicing shooting layups all day long. I brought this editorial proficiency into my next project, my second film, an action picture called *Back to Back: American Yakuza 2* (1996), and then to *Trekkies* (1997), a documentary about *Star Trek* fans. Both are fast-paced, with experiments in radical editing, as I was creating my own style of "coloring outside the lines." Imagine if teachers let children color however they are inspired and praised them for expressing themselves. Who knows what they might come up with? In *Back to Back*, I played with jump cuts, wipes, and repeated action to maximize footage in gunplay and car-chase set-pieces. To shape *Trekkies*, I established what would become a signature documentary technique, asking the same thematic questions

Courtesy of Trekkies Productions.

Star Trek fans Brian Dellis and Paul Rudeen in 1996.

Courtesy of Trekkies Productions.

Denise Crosby with director of photography Harris Done, interviewing *Star Trek* fans in 1996.

of all interviewees and assembling like with like, building sound-bite trains, where everybody answers the same question. I arranged their fractured responses so interviewees finished each other's sentences.

As I continued to navigate the independent film world. I took my fourth film, *Suckers* (2001, a dramatic comedy about car salesmen) to film festivals. Comedian and filmmaker Mike Binder attended a screening of *Suckers* at the U.S. Comedy Arts Festival in Aspen. He noticed my editing style and offered me a job editing his HBO pilot *The Mind of the Married Man* (2001–2002), which became my first professional editing job, where I was editing somebody else's project. That also led to working with a post-production supervisor named Gregg Glickman. Several years later, in 2007, I was in India shooting footage for my fourth documentary, *The Nature of Existence*—a humorous exploration of existentialism, if you can imagine that. Gregg Glickman, now a vice president supervising post-production at HBO, called to ask if I was available to meet with *Seinfeld* (1989–1998) co-creator Larry David, who was currently shooting season six of his HBO series, *Curb Your Enthusiasm* (2000–TBD). They were about to lose an editor and needed a replacement. I replied that due to being in Mumbai, India, I was *not* available, but I would be back in three weeks if the position was still open.

Courtesy of Blink, Inc.

Roger Nygard interviews a Hindu sadhu and disciple for *The Nature of Existence* in 2007.

When I returned to Los Angeles, I was surprised to find the position was still available. According to post-production producer Megan Murphy, I was the twenty-fifth editor they considered; twenty-four top editors had been found lacking in some way or had declined because of the daunting amount of footage and the level of difficulty due to the use of minimal story outlines. Megan Murphy and editor Steven Rasch met with seven editors and then narrowed the field down to three, including me. I went to one of the trailers on the *Curb Your Enthusiasm* set and chitchatted with the producers until Larry showed up between scenes.

Larry asked, "Why do you want to work on this show?"

I said, "I want to learn from you, Larry. I want to see how you do what you do from the inside."

He chuckled, pretended he wasn't flattered, and said, "You can't learn anything from me."

I also said that working with him would be like an opportunity to work with one of the greats like Ernie Kovacs or Phil Silvers—except those guys are dead. He loved the comparison to Phil Silvers, who it turned out was a comedy hero of his.

Our conversation up to that point took only four minutes. In the fifth minute, Larry turned to his producers and said, "He seems fine." He thanked me and walked out.

They offered me the job. Maybe they were tired after so many interviews. But I learned that the editing of improvised dialogue is one of the most difficult challenges, and that makes the choice of editor crucial to a show's success. Plus, Larry had called Mike Binder to do the usual, thorough background check consisting of a version of, "Nygard's not a psycho, right?"

Larry said of his interview process, "For me it's enough to see that I have some kind of rapport. I'll walk into the room and say, 'hello.' And I'll get a vibe and I'll leave." His instinct meter is well tuned. Larry David makes his hiring, casting, writing, and editing decisions by instinct. Once during an episode called "Funkhauser's Crazy Sister" (season seven, episode one), there was a scene where Catherine O'Hara plays Marty Funkhauser's sister, and she seduces Jeff Green (Jeff Garlin). I finished cutting the scene and Larry said, "It's not funny. I don't know why, but it's not funny." He decided to do a rare reshoot. Everybody tried to analyze why the scene was not funny. Who would be blamed for this failure? Was it the editor's fault? What should be done differently? How elaborate of a rewrite would satisfy Larry? Finally, as the reshoot date neared, they asked Larry how drastic the changes to the scene would be and he said, "Get rid of her hat." They changed Catherine O'Hara's wardrobe. Her hat was killing the comedy. I cut together the hatless reshoot and it was brilliantly funny. My reputation was saved.

When I was in school, I had no specific intention of becoming an editor. I never had considered being a documentarian. I had simply wanted to make funny films. Somehow. My dad could make people laugh, and I had always wanted to be like him. I was not a joke teller or an extrovert like he was, but I channeled into short films my desire to make people laugh, and later into features and television shows. Post-production producer Megan Murphy's theory is that people come home after work and rely on folks like Larry David and Sacha Baron Cohen and Julia Louis-Dreyfus, and all the people behind the scenes, to provide moments of happiness, to make them feel a little bit better in their lives, so they can do it all over again the next day. If you get to be a part of the process of making people laugh, it's supremely rewarding. We watch movies and television shows to get a dose of emotion: suspense, fear, anger, tears, laughter. We gravitate toward entertainment that allows us to (safely) feel emotions we have a deficit of in our own lives. When you pay attention to films, you begin to notice an abundance of romance stories, superman themes, and revenge plots.

This book is about learning how to find the funny in any project. If you follow these guidelines, your end product is going to be 15 percent funnier on average than the next person's. (This figure is supported by no actual scientific data.) It's a challenging industry, there is intense competition, so you need to be at your best. A showrunner is going to observe your work and compare it with others. Which editor is easier to be in a room with for several weeks? Whose cuts are funnier? Who works faster? In this book I will offer the secrets from my essential bag of tricks. This is not a lofty meditation on editing theory, it is a practical guide on how to prosper as an editor in the film business. It's like an editor's cookbook. I have included wisdom from many of the funny people, showrunners, and editors I've worked with or learned from, adding their insights to this crucial question of how to cut to the monkey in any situation. "Monkey? What monkey?" Don't worry, all will be explained.

—Roger Nygard

CHAPTER ONE

Is This Funny?

Defining Comedy Is a Fool's Errand, but One Thing That's Definitely Funny Is the Antics of a Fool

When I was editing Mike Binder's Showtime documentary-series *The Comedy Store* (2020), comedian and former *The Tonight Show* host Jay Leno said he's always trying out jokes on everybody, always asking, "Is this funny?"

How do we know if something is as funny as it can be? Is there an instinct for comedy? Psychologists have studied humor and found that humans aren't the only species who laugh. Researchers have observed chimpanzees laughing with each other during social play.[1] Even rats have been observed vocalizing during positive, playful social situations.[2]

What is funny and what is not funny almost can be constructed mathematically. Two adept comedy mathematicians analyzing the same comedic question will arrive at a similar quotient. There may be personal differences in which punch line feels strongest. But typically, comedians generally agree on what's funny.

Is Comedy Innate?

Can anybody be taught to run as fast as Usain Bolt? Obviously Bolt started out with inherent natural abilities that he trained to improve until he was the fastest in the world. But no matter what someone's baseline is, you *can* teach them to run faster. That's why an Olympic runner has a coach. You can also get better at being funny, and at editing comedy. Some skills must be learned and practiced.

At the season seven wrap party for *Veep* (2012–2019), showrunner David Mandel said to the assembled crew, "Is it funny? Honestly, I'm a damaged human being and that's all I care about." Jeff Schaffer, showrunner of *The League* (2009–2015), said ten people could look at the same thing, but the comedy writer will figure out what's funny about it and make an audience feel, "Oh yeah, that happens to me."

I asked Larry David, "How do you know something is funny?" He said, "You have to have faith that if it's funny to you, it'll be funny to other people." Larry doesn't intellectualize comedy. He feels it. When I asked Larry about the casting of J. B. Smoove, who plays Leon Black on *Curb Your Enthusiasm*, Larry said when J. B. Smoove came in to read for the part, "He gave me that look. He had the part as soon as I was laughing, before he even opened his mouth and spoke." When Larry *feels* something, that's what works. Luckily for me, I also enjoy what Larry finds amusing, and he is one of the funny people I have been fortunate to learn from.

Larry David

Larry David didn't know comedy would be his thing when he was young. He didn't even begin to pursue comedy until he was twenty-seven, after all other avenues were closed. "I really wasn't suited to do anything. Nothing appealed to me," said Larry. "I had jobs that didn't require a college diploma. I don't have the patience to be a kindergarten teacher. I think I could have been a postman—in the field, not sorting. I was a paralegal. I was a cab driver. I was a private chauffeur. I would've been a limo driver, there's no question in my

Larry David and Roger Nygard at a *Curb Your Enthusiasm* wrap party in 2010.

mind, because that's all I could do." Perhaps that's another reason he's so convincing as John McEnroe's driver in the *Curb Your Enthusiasm* episode "The Freak Book" (season six, episode five). "But people always told me I was funny. And then one Saturday night I went to the Improv and watched the comedians and thought, 'Maybe I could do that.'" Larry approached owner Budd Friedman and asked to go on stage. Friedman peered at Larry over his famous monocle and said, "Who are you?"

Larry said, "I'm in the audience."

"Are you a comedian?"

"No, I've never done it."

Friedman waved that night's nutcase off. "No, you can't."

In hindsight, Larry was glad he'd been turned down, because he was completely unprepared. "If I had gone on that night, I probably never would have set foot onstage again."

After that momentous non-occasion, Larry slowly eased into comedy. What really affected him was a three-hour improv class taught by an actor named J. J. Barry. "There was something about improvisation that stayed with me. I never did it again until *Curb Your Enthusiasm*. But I always felt like *that's* something I can do. I don't like memorizing; I want to make it up. That's how the show came to be."

I said, "This whole show is so you can avoid memorizing dialogue?"

Larry nodded. "Yeah."

I never had asked any of the people I work with why they made such an insanely difficult career choice like comedy. I wanted to know what had motivated them. I asked Larry what television shows or movies inspired him when he was a child. He said, in addition to Phil Silvers, he was a fan of Abbott and Costello, Amos and Andy, and Woody Allen. "When I saw *Take the Money and Run* (1969), I had never laughed so hard in my life. And Mel Brooks and Carl Reiner's recording of their routine *The 2000 Year Old Man*. I remember listening to it with Richard Lewis, over and over, when we first met."

Alec Berg, David Mandel, and Jeff Schaffer

Along with Larry David, his *Seinfeld* and *Curb Your Enthusiasm* writer-producers, Alec Berg, David Mandel, and Jeff Schaffer, became comedy mentors for me. Jeff Schaffer is the million-miles-per-hour joke-wunderkind, willing to make it up on the day if necessary:

Photograph by John P. Johnson. Photograph courtesy of HBO®.

Jeff Schaffer (center) with Larry David (left) and John Hamm (right), on the set of *Curb Your Enthusiasm* in 2021.

"We're all funny people here. We're gonna figure it out." Jeff Schaffer and David Mandel characterize Alec Berg as the logical, Vulcan assassin of comedy—which is appropriate, since he co-created *Barry* (2018–TBD), a show about an assassin. Alec and Jeff describe David Mandel as the one who likes to push things into offensive absurdland as far as possible.

Jeff Schaffer said his first impression as a child growing up in Warren, Ohio, and watching television was that he hated sitcoms. But one day he chanced upon *Monty Python's Flying Circus* (1969–1974) coming in with static from a station in Pittsburgh. He became obsessed and rented *Monty Python and the Holy Grail* (1975) and *Monty Python's Life of Brian* (1979) on Betamax. "I would rewind those tapes over and over, memorizing the films. I wrote the sketches down, just to have the words, because there were no scripts available."

Alec Berg's interest began around age seven. "What got me into comedy was listening to my parents' albums. It's where I learned those rhythms. Steve Martin and Bob Newhart. I could do two hours of Bill Cosby word perfect. It was a weird thing to see this little kid in Boulder, Colorado, talking about growing up on the streets of Philadelphia."

David Mandel was a comedy nerd. He became obsessed with the original-cast years of *Saturday Night Live* (1975–1980). He was a hardcore fan, memorizing sketches. He also discovered his mother's old comedy albums by Woody Allen, Steve Martin, and Mort Sahl.

Alec, David, and Jeff became a throuple when they met at Harvard University. Alec was a visual arts major. David was a government major on his way to becoming an attorney: "I always imagined I'd just be a funny lawyer somewhere." Jeff was a biological anthropology major on a course toward pre-med, thinking he'd be a doctor like his father and grandfather. But then they discovered *The Harvard Lampoon*, a satirical humor publication. In 1991, David Mandel, Jeff Schaffer, and Alec Berg wrote a fake, one-hour tenth-anniversary-celebration of MTV for Comedy Central, called *MTV, Give Me Back My Life: A Harvard Lampoon Parody*, starring Louis Black, Al Franken,

Roger Nygard and Alec Berg in 2020.

and Daisy Fuentes. David recalled, "The show was a bit of a disaster. No one was listening to us, but we were there! We were on the set! After that, there was no turning back." Alec Berg said, "It occurred to us that writing was a much more enjoyable way of making a living."

Jeff and Alec drove to Los Angeles in 1992. Proctor and Gamble wanted to fly David to their corporate headquarters for an interview. But to David, writing comedy "seemed better than selling toothpaste in Cincinnati." Instead, he joined Al Franken at Comedy Central to do coverage of the Democratic and Republican conventions. That led to a three-year stint writing for *Saturday Night Live*, the show David had idolized.

Meanwhile, Jeff and Alec landed story editor and writing jobs on such shows as *Herman's Head* (1991–1994) and the early days of *Late Night with Conan O'Brien* (1993–2009). That led to joining *Seinfeld* for season six in 1995. David caught up with his friends on *Seinfeld* for season seven.

When *Seinfeld* ended, they landed deals that didn't lead anywhere: Alec and Jeff at DreamWorks Pictures and David at Touchstone Pictures. Finally, as a three-person team, they made the sex-comedy

David Mandel surrounded by his trove of movie collectibles in 2019.

Eurotrip (2004). After that, they were reunited with Larry David in 2005 on season five of *Curb Your Enthusiasm*. Alec Berg said, "There's no more affirming sound in the world than hearing that man laugh. If you can crack him up, you feel like you're twenty feet tall." I met them all when I joined *Curb Your Enthusiasm* for season six in 2007. That was the beginning of an exciting comedy tutorial for me.

After a few seasons together on *Curb Your Enthusiasm*, Jeff, Alec, and David began to realize that a one-way payday is more lucrative than a three-way split. Jeff said, "It was three people who loved working together and each of us was absolutely sure we didn't need the other two. We didn't do it because we had to. It was more enjoyable. We got stuff done faster. It was fun to be our own little writers' room." But soon they began to follow separate paths.

Jeff Schaffer co-created *The League* (2009–2015). Alec Berg took on executive producer duties at *Silicon Valley* (2014–2019), while creating *Barry* in 2018 with Bill Hader. In between pursuing his hobby of collecting rooms full of movie memorabilia, David Mandel took over *Veep* in 2016 as the new showrunner, beginning with season five, with the approval of the show's star, Julia Louis-Dreyfus.

Brad Hall and Julia Louis-Dreyfus

Julia Louis-Dreyfus and her husband, Brad Hall, are both performers. They worked together as cast members on *Saturday Night Live* from 1982 to 1984, then moved to Los Angeles, where they were married in 1987. I worked with Brad on an episode of *Veep*, which he directed, titled "A Woman First" (season six, episode nine). Brad believes the comedy instinct begins with "trying to make your parents or your brothers and sisters laugh. As you begin to enjoy live performing, you develop a sense of holding for a laugh. You learn by experience."

Julia Louis-Dreyfus and Roger Nygard in 2019.

Julia and Brad were both theater majors at Northwestern University, though at different times. According to Brad, "We gravitated toward improvisation, where you learn about the concept of 'yes-and'—that's a really important lesson as an actor."

Julia agreed. "And not just as a comedian. It also applies to drama."

The rule of improvisation is to always agree with what your partner tosses at you. If you say, "I'm holding a duck," and then if I respond with, "no you aren't," disagreement shuts down forward motion. Say "yes," add details, and toss it back. Such as:

"I'm holding a duck."

"Yes, and it just shit on your new chinos."

This is a good rule for the editing room as well. Try any suggestion, run with it, and then add your ideas. "*Yes*, let's try that. *And*, we can also try this."

Roger Nygard and Brad Hall in 2019.

Never say, "No, that won't work," or you are shutting down forward movement.

When I asked Julia what triggered her love for comedy, she credited Barbara Streisand in *Funny Girl* (1968). "I related to her. She was funny. She was desperate. She was not standard good-looking. I felt aligned with her as a result." *All in the Family* (1971–1979) was also an influence. "Carroll O'Connor's performance was incredibly instructive. He was playing a vile human being. And yet you loved him."

Brad agreed. "That was new in sitcoms. Everything else had been idealized versions of life like *Please Don't Eat the Daisies* (1960)." Brad grew up loving musical comedies such as *Singin' in the Rain* (1952). His earliest comedy memories were of watching Tex Avery cartoons with his minister father, who would be helpless with laughter. I remembered having the same experience, watching Tex Avery's animated shorts. If you track down "Rock-a-Bye Bear" (1952) and don't laugh yourself senseless, I'll eat my hat. Later Brad discovered Monty Python. "I knew every word of every Monty Python sketch, as did all my friends in high school."

Sacha Baron Cohen

Sacha Baron Cohen also indicated Monty Python as one of his early inspirations, as well as Phil Silvers. "My father would force us to watch *Sergeant Bilko* (a.k.a. *The Phil Silvers Show*, 1955–1959). And then it

Photo Courtesy of Amazon Studios.

Sacha Baron Cohen, in a still from *Borat Subsequent Moviefilm*.

was Danny Kaye, and Peter Sellers's Inspector Clouseau that made me love comedy." Working with Sacha was different from every other comedian I'd worked with. Sacha has a Peter Sellers–type dedication to fully inhabiting a comedic character, as in his alter egos Erran Morad or Borat Sagdiyev.

Sacha began writing sketches when he was six years old while in a scouting youth group for end-of-summer camp performances. He would prepare the whole year for it. "I loved the sound of hearing people laugh. After that, whenever I had a funny idea, I'd write it down." In college Sacha studied history, while dabbling in theater at the Cambridge University Amateur Dramatic Club. "When I was twenty-four, I remember what was in a way the beginning of me entering the world of comedic satire. I was in a store in Dublin and doing this whole bit with a banana in my hand, pretending to hold up the store in front of the shopkeepers, and they were really laughing."

Krista Vernoff

When Krista Vernoff studied acting at Boston University's College of Fine Arts, she happened to take a playwriting class during her senior year, and that changed everything. "I fell deeply in love with writing. Acting had always made me feel insecure and neurotic, but writing was joyful and came relatively easily to me." She didn't have the confidence to consider herself a writer at first. "It took me several years to give myself permission to pursue it."

When Krista hired me during season fourteen on *Grey's Anatomy* (2005–TBD), I saw firsthand how focused she gets as she is creating heartfelt, quality stories, while at the same time supervising writing, directing, editing, music, and sound mixes. I asked her how she manages so many simultaneous tasks, yet stays original and creative. "I suspect it has something to do with the chaos of my childhood and

Photo by Emily Culver.

Script supervisor Lindsay Cohen, Krista Vernoff, and writer Elisabeth Finch, on the set of *Grey's Anatomy*.

how my brain was wired, plus twenty-six years of therapy and twelve-step work, giving me a deeper understanding of the human psyche, which helps in writing and managing people." As a child, she survived being raised by alcoholics and drug addicts, in an environment that included emotional, verbal, and physical violence. Krista said she "learned to escape the insanity of her childhood by disappearing into imaginary worlds; both fictional worlds created by brilliant authors and the imaginary worlds I created for myself. In my real life I had no control, but I always imagined that if I could just be in charge and script everyone's behavior, then somehow everything would be okay. So, showrunning is kind of a beautiful combination of all of that." She now has an avenue as a writer to express the darkness she experienced. "I have to believe the reason that we survive a thing is so that we can help other people survive that thing."

What triggered her love for movies and television was the series *M★A★S★H* (1972–1983). "I was very young when I was watching it—too young probably. I was twelve years old when it ended and I still remember the impact the finale had on me. I cried for what felt like hours, because of the storytelling, and because the show was ending. It felt like leaving really good friends behind." Her drive to succeed in the business of storytelling is now fueled by her competitiveness and ambition, plus the knowledge that "Hollywood has never been harder or scarier than my upbringing!"

Judd Apatow

I met Judd Apatow when we were both frequenting comedy clubs in the late 1980s. Judd doesn't like mean-spirited comedy. His movies, such as *The 40-Year-Old Virgin* (2005), *Knocked Up* (2007), and *The King of Staten Island* (2020), gravitate toward moments that are emotionally connected. "Life is about suffering and I'm interested in how people try to do better and move forward in spite of that. The obstacles are what make me laugh. I root for the person because they keep trying."

Judd became enamored with stand-up comedy early, and at age seventeen, he moved to Los Angeles and started looking for open-mic nights. "I was so terrible. I finally cobbled together enough material to be the emcee for fifty bucks at a bar in Rancho Cucamonga." When Judd realized that comedians would buy jokes for fifty bucks each, he started writing for Jeff Dunham and George Wallace. "I came at it as a fan, so the idea of writing jokes seemed like the most fun in the world."

That led Judd to helping Jim Carrey write sketches for *In Living Color* (1990–1994). Jim paid him out of his own pocket to brainstorm during the show's hiatus, so Jim could return the following season

Judd Apatow

with ideas ready to pitch. I was amused to hear this, because I had taken a turn doing the same thing one summer with Jim Carrey. We wrote a sketch called "The Teamster Psychic," about a blue-collar guy who reads palms, but only when he's not on break—which is a lot. Jim and I went to a pair of psychics in a storefront on Melrose Avenue for research. Jim had already been on *In Living Color* for a couple of seasons, and their eyes lit up when we walked in. Jim's psychic boldly predicted, "You will be very successful." How many psychics stay in business telling clients they will fail? My psychic told me listlessly, "You'll be successful too, but not as successful as him." Thanks a lot.

Soon Judd was writing for Garry Shandling, and Tom Arnold, and then when Judd met Ben Stiller, they created and sold *The Ben Stiller Show* (1992). Judd felt like he had been thrown into the deep end of the pool. "The next thing you know I was running a TV show with almost no experience." Oddly enough, *The Ben Stiller Show* replaced another FOX sketch-comedy series called *Haywire* (1991), which I had worked on as a segment director. Many years later Judd's and my paths crossed yet again when we worked on *Crashing* (2017–2019), the HBO series he executive produced with Pete Holmes.

Ivan Ladizinsky

In 1996 I met editor Ivan Ladizinsky while I was directing and editing my second movie, an action picture called *Back to Back: American Yakuza 2*. Ivan was in the next room cutting Steve Wang's 1997 action film, *Drive*. A few years later, Ivan took a job editing the pilot for a new reality show called *Survivor* (2000–TBD). Ivan stuck around for thirteen years (twenty-six seasons and eight Emmy nominations) and helped create a new style for reality shows.

When I asked what Ivan's first influence was, he said he grew up loving *The Twilight Zone* (1959–1964), *The Outer Limits* (1963–1965), *Star Trek* (1966–1969), the Three Stooges, and Abbott and Costello.

Photo by Elizabeth Ladizinsky.

Ivan Ladizinsky on location in 2001 for *Survivor: Africa*.

"Costello cracked me up the way he would lose control and scream in *Abbott and Costello Meet Frankenstein* (1948). I loved monster movies when I was a kid. I would think, 'Look at how those grown men are as scared of the monsters as I am.'"

While at Canoga Park High School, Ivan met other kids who liked to make crazy little movies, one of whom was John Ryman, from Cleveland High School in Reseda. According to John Ryman, "Everyone acted in each other's movies, and Ivan and I met on a friend's Super-8mm remake of *Planet of the Apes*." Ivan added, "I was cast as a gorilla and John was cast as a mutant. Type casting?" Their comedy interests expanded to include Woody Allen, Mel Brooks, and Monty Python. (Monty Python turns up again.) In college Ivan got a job as a gofer at a special-effects company that happened to have a three-quarter-inch RM440 convergence editing system. Ivan taught himself how to use it and was soon cutting the company's demo reels. At the same time, he began studying music at Pierce College and sang in the L.A. Jazz Choir for three years, which included a gig singing with Rosemary Clooney in a George Gershwin show at the Hollywood Bowl. He might have continued the singing career, but in 1990 his high school pal John Ryman hired Ivan to edit his first feature, *Galaxies Are Colliding* (1992), on a Moviola, a machine that was invented in 1924 specifically for motion picture editing. Later they upgraded to 1930s technology, using a K-E-M (Keller-Elektro-Mechanik) and a Steenbeck flatbed editor. Working on that project is when Ivan realized editing was for him.

Grady Cooper

Another *Survivor* editor-alumnus is Grady Cooper, who I worked with on *The League* (2009–2015). Grady remembered being enthralled with such Mel Brooks movies as *Blazing Saddles* (1974), *Young Frankenstein*

Photo by Bill Martin, courtesy of Peter Turman.

Grady Cooper, between episodes.

(1974), and *Silent Movie* (1976), as well as *SCTV* (1976–1984) and *Monty Python's Flying Circus* (yet again!). After seeing an animation festival at the local art museum, he borrowed his neighbor's Super-8mm camera and started making claymation films. His first film was about an antagonistic creature who harassed a real-person roommate.

Grady Cooper had performed magic for neighborhood parties—something else we had in common, as I had done the same as a kid. And in high school, Grady convinced his teachers to let him and his friends make short films to act out scenes instead of writing papers. I recognized another parallel to my own early years. I had sometimes made films instead of doing book reports, like a dramatization of a cyclops menacing toga-clad folks for Greek literature studies in my humanities class.

After high school Grady went to the University of North Carolina at Chapel Hill with some of his friends from high school, one of whom was Peyton Reed (*Ant-Man*, 2015), and they upgraded to three-quarter-inch video and kept making films. When Grady moved to Los Angeles, he got a job as a post-production assistant for documentary producer Andrew Solt. One day Grady was hanging out in the editing room observing. The editor sensed his presence, turned around, sized him up, and said, "You don't have what it takes to be an editor, kid." Grady vowed he would prove him wrong, although he didn't know how.

Not long after, Grady went to lunch with friends who were working at a company that produced behind-the-scenes documentaries. The owner, George Zaloom, walked by and they said, "This is Grady. He's an editor." He wasn't, but he didn't deny it.

Zaloom said, "We need another editor for a project. Are you available?"

Grady recalled, "I heard myself saying, 'Yes.' I had no business taking that job. I kind of knew the basics, thanks to cutting zany college videos, but I had a lot to learn." Grady felt like he was way in over his head. "I would leave when everybody else did but then sneak back in and keep working, to try to learn how to do it better." He was frustrated and panicking, but he persevered. And then one night, after a couple of weeks, he finally had an epiphany, "Oh! I know how to do this!"

A few years later, Grady was editing the stand-up special *Chris Rock: Bigger & Blacker* (1999), and the producers recommended Grady to edit a new show just starting its first season, called *Curb Your Enthusiasm*. After six weeks, Larry David came into the editing room and said, "Hey Grady, we're gonna keep you." Grady had no idea he was auditioning. "I was terrified, but I was just glad I fit in." After this first season on *Curb Your Enthusiasm*, Grady Cooper decided to start his own editorial company, hiring young employees. That took him out of the editing marketplace for several years. It turned out to be a bad choice financially, but it introduced him to directing promos and commercials, which he loved. Grady's departure from *Curb Your Enthusiasm* opened up an editing chair for another young editor.

Jon Corn

Jon Corn thought he'd become a lawyer like his dad. But when his dad found this out, he said, "Don't be a lawyer because I am. Only do it if you really want to be a lawyer." Jon's dad was a comedy fan and together they watched movies such as Stanley Kubrick's *Dr. Strangelove* (1964) and Mel Brooks's *Young Frankenstein* (1974). "I remember as a seven-year-old watching the monster sing 'Puttin' on the Ritz.' My dad still talks about how he's never seen me laugh so hard." They also watched *Monty Python's Flying Circus*. (There it is again!) "There

Photo by Steven Rasch.

Jon Corn (left) and Larry David (right), working on *Curb Your Enthusiasm* in 2002.

was a bit called 'Confuse a Cat.' I still think it's the funniest sketch I've ever seen." In 1983, when he was in junior high school, he discovered *Late Night with David Letterman* (1982–1993), with all the bizarre characters, such as Chris Elliot as "The Guy under the Seats."

In college, Jon started out as an architecture major. He did well with an assignment to make a collage within a strict set of parameters: exemplify a subject or a word like "surface." But when he was assigned to draw a simple perspective, like a three-dimensional line drawing with vanishing points—a simple enough task for those with the goods—he had trouble. "It was me being weeded out of the architecture profession—appropriately." He switched his major to English.

After college, having no particular media skills, just a love for comedy, he thought, "I'm going to give Los Angeles a try. If I fail, I can always go to grad school and have a miserable life as a lawyer." He got a job as a production assistant on music videos. Then, while working on *Mad TV* (1995–2016) as a post-production assistant, he met editor Matt Davis, who would let Jon sit in his edit bay and watch and learn. "Matt taught me not to be afraid of the machine. It was then I realized editing was a confluence of my three top interests: computers, graphic design, and storytelling."

In 2019 I shared a limo ride with Matt Davis (thanks to our co-Emmy nominations for *Who Is America?*), so I asked Matt if he remembered Jon Corn being a pest during those early days. Matt laughed and recalled how Jon showed interest. "He compared editing to making collages. He liked to learn, and I wanted to pontificate— and there should be more of that! When a post supervisor walks in on that sort of dynamic, their first instinct is to dispatch everybody to do their individual jobs. But overlap and interaction should be encouraged; it's where we improve each other's skill set."

When I worked with Jon Corn on *The League* (2009–2015), every few days, around 3 p.m., Jon would plop himself down on my couch. I didn't ask him in. He would just turn up. Years later when I asked him why he did that, he said, "You were so focused. I was enjoying coming in and talking at you for a little too long. I wanted to see, was there a breaking point where you would go: 'Jon, I have to work, get out!' But you never did."

I said, "It's because you're a likable guy."

"I can be bothersome."

"You're still likable even when you're bothersome."

Being in a room alone, I occasionally need a people break. We all need personal contact. Even super-focused madmen. There is a tendency to remain insulated in an editing room all day. And as Matt Davis had done, Jon was continuing a tradition of being interactive with other editors, which led us to improving each other's work.

In 1997, Matt Davis hired young Jon as his assistant on an MTV show called *Austin Stories* (1997–1998). "Matt let me share an 'additional editing' credit. I took that credit and ran with it, telling anybody who would listen I was an editor." Jon found work editing an MTV show called *2gether: The Series* (2000) about a fake boy band. Then he got a call from Steven Rasch, who said, "We got your name from Matt Davis. I'm editing a show called *Curb Your Enthusiasm*. And we're looking for an editor."

For the next six seasons, Jon Corn and Steven Rasch worked well together. Jon said of Steven Rasch, "I called him 'Even Steven,' always calm, cool, and collected. While I'd be pounding my fist complaining, 'Why didn't they shoot this? Why didn't they do that?' he would calmly say, 'Well, they probably didn't have time to get it.' Then I'd calm down. 'Argh, you're right. What can I do to make this work?'"

Steven Rasch

Steven Rasch has been editing *Curb Your Enthusiasm* since the beginning. Steven's father was a salesman, jocular, verbal, and amusing. His

Photo by Jon Corn.

Steven Rasch, working on *Curb Your Enthusiasm* in 2002.

mother was a great laugher. They had five children and dinner was fun-time. They would compete for the funny "rip" on whoever was going to get it that night. "It was open season on each other. I thought that's how you relate to people generally."

In high school he felt like he couldn't take part in theater because, being a jock, his friends would make fun of him. But that didn't stop him from buying a Kodak 8mm camera. He was influenced by the Marx Brothers, Benny Hill, and Monty Python (ibid!!). In a story that was continuing to sound familiar to me about comedy editors, Steven began making humorous short films when he was young. He animated a Barbie doll in his basement, much like I had done with my Linus and Charlie Brown dolls.

Steven chose Colgate University in Upstate New York and majored in English. After college, Steven got a series of jobs as a salesman, like his father, retailing cameras, televisions, and videotape machines. But when he decided to take a six-week comedy-improv class in Boston, it was pivotal. He got the bug. But he didn't quite know how to make something happen from it, because he didn't want to be a stand-up comic. He got a job as an assistant editor at a Boston post-production house. Now that he had access to nice equipment, he made a 16mm, comedy short film, which won a handful of film festival awards. That film helped get him into the American Film Institute (AFI), which is what brought him to Los Angeles. After a year at the AFI, Steven found some online editing work, followed by a job editing stand-up shows for Comedy Central, and then a job cutting twenty-two-minute episodes of a series called *The Hogan Family* (1986–1991) down to twenty minutes, to make room for more commercials in syndication. "I had to figure out how to tighten everything and make edits that made sense and were still funny." This exercise sharpened Steven's editing chops; it's what prepared him for his next challenge: a one-hour special called *Larry David: Curb Your Enthusiasm* (1999). To get the job, he had to cut three scenes for the director, Robert B. Weide. He passed that test and got the job. (In another case of paths crossing, Bob Weide also had begun his show business career working at Rollins, Joffe, Morra and Brezner.)

Because *Curb Your Enthusiasm* was very low budget, they had only one camera to get all the coverage. "They would try to re-create improvised bits, but it was not easy. They realized, with improv, you're screwed without an opposing camera." Producer Mark Farrell got a home DV camera and held that as the B-camera wide shot. They filmed the pilot in scene order because Larry wanted to be able to zig and zag with the storyline as ideas came up.

About a year after finishing that one-off job, Steven opened the door on Halloween night to see Larry David trick-or-treating with his five-year-old daughter. Steven recalled, "He was just wearing what he wears on the show. He's always dressed as 'Larry.'" Larry didn't know Steven lived there. They hadn't spoken in months.

Steven said, while tossing a fistful of candy in the young girl's bag, "Well, hi, Larry. How's it going?"

Larry said, "Pretty good." And then as he turned to leave, Larry turned back and said, "Oh, HBO wants to make a series."

Steven replied, "Great. Well, I do, too."

Steven still isn't sure if he would've been hired back if it hadn't been for Halloween.

Mike Binder

Another filmmaker who got into show business via family dinner-time comedy was Mike Binder. Mike loved to make his dad laugh.

Author's collection.

Roger Nygard, cinematographer Walt Lloyd, and Mike Binder on the set of *The Mind of the Married Man* in 2001.

It was also a way to get out of trouble and get attention from girls. Mike's earliest comedy influences were such television series as *The Monkeys* (1966–1968), *Batman* (1966–1968), and especially *Get Smart* (1965–1970). "I loved the opening doors. I loved the secret devices, like the cone of silence. And the way they would do jokes upon jokes." There was also a show called *That's My Mama* (1974–1975), which motivated Mike to write a spec script when he was in ninth grade and send it to Hollywood. "I never heard a damn thing back. But I loved that show, because everybody was so perfectly delineated. You could write any story for them and you knew what every character was going to do."

I asked Mike what made him think he could send a script to Hollywood. He said, "I always had a lot of confidence."

I said, "So, you were delusional. That's worked to your advantage. I had the same thing, thanks to my mother."

Mike nodded. "I got it from my parents too. They would always tell me I could do anything I wanted—until I wanted to go into show business. Then they said, 'No, you can't do that.'"

When Mike was eighteen, he lied to his parents and said he was going to Los Angeles for college. In reality, he went to audition at The Comedy Store. He got a job as a doorman. He wanted to be a stand-up comic because he'd always loved Bob Hope, George Carlin, and Cheech and Chong. "The first joke I wrote when I got to Los Angeles was: The big thing out here is jogging on the beach. I tried it. I lasted ten seconds. You hit the water."

Punch Upward

As I talked with all these comedic geniuses, the Marx Brothers and Monty Python kept coming up. I wondered why these two comedy troupes were such big influences on modern comedy. When I asked

Judd Apatow, he said as a little kid he was often picked last in gym class, which pissed him off and made him think life was unfair. "I loved that comedians were mad about systems they thought were corrupt. There's a direct correlation between me loving the Marx Brothers and me feeling like I was being mistreated in school. [In the Marx Brothers movies,] there were people in suits who were in power, and someone would beat up Harpo, and that gave the Marx Brothers permission to torture that person for the rest of the movie. I was attracted to that."

After the Marx Brothers, why did Monty Python become the gold standard? Alec Berg said comedy writers reference Monty Python all the time, saying things like, "This is sort of a dead parrot thing." Everybody immediately knows what that means. To solve the Monty Python mystery, I tracked down Julian Doyle, who was the editor of the Monty Python movies. Julian said he and the Pythons were all fans of the Marx Brothers, and they also loved Spike Milligan and Peter Sellers on *The Goon Show* (1951–1960), a BBC radio program that was all voices and crazy ideas: "They're going to fire pancakes from France to England! We must protect ourselves!"

Julian said of Monty Python's secret to success, "They take the piss out of everybody, especially the upper class, the judge, the Queen, the people in power. Nobody is safe." That is the same winning formula utilized by the Marx Brothers, to punch upward, to take on the bigger targets. Julian also believes another secret behind Monty Python is the intellect underneath the comedy. The ideas they examine are complex. "They're not playing down to people; they're playing to an intelligent audience."

Julian Doyle

Julian Doyle did not begin as an editor. He came out of film school doing every job, making commercials and short films. After he gave

Julian Doyle on the set of *Chemical Wedding* in 2008.

the Pythons a hand with a couple of shorts, they asked him if he would work on their first feature, *Monty Python and the Holy Grail* (1975). From that point forward, Julian's life diverted to the Pythons' comedy career. Julian's first foray was to work on some of the problem scenes, production managing, shooting, special effects, props, editing, and anything else that was needed. "We didn't have proper footage of the rabbit fight. To get the missing shots, I got a hand puppet and put blood on it and filmed it in my garden over Hampstead Heath in London. That's how the film was put together, bits and pieces that I shot with bits and pieces they shot." The film was such a huge success that Julian still receives royalties from his little percentage.

When they were preparing to do the next Monty Python movie, Terry Jones said to Julian, "You must come and do *Monty Python's Life of Brian* (1979)." Julian agreed, but only as editor. Julian had not yet edited a full feature, but he had learned that he loved editing most. He also discovered he had a knack for knowing what was funny on screen.

What's So Funny about That?

Let's get specific. Why exactly is something funny? E. B. White once said, "Humor can be dissected, as a frog can, but the thing dies in the process. . . ."[3] But let's choose to be foolish and try to explain humor. I had all these hilarious people around; I figured they must be able to tell me what "funny" is.

Julian Doyle said he breaks comedy down into two types: verbal humor and clowns. And he said Monty Python mines both veins. "Terry Gilliam always accused John Cleese of being a clown. He's funny by the way he moves. Eric Idle is quick witted. A typical quip from him is, 'American beer is like making love in a canoe. It's fucking close to water.' Terry Jones is about being silly. He and Mike Palin write the silly stuff, like the 'Biggus Dickus' scene." In that classic scene in *Monty Python's Life of Brian*, if anybody laughs when Pontius Pilate mentions the name of his friend "Biggus Dickus," they get thrown to the lions. Everybody's trying to hold in their laughter, which becomes increasingly difficult when they find out his wife's name is "Incontinentia Buttocks." That scene alone is reason enough to check out *Monty Python's Life of Brian*.

Judd Apatow finds comedy hard to quantify with rules. But he tried. "It's always about creating surprise or suddenly moving in a direction an audience doesn't expect. But my brain melts when forced to be in those conversations. It's almost like if you play the piano and think, 'Oh my god, I'm playing the piano.' Suddenly you can't do it and you crumble. You have to go into a sort of flow state. It's intuitive. Every time a joke works, it works for a different reason. It's like Bono wanting to write another song like 'One.' There are no rules to help him. Something magical has to happen with the melody, the orchestration, the feeling, and the words."

Sacha Baron Cohen's goal is also to be unexpected, to show the audience something they've never seen before. "Even if the comic principles being used may be familiar, the scene itself should be original. I think Ali G made an impact because no one had seen that style of comedy before, in England at least, where somebody is asking ridiculous questions to a real person, who is an expert and answering seriously. So, it felt new and surprising. With *Borat*, there hadn't been a film where real people were moving the plot along."

Alec Berg sees rules as advisory, not hard and fast. "It's a rule until you break it and it still works fine." But I think we can all agree, on a basic level, some choices are indeed funnier than others. In the spirit of exploration, I have made a list of what is funny. It is by no means exhaustive. It's more like a periodic table of comedy elements, to which new entries can be added as more data comes in.

The Periodic Table of Nonsense

1. Surprise

The classic joke structure is: set up a premise, establish a pattern, then deliver an unexpected variation. Surprise is so important it's at the top of the list. Sacha and Judd went immediately to this concept. Comedy is a cycling of tension and release, triggered by unexpected turns. Humor is born in the difference between expectation and reality. The greater the difference, the bigger the laugh. Double entendre, for example, is when a listener realizes there is a second meaning and suddenly comprehends a seemingly benign statement in a new, outrageous way. Steven Rasch has a theory he calls the three S's of comedy: It has to be smart, sophomoric, and surprising. A pratfall comes as a surprise. Plot twists must be surprising. Misunderstandings and mistaken identities are common comedy plots that set up surprises.

One summer, a few years after my father died, I was in the basement browsing through his old sci-fi books. I noticed a title by A. E.

van Vogt called *The Voyage of the Space Beagle* (1950). I opened randomly to the middle, intending to kill a few minutes. I became so absorbed in the story that I read to the end of that book in one sitting. I went back to the first page and read to the end again. The story is about a spaceship with scientist and military personnel that goes from planet to planet investigating the universe and battling hostile aliens. Gene Roddenberry must have been a van Vogt fan. Chapter 1 is very similar to the first episode of *Star Trek* called "The Man Trap." The Space Beagle's crew encounters an alien called the Coeurl, which sucks phosphorus out of humans (they made it sodium in *Star Trek*). Chapter 3 is about a creature called Ixtl, the last survivor of an ancient civilization from a prior universe. It has been stranded in deep space since before the Big Bang, waiting for anybody to happen by. The Space Beagle does, and Ixtl beams itself on board and implants eggs into the abdomens of human hosts. The hatchlings emerge hungry. Does that sound like a possible inspiration for the film *Alien* (1979)?

A. E. van Vogt was popular during the 1940s and early 1950s, the "golden age" of science fiction. The legend of van Vogt the writer is that he believed surprise to be paramount, that he would consider, every few pages, what would be the opposite of what was currently happening, and then send his character into a new direction. When I searched for the source of van Vogt's inspiration, I discovered what he was really doing was following advice from his treasured writing manual, *The Only Two Ways to Write a Story* (1928), by John W. Gallishaw, who suggested that the best writers wrote stories in a series of eight-hundred-word scenes, broken down into five steps: meeting, purpose of scene, interchange, conclusive act, and plot crisis. Just as a story has a progression, so does each scene.[4] In a 1979 interview, van Vogt said, "And this system I also did in my disciplined way. No piece of music was ever more rigidly organized than the five steps of these scenes—the wordage could vary slightly, but not much."[5]

Now that you are intent on surprising your audience, keep in mind that all your surprises must be properly set up. Lay the groundwork early, so no twist, no gag, nothing comes out of nowhere. A surprise without groundwork is a cheap shock. When done successfully, the more you surprise an audience, the harder they laugh. When Mike Binder is writing, he said his goal is to have an audience reaction be: "Wow. I didn't expect that character to say that—*and it's true*." A double win. Surprise and truth.

2. Truth

A punch line is often a simple statement of truth; things that are supposed to remain unspoken, the embarrassing thing, the way things really are, particularly when our culture tells us not to say these things. Observational humor is processing everyday life through your own lens and finding humor in it. There are old sayings such as "there's a grain of truth in every joke," or alternately, "many a true word is spoken in jest," or "a joke is truth wrapped in a smile."

When writing dialogue, Mike Binder asks, "What really is the truth of this moment? It'll either be really dramatic or really funny. It could be both." When I was editing Mike Binder's documentary-series *The Comedy Store*, Mike asked comedian Whitney Cummings about her writing, and in one of the outtakes she said the secret to understanding comedy is simple: "Tell the truth." She asks herself, "What's the elephant in the living room? [When you were growing up,] what was the thing you weren't allowed to say? The taboo things, the things that were off limits, the things that we all experience but keep in the shadows. That's where all the meat is."

Sigmund Freud suggested jokes function as a way to release forbidden thoughts and desires.[6] Forbidden things become funny when the work we do repressing them is released. Humor breaks down the barriers we build against truth. Truth is a bitch; we work hard to avoid it, because it's painful.

3. Pain

Steve Allen (comedian, writer, and the first host of *The Tonight Show* in 1954) once said, "Tragedy plus time equals comedy."[7] When somebody falls down, we laugh. The more it hurts, the funnier it gets. Julian Doyle lamented, "My wife laughs any time I get hurt. I don't know what she's got against me, but if I fall over, the first thing she does is laugh. She finds that hysterical, me hurting myself."

I said, "I hope she won't be at your funeral cackling wildly."

Julian replied, "She'll think it's very funny."

In *Veep*, when Jonah hit his head on the ceiling, the louder and more solid I made the sound effect, the funnier it got. I also removed a single frame to speed up each hit to make the bumps appear even more violent. Watching awkward or clumsy behavior, we laugh and think, "I'm glad that's not me." The English language borrowed a word the Germans have for enjoying someone else's misery: schadenfreude. The literal translation is "harm joy." Philosophers all the way back to Plato recognized how we laugh when we suddenly feel superior to others. However, there has to be a benign aspect to the injury. Seeing somebody we care about sustain a fatal head trauma is not so funny. But if a bump to the noggin is set up in such a way that the audience knows there is no real damage, it's just about the funniest thing there is.

The more serious a situation gets, the more we need to make jokes about it. Death is the most serious misfortune we face, therefore, by definition, as a topic, it's also the funniest. As you go through life, facing one ordeal after another, if you can't laugh, you'll go crazy. Looking back, I realized that many of my works ponder the abyss of death. My documentary *The Nature of Existence* (2010) dives directly into the subject. In the episode "Grief Counseling" (season three, episode four) of *The Office* (2005–2013), Michael Scott deals with his fears of mortality. In the *Veep* (2012–2019) finale (season seven, episode seven), Julia Louis-Dreyfus fully embraced the death of her character Selina. Julia said, "Everything feels so *meaningful*. And guess what? It ain't. It's meaningless. All this stuff we're thinking about all the time, this conversation, everything, it's meaningless. It's fun to consider that."

4. Absurdity

In philosophy, existentialism gave birth to absurdism, which holds there is a natural conflict between the human tendency to look for meaning in a purposeless, chaotic universe. If you create characters and set them against an impossible task, like trying to beat back the ocean, or push a boulder up an endless hill, or find and marry Pamela Anderson's (nonexistent) television character, the attempt becomes ridiculous. Religion, superstition, mythology, and stories told around the campfire are defenses humans have put up in opposition to a purposeless universe. The more sacred something becomes, the greater a target it becomes for humor. I could see no topic that was off limits to Sacha Baron Cohen. He will work with his writers and ask, "What's the funniest thing there is? How can we make this funnier?" He will continually rethink a premise. "Have we got what would be the most ludicrous thing to show an audience? And then how can we achieve that?" If they haven't reached total absurdity, they keep pushing.

Jeff Schaffer and I had a mini-bonding moment over a British film called *Withnail and I* (1987). I asked Jeff if he had seen the movie, and his eyes lit up and he exclaimed, "Yes!" It had been a pivotal inspiration for both of us. The film is about the ridiculous meanderings of two out-of-work actors in 1969 London, like

34

an updated version of Samuel Beckett's absurdist novel *Waiting for Godot* (1952). The film has dialogue that still had me laughing many years after seeing the film.

For example, as Withnail is cold, wet, miserable, and begging for firewood, he shouts for help to a passing farmer: "We've gone on holiday by mistake!"

Marwood, the narrator, suggests about a live chicken they want to eat, that is staring at them: "I think you should strangle it instantly, in case it starts to make friends with us."

Danny, their perpetually stoned drug supplier, waxes about the future: "I'm thinking of retiring and going into the toy industry. My partner's got a really good idea for making dolls." He indicates his partner-friend nearby. "His name's Presuming Ed. His sister give him the idea. She got a doll on Christmas what pisses itself. And you gotta change its drawers for it. It's horrible, really. But they like that, little girls. So, we're gonna make one that shits itself as well. He's an expert. He's building the prototype now."

It's the type of dialogue that could come only from two drunken nitwits experiencing the absurdity of life. And thankfully, one of them was jotting it down, as director Bruce Robinson based the story on his own experiences as a young actor.

5. Contrast

When you have a clash of opposites, of two different worlds or two different societies, on one side is the establishment, and on the other side are those who want to change things. The establishment is rigid, serious, dignified, and resistant. The change agents are fish out of water, they don't fit in, they don't follow the rules, they cause disruptions, often by absurd means. Comedy is richest in the contrast between these worlds, when the upstarts attack the status quo and those in charge. The Marx Brothers were experts at the approach of ridiculing the pretensions of those who consider themselves socially superior. At the end of this sort of comedy, the two sides often come together, sometimes at a wedding or a party, where social unity is restored. The French film *La Cage aux Folles* (1978) is a prime example of this formula. When a young couple decides to marry, the two worlds collide when their parents meet: One set is the gay owner of a scandalous night club and his cross-dressing lover, and the other pair are ultraconservative.

Outsiders are good at seeing contrasts. When I choose a topic for a documentary, it's a subculture I am outside of. If I was a part of it, I wouldn't be able to see it as clearly. Alec Berg told me he felt like an outsider when he was growing up because he is left-handed: "I remember vividly in first grade when the coffee can of scissors came around the room. I had to take the ones with the green handles. In that moment I had this feeling of being different. And since so much of comedy is about standing outside of a system and analyzing it, if you feel like you're not part of something, it makes you conscious of being outside of it and you can take it apart and examine it."

Alec Berg has a comedy casting formula that highlights the outcasts: "Nobody who has washboard abs is funny. You see comedians who suddenly become fitness buffs and they're not funny anymore. I think it's because they start taking themselves seriously and buying into their own masculinity or fitness. I've worked with actors who lose weight and they're not funny anymore. I'm sure some vain, fit comedian will be upset I said that, but keep it in anyhow."

6. Language

Witty dialogue is the currency of comedy. Plays on words, puns, double entendres, clever insults. Word choice is crucial. Some words are funnier than others. Chicken is funnier than hen. Why? Probably because it has a K sound in it. Hard consonants are funnier.

Words with B, P, and K are funnier than F, H, M words. Duck is funnier than dove.

Specific is funnier than general. Camaro is funnier than automobile. Waffle is funnier than breakfast. Mallard or woodpecker is funnier than bird.

Commonly used, imprecise phrases are the enemy of comedy. Be specific. Avoid: "a number of things," "back in the day," "at the end of the day." Tell us when, where, and how many.

When Ricky Gervais hosted the *77th Annual Golden Globe Awards* in 2020, he needed the right funny-sounding words for this bit:

> The world got to see James Corden as a fat pussy. He was also in the movie *Cats*. But no one saw that. And the reviews—shocking. I saw one that said this is the worst thing to happen to cats since dogs. Dame Judi Dench defended the movie saying, it was the role she was born to play, because she likes nothing better than plunking herself down on the carpet, lifting her leg, and licking her own minge.

The network standards and practices lawyers review the jokes in advance, and they objected to his use of the British slang for vagina, "minge." They suggested using vagina.

Gervais said, "I'm not going to say vagina, that's so much worse. . . . She acted like a cat, and cats lick their own bits. . . . There's got to be some sort of funny twist and silliness to it. Minge is a funny word."

The brain trust of lawyers threw out more suggestions, such as "box."

"I'm not going to say box!" Gervais said. "They were coming up with much worse things. So I said, 'What about flange? We say that as well.' . . . Minge and flange, I like those 'nge' words. . . . 'Nge' is a funny syllable." Gervais went with minge, and the network bleeped it. He was ready though. "I knew they would, so I pointed, and I still won."[8]

Some numbers are funnier than other numbers. When Douglas Adams needed a funny answer in *The Hitchhiker's Guide to the Galaxy* (1979) to "the Ultimate Question of Life, the Universe, and

Inspector Clouseau argues whether a beggar or his monkey is breaking the law, in *Return of the Pink Panther.*

Everything," he chose forty-two. A round number would not have been as funny, and forty-two sounds funnier than forty-four because "ooo" is a funny syllable.

Unusual accents and bizarre ways of speaking elicit laughs. Inspector Jacques Clouseau constantly violated linguistic norms.

In *The Return of the Pink Panther* (1975), Chief Inspector Charles Dreyfus sputters: "Minkey? You said *minkey!*"

Inspector Clouseau nods, nonplussed: "Yes, a chimpanzee minkey."

Larry David often finds combinations of words that become funny: "Pretty, pretty, pretty good." But Larry admitted, "I don't even know why that's funny."

7. Abnormal Behavior

Clowns, buffoons, lunatics—these people do idiotic things, yet they somehow come out on top. Peter Sellers was doing Jerry Lewis who

38

was doing Buster Keaton who was doing what clowns have been doing since 2400 BC.[9] None of the world's top assassins could kill Inspector Clouseau in *The Pink Panther Strikes Again* (1976). Jerry Lewis could destroy an entire department store with a vacuum cleaner and still win the owner's daughter in *Who's Minding the Store?* (1963). In *Steamboat Bill, Jr.* (1928), an entire building collapsed onto Buster Keaton, leaving him unscathed.

Society mandates that we live within social and moral rules. Crazy or unexpected conduct violates norms. But what is normal? By definition, what most people do is what's considered normal. If 80 percent of a society is delusional, then delusion seems normal. But as soon as one person points out the emperor has no clothes, delusion is threatened and destroyed by gales of laughter.

John Cleese once said, "Humor is about things going wrong and people behaving inappropriately." In his series *Fawlty Towers* (1975–1979), Cleese's character Basil Fawlty begins each episode calm and gets progressively angrier. "He's frightened that somebody will find something out—that's the basis of all farce. . . . As the cover-ups become more ineffectual and fail, it forces him to do another cover-up, which explodes in his face and things get worse and worse and the frustration leads to the anger."[10] Basil Fawlty's rage builds until he is whipping a stalled car with a tree branch as punishment, a climax so absurd it is undeniably hilarious (season one, episode five, "Gourmet Night").

Clowns often give mixed signals, like pointing one way while looking another. Julian Doyle gave an example. "You have a drink, you put it down, you look away, somebody takes your glass, and you look back and go, 'Who's got the glass?' That's not funny. But if a clown takes a drink, puts it down, looks away, looks back and it's not there. Then he's looking for it up in the sky. Has it gone through the table? He's feeling under the table. 'Where is it?' Idiocy makes it funny."

8. Reproduction

The opposite of death is the creation of life. Sex and the pursuit of sex is funny. It's quite ridiculous when you think about it. At a biological level, the sperm chases an egg, but only one out of millions will be allowed in. How absurdly funny is it that so many fail? On a societal level, men court women. The suitor must prove he is worthy, that his ardor is genuine, in order to be chosen above all others. The suitor must be charming—which means *funny*. Sense of humor is high on everybody's list of requirements on dating profiles. Humor is a great way to test the intelligence of potential mates. If neither partner has the ability to deliver or appreciate humor successfully, they are at a distinct disadvantage against more likable suitors. Romantic comedies are full to the brim with charming, amusing banter and funny courtship behavior.

9. Do It Faster!

The more concise a line, the funnier it gets. Cut down a joke to as few words as possible. Long windups are death to comedy. A writer should think economically. Even though a screenplay has ninety minutes to fill, treat every second as judiciously as if you were making a thirty-second commercial.

Larry David is always trying to find a quicker way through scenes. "Shorter is funnier. Quicker is funnier. If we don't say a line in a concise way, we'll rewrite it shorter and replace it with ADR." (Automated dialogue replacement, rerecording it after the fact.) It's about increasing impact through compression, making it tight without making it feel cutty, or rushed.

When he was supervising editor on *Survivor*, Ivan Ladizinsky would pick a number and then tell editors something like, "Compress it 70 percent."

They would ask, "Where?"

"Wherever you think it should be done. Do it any way you want." He would let them figure it out. "Once an editor got mad because I removed a perfectly good scene. I said, 'It's a fluff piece. It's something that doesn't have any relevance to this show other than it's nice. It's gotta go.' You want to make the episode move fast while keeping track of the story and the characters and the emotional arc."

When I asked Brad Hall and Julia Louis-Dreyfus about their philosophy of editing, Brad said, "Faster, faster, faster—"

Julia overlapped him. "Faster, faster, faster. Yes! Forget comedy. Faster, faster, faster applies to everything. Because then slowing down has enormous significance. It becomes more impactful."

"There's a thing in acting school where you learn about 'arresting,'" Brad said. "Let's say you're having a conversation, you've picked the business of drinking coffee, then suddenly you stop. The stopping has so much impact. The *arrested activity* is the whole thing. If you create motion in a scene editorially, and then hold for that beat when she's listening, all of a sudden, you've created a moment."

Julia nodded. "Think about it musically. You create a beat. And then it all stops. And then you come back in. The coming back in is fucking erotic. It's so good."

Judd Apatow offered up a contrasting opinion on faster versus length. He likes to have the time to go deeper with his characters. "With comedies people sometimes want them to be shorter. But I never think of them as comedies. I think of them as stories that are both emotional and funny. When you have a ninety-minute movie it's all plot. You can't slow down and just be with people. I've done movies running an hour forty-five to two fifteen. That's usually the range. If I'm into it, I don't care how long it is; the longer the better, because I am enjoying it so much. If it's working there's no reason to rush through it. People will sit at home and watch eight episodes in a row of a television show, yet they'll complain about a movie being eight minutes too long."

Now You Know What's Funny

Apply these principles to your analysis of a television episode or a movie and it should help your search for editorial solutions. I can't make a list, though, without a bonus list.

When I was at the 2020 Barbados Independent Film Festival—one of the most enjoyable festival locations ever—I met screenwriter-director Edward Neumeier, who co-wrote *Robocop* (1987) and wrote *Starship Troopers* (1997). Both are action films that are also comedies. Neumeier told me that one of his inspirations was filmmaker Preston Sturges, who had one of the most prolific bursts of screwball comedy filmmaking ever, writing and directing seven classics within four years: *The Great McGinty* (1940), *Christmas in July* (1940), *The Lady Eve* (1941), *Sullivan's Travels* (1941), *The Palm Beach Story* (1942), *The Miracle of Morgan's Creek* (1944), and *Hail the Conquering Hero* (1944). Sturges once offered advice for writers and filmmakers about what works best.

> *A pretty girl is better than a plain one. A leg is better than an arm. A bedroom is better than a living room. An arrival is better that a departure. A birth is better than a death. A chase is better than a chat. A dog is better than a landscape. A kitten is better than a dog. A baby is better than a kitten. A kiss is better than a baby. A pratfall is better than anything.*

> —Preston Sturges

CHAPTER TWO

Keep It Real

Comedy Needs the Sharpest Scissors

W̲hat's harder, drama or comedy? When I surveyed the showrunners, there was unanimity.

"We do drama every week—plus we're adding jokes on top of it,"
argued David Mandel. "A good story is inherently dramatic, so we're
telling a good story *and* trying to get the comedy right."

Alec Berg seconded him. "With comedy, either it works or it
doesn't. And it's obvious."

Judd Apatow agreed. "It would be easier if we didn't have to add
the jokes."

Julia Louis-Dreyfus said, "You can't fake comedy. I think you can
pull the wool over somebody's eyes with a dramatic performance in a
way that you absolutely cannot with a comedic performance."

Sacha Baron Cohen pointed out how two people can sit next to
each other in a cinema for an entire drama and afterward one says,
"I thought that was great," and the other one says, "I thought it was
terrible." But with comedy, when two people sit next to each other,
they agree whether it's funny, because there is a very clear metric:
You can hear the audience laugh or not.

Larry David was on board. "Drama only requires you to concen-
trate and listen, and perhaps be moved somewhere along the line.
Comedy writers probably could write a drama. But if you asked a
drama writer to write a comedy, I think they'd have more problems. If

you took one of these *Curb Your Enthusiasm* episodes and told every-body, 'This is a drama. Don't be funny,' you could still do the show." He laughed as he considered that idea. "I'm wondering how that would go. I'd like to try that as an experiment."

I said, "I hope you do!"

"That would be interesting, don't you think?"

Editing Drama and Comedy

While the majority of my editorial hypotheses herein apply to both drama and comedy, with comedy, if your skills aren't razor sharp, it's obvious. Hence, the need for a dissection of *comedy editing*. If some-body can edit comedy, they can probably also edit drama. But not necessarily the reverse. Typically, comedy series pay editors more than drama series, because good comedy editors are scarcer. It is a particular skill to be able to make the funniest version from a pile of footage.

The Level of Reality

What's funnier overall, broad comedy or reality-based humor? They both work, but it's about context. A funny moment is funnier when it seems like it could really happen. Good dramas season serious sto-rylines with humor. Somebody trying to be funny is not as funny as somebody trying to be serious while caught up in a crazy situation. Whether broad or serious, once you set the tone, you cannot violate the reality level or the audience will object. I often sacrifice comedy for drama, removing jokes to keep things as dramatic as possible. Then the remaining jokes play funnier. The more believable and grounded a story is, the stronger the jokes land.

Jeff Schaffer loves to push the envelope of outlandishness. I often try to cut Jeff's most over-the-top bits. But he puts back his favorites. Some of them he forgets about, and I get rid of them. But when broad works, it's brilliant. There's a scene in *The League* (season seven, episode two, "The Draft of Innocence") that is probably the most ridiculous thing I have ever edited. Rafi (Jason Mantzoukas) is in love with Margaret, who happens to be a watermelon. "My very serious girlfriend, Margaret, and I have been trying." But he's worried she might be seedless. Sadly, Taco (Jon Lajoie) "murders" Margaret, sending Rafi over the edge. This scene is way past broad, it's beyond insane, but it works. I laughed so hard at Rafi's idiocy I was gasping in the edit bay. But as crazy as the moment was, the actors played it straight.

On *Curb Your Enthusiasm*, one of the broadest things I tried to rein in was when Larry would instigate a stare down to determine if somebody was lying. This back-and-forth came with long pauses, as they eyeballed each other, drawing out the moment. I reduced the intercuts to what felt to me like a realistic back-and-forth. When Larry watched my cut, he asked me to lengthen the stare downs. I felt like this heavier emphasis violated the reality of the scene. But when we played the longer version, people laughed. It's incredibly broad. But it is indisputably funny, and ultimately funny trumps all. Sometimes you don't really know what you've got until you test it. Alec Berg recalled that with each successive take, Larry and his nemesis would ramp up faster and faster. "You have to remember when you're cutting it that these guys both know where they're headed and they can't wait to get there. So sometimes you have to rely on the earlier takes that have a bit more natural pace to it."

Despite the successful over-broad moments, I stand by my contention that the more real a scene plays the more invested the audience becomes in the characters, and the stronger the release is in the comedic beats. Remove any line if it violates the story's level of reality, or if it is untrue to the character. Anything that takes viewers out of a story will make them less engaged. You want people to forget they are watching a screen. Eliminate anything that reminds them. Referencing other movies in dialogue is a dangerous choice, to be avoided when possible, because it breaks the spell and takes viewers out of the story. Speaking directly to the audience is a technique that can kill dramatic grounding. It takes a lot of skill to successfully break the fourth wall. Musicals, with characters bursting into song, are a fourth-wall violation that can work if set up properly.

If you are going off the deep end, first help people identify with the characters by giving them things they are used to seeing before having everything go insane. The movie *Jaws* (1975) spends a lot of time allowing viewers to get to know the three main characters, Police Chief Martin Brody (Roy Scheider), Oceanographer Matt Hooper (Richard Dreyfus), and Captain Sam Quint (Robert Shaw). The tension skyrockets when Brody sees the massive shark up close for the first time. As he stumbles backward, in shock, he says to Quint in all seriousness, "You're gonna need a bigger boat." It's not meant as a wisecrack, but it gets a huge laugh because it follows such a serious moment. That may be why it's one of the most famous lines in film history.

Keep It Grounded

I once asked Sam Raimi how he directed the actors in *Evil Dead II* (1987), and he said he told them it was a serious film so they would play it totally straight. In reality, it's an outrageous comedy where everybody deadpans while a maelstrom of ghostly mayhem swirls around them. Raimi's approach made the film all the funnier. Silent-film master-comedian Buster Keaton similarly discovered the more serious he looked, the more laughs he got, so he became known for his deadpan expression.

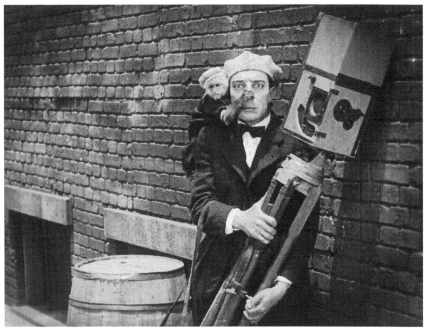

Buster Keaton and Josephine, a capuchin monkey, in *The Cameraman*.

The series *Barry* (2018–TBD) is an unusual combination of moments that are dark, sad, graphic, violent, and real, interspersed with scenes that are incredibly broad and silly. Some reviews said the combination of *The Bourne Identity* (2002) meets *La La Land* (2016), a show about an assassin who wants to act, shouldn't work, yet it does.[1] Why does this combination work? According to Alec Berg, "It's because there is a huge amount of experimentation and tweaking that goes into every moment. 'Can it be broad here? What if we were broader? Nope, that's too broad. Pull it back.' We didn't just guess. An enormous amount of trial and error went into it."

David Mandel believes broad jokes have their place, but he favors a more realistic tone, pseudo real life. When doing a broad joke, he prefers to slip it past the viewer, by throwing it away matter-of-factly. "When I think of what going broad typically means, I think of a joke getting tremendously emphasized. I'd rather have less underlining. If the viewer misses it, let them come back. A lot of what we did on *Veep* is flying so fast and furious that great jokes are often playing in the background, or as asides, in these little holes that we find for them."

Jokes about Jokes

David Mandel loves commenting on the comedy form itself. A lot of his bits are jokes *about* jokes. Alec Berg recalled an unproduced script called *Aftermath* that he, Jeff Schaffer, and David Mandel wrote, where David came up with a guy who was trying to break into an office to rig an elevator to do something ridiculous. But the security guard says, "I'm sorry, I can't let you in."

David's character responds, "I'm from the elevator repair company."

"If you're an elevator repairman, where's your credential?"

And the guy goes, "Oh."

And then David wrote a long, crazy montage of the guy going to elevator-repair school for six months. And then he comes back and shows his new credential to the security guard, who doesn't care about seeing it and waves him through, saying, "Whatever. Go ahead. Keep it movin'."

Not yet finished with examples of jokes about jokes, Alec offered another favorite:

> A guy is sitting at a bar and he has a stop sign for a face. Another guy sitting at the bar notices and says, "Listen, I'm sorry to bother you, but I have to ask something. You have a stop sign for a face. What happened?" The guy replies, "Well, it's an interesting story. I was walking on this beach and I stepped on something. I looked down and it was a brass lamp. I polished it and this genie came out and said, 'I'm a genie and I'll grant you three wishes.' I said, 'Wow, this is amazing.' And with my first wish, I wished for eternal health. All of

a sudden, my back problems cleared up and my sciatica went away. My teeth were straight. I had my cholesterol tested and it was fantastic. And then with my second wish, I wished for infinite financial resources. Suddenly my bank account was full. Every time I spend a dime, it fills up again. I'm never gonna run out of money for the rest of my life. And with the third wish—and here's where I think I went wrong: I wished that I had a stop sign for a face."

I laughed as Alec went on. "If you tell that joke to people who write jokes for a living, they laugh. They think about the construction of jokes. If you tell that joke to somebody who doesn't think about jokes, they go, 'That's not a joke.' But it is; it's a joke about jokes." In hindsight, I'm glad I found that joke funny.

Reality

With documentaries and reality shows, producers rely on editors to find or create a believable story from tons of raw material, often from a shooting ratio as high as three hundred to one. On the first season of *Survivor*, episode one went through roughly twenty versions during approval. As the show started to progress into episodes two, three, and beyond, the network started to panic over the series arc, instinctually wanting to find a more familiar dramatic form. As a result, CBS insisted that executive producer Mark Burnett bring on a CBS-approved scripted-series editor to "fix" the show.

The big-credits veteran came over and dug into the footage. But he became increasing frustrated by the volume of material. According to editor Sean Foley, when the veteran was watching one of Sean's transitions, he asked, "Who creates those? Who finds the B-roll? Who chooses the music?"

Sean explained, "We do. You've got to dig through the footage and pull selects yourself. The same goes for score. There's no music editor—we cut everything." The big-time guy gave up two weeks later. These early-days reality editors had no script, no director, and a mountain of footage, all of which increased the level of difficulty. Field producers brought notes from the location and helped dig through interviews, but the biggest challenge for the editors was finding the right footage to tell the story.

Whenever editor Ivan Ladizinsky got what he thought were silly notes, Ivan said it reminded him of a scene in *Amadeus* (1984): After the premiere of Wolfgang Amadeus Mozart's first opera in Vienna, Emperor Joseph II is in attendance and says, "My dear young man, don't take it too hard. Your work is ingenious. It's quality work. And there are simply too many notes, that's all. Just cut a few and it will be perfect."

Mozart replies, "Which few did you have in mind, Majesty?"

Experienced producers know you can't micromanage a good editor. The *Survivor* filming process is managed by the field producers. They create a six-act outline of a well-conceived game with rules. Each episode has two challenges: one for reward and one for immunity. And then stories are built after the events took place. Sean Foley described how editors typically reverse-engineered scenes to illustrate the need for reward (food, comfort, etc.) and the need for immunity (vulnerable cast, alliances, etc.). Then the final structural piece—the Tribal Council—pays off the episode's story arc by sending someone home. To prepare for the Tribal Councils, Jeff Probst worked daily with the producers to outline the key themes that emerged, to come up with his questions for that segment.

To find the beginning of a structure, the producers would put note cards on the wall with a short description of a scene. A producer might only recount that, "two characters on the beach got in a fight," or, "someone fell in a fire," or in one case there was an unexpected storm that destroyed the camp—there was no way to script that story in advance. Ivan Ladizinsky's approach was to watch everything and fill a notepad with ideas for story possibilities. He identified the heavy interactions and the beautiful moments, plus made notes on characters, funny dialogue, and great camerawork. Reviewing all the footage took him two weeks. First, he crossed out what was not going to make it into the show. Then Ivan began "writing the script" by editing down the footage. He said, "I preferred using fewer confessional interviews, to try to make it more real. I looked for a three-act structure. The secret to really good reality cutting is organization, because there's so much to watch—so you know how to find things."

The toughest challenge was when producers wanted to tell a story that didn't get shot. Ivan still had to try to create that. "The producers might say, 'These two guys got in a fight.' You might look at the footage and find they're not fighting. They're having a slight discussion. It's barely an argument. The production team is shooting guerrilla style, so they don't really know what they have until you evaluate it in the editing room."

If Ivan decided he wanted a reaction shot but there was only one camera and they didn't get it, he scoured the footage from other mornings with the same light to find the person he needed. The best camera operators understand editing. They act like three cameras in one, picking up coverage and inserts. Ivan liked to call the editors "post-production directors" because they chose the footage, constructed the story, created the tone, scored the show from the music library (unless they commissioned something from a composer), and supervised the on-line edits and the sound mix. Ivan said, "It was a lot of fun. It was total freedom. I felt like I was directing the show." Times have changed since the early days, with producers now exercising more control.

Each editor on *Survivor* brings their own storytelling sensibilities. Ivan's goal was to try to create a cinematic style for the episodes, inviting the audience to "experience" the show, more like a movie, not just present a recitation of events that took place. That approach required a knowledge of cinema history, which came from Ivan's love of movies by filmmakers such as John Cassavetes, Bob Fosse, and Sidney Lumet.

An editor has to have a passion for editing to put in the effort it takes. By year thirteen on *Survivor*, Ivan was starting to wonder how to avoid copying himself. "I would try to break the format. But as time went on, the format screws got tighter. When somebody from the tape library becomes a producer and all of a sudden says, 'This is how we do it,' I didn't want to hear it because I was one of the people who had created how it was done. I had had enough and they had enough." That's when Ivan moved on to other work, to keep his palate fresh.

When *Survivor* began, nothing was staged. "I don't think pure reality exists as much anymore," Ivan said. "To attempt to create more story, some shows stage incidents." Later when Ivan worked on other reality shows, he found them to be more manipulated. "Producers would respond to what people were doing and inter-ject, which is a mistake. If the participants have any kind of organic energy and someone goes, 'Wait a minute, don't you think you should talk about this and that?' Now you've killed any kind of realism that could have happened."

Test Screening

How do you know if your cut is actually funny? Ivan Ladizinsky said he never listens to one person's opinion. "But if *three* people tell me something's wrong, they're always right." Julian Doyle tests everything because first cuts are always too long. He recalled difficult screenings, when he was invited to other filmmakers' viewings, where all he said was, "Yeah, it's great, very good," because he thought, "There's noth-ing I can say that's going to save this film."

Steven Rasch finds test screenings essential for comedy. "Even though you think you know where the laughs are, I've been doing this for thirty years and it's always a surprise when you bring people in the room and hit play." You might intellectually know something is funny, you feel it might be funny, but you don't really know how it will play until you're in a room experiencing it with an audience. Then it becomes clear where you were wrong about some things and right about others.

Krista Vernoff multitasks by using the music-spotting session as a test screening. She gathers the composer's team, the editing team, and assistants. "It's the one time in the process that I can watch the episode with people who weren't on set, haven't seen the dailies, and haven't read the script. If they don't laugh and cry in the right places, I can rework the edit."

Feature film schedules allow more time to tinker. Mike Binder repeatedly tests all his films. Studios insist on testing. They want to know as soon as possible what they've got, to figure out how to market it. Films get numerical scores, based on an average of how the entire audience scored it. "Getting your numbers up" is a goal on studio films; they love scores in the nineties, the higher the better.

Despite all the pressure from testing data, Judd Apatow tries to maintain his comedy core. "At one of my screenings, a famous, well-respected filmmaker gave me helpful notes," said Judd, "but I realized if I took all of them, the film would feel exactly like the kind of movies they make. The notes exemplified *their* approach. The dangerous part of taking notes is, what if you're influenced by the wrong one?"

Judd Apatow's test-screening process begins with a three-hour, first-assembly test for forty or fifty people. And then Judd and his team trim it down to a two-and-a-half-hour version to screen for a group of a hundred friends and family. After making further trims, they have the first showing for the studio at two hours, fifteen minutes. And then they will do three to four test screenings with four hundred people, which provides favorability numbers and feedback from focus groups. They ask the audience: "Did you find it poor, good, very good, or excellent?" The main question is, "How many people thought the movie was very good or excellent?" A score of fifty means 50 percent thought it was very good or excellent. Judd is pleased when his type of comedy scores in the eighties. Every once in a while, a big crowd pleaser such as *Bridesmaids* (2011) gets a ninety. But Judd worries when it's too high. "It's just as bad to be at ninety-eight as it is to be at fifty. If you're pleasing everyone at the highest possible level, if no one has an issue with it, you may have accidentally made garbage." He is aiming for a sweet spot. Somebody has to hate it somewhere for it to be working.

Test screenings are not for finding solutions. The audience cannot tell you how to fix your film. What they can do is show you where the problems are, where it is not working. And then *you* have to fix it. The best data comes *during* the screening and in the first five minutes of a discussion afterward when initial reactions are expressed. After that, as viewers begin offering suggestions for what to change and fix, it becomes less useful. A filmmaker's inclination is to stand up after a screening and debate the audience, to defend creative choices. That's a waste of time. The only suitable course of action is to listen politely, thank them, and send them on their way. Ask specific questions about the weaknesses you suspect your film to have. Where their criticisms are in sync with your doubts, work on fixing those problems. If you disagree with their criticisms, go with your gut and stand firm. The film is your vision, not anybody else's.

Describing Larry David's testing process will be quick, because it's minimal. He screens each episode of *Curb Your Enthusiasm* for a small audience of seven or eight people. The most helpful aspect is to identify any plot points that an audience is missing. He and Jeff Schaffer gather a list of questions about various story points to see if they were made strongly enough. Larry may ask, "Did you understand why I went into the other room and came out with the cake?" But mostly Larry and Jeff simply feel the room while the episode is playing. The energy from the audience makes it painfully clear when jokes are falling flat, where the story drags, or when something they thought was insignificant is a big laugh.

Larry David doesn't care what a test audience *says* is funny or not funny. "I never ask them if they like this line or that line, because we already know we like the line. It's more about getting a sense of the pacing. But if there's something I am unsure about and it doesn't get any laughs, then I'll get rid of it." I asked Larry how much he trusts his instincts when he feels the energy of the room. He said, "I'm an extremely indecisive person in my own life. You could put a menu in front of me for lunch and I'm flummoxed. I don't know what to do. And that's throughout everything in my life. Any decisions you give me I can't make. But here in this room I am extremely decisive. I feel like I know what I'm doing. Outside of this room I'm lost."

On the four seasons of *Curb Your Enthusiasm* when Alec Berg, David Mandel, and Jeff Schaffer were all on board, there were often debates about jokes in the editing room. Larry is the final arbiter, but if all three guys were on the same page, it was a three-to-one tie. Then it's up to the test audience. In "The N Word" (season six, episode eight), when Larry was dating a woman who was a doctor, who acted very clinical even outside of work, the guys put a medical scale visible in the background in her home as a sight gag. Larry objected, saying, "What is the scale doing here? I don't like this." The guys petitioned on behalf of the scale, begging, "Trust us, it'll be fine." Larry is willing to try anything, so they did some takes with it in and some with it out; they could have cut around it and done it either way. They persuaded Larry to keep it in for the test screening, and two people actually pointed to the scale, exclaiming, "Ha ha, there's a scale!" They all looked at Larry, who shook his head, accepting the outcome. Jeff said, "I remember feeling like, 'We won. We won.'"

Larry David waits for his date, medical scale in the background, in *Curb Your Enthusiasm*.

In the episode "Insufficient Praise" (season ten, episode five), there's a moment when the maid bends down to clean a blow-up doll that Larry is holding. The cleaning gag was a very broad joke and Larry wanted it out, and I agreed. Jeff liked the joke and lobbied on its behalf. "Let's just screen it and see what the audience does." Well, the audience laughed, so the gag stayed in.

But Larry is wise to that tactic now. He will counter with, "Yeah, we'll screen it and it'll get a laugh, but it still shouldn't be in the show." Or his new counter is, "But it's not the *right* laugh."

Jeff persists. "Well, let's see how you feel when you actually hear the laugh." But with that game no longer working reliably, Jeff's strategies have had to grow more sophisticated. In the episode "Happy New Year" (season ten, episode one), there is a montage of Larry wearing a MAGA hat to discourage people from bothering him. The last bit was a confrontation with a biker screaming, "What are you doing, ya little fucker?!" Larry puts on the MAGA hat and the biker changes his tune, now being more genial. "Oh. Just be more careful next time, okay?" As the guy drives off, Jeff Schaffer persuaded Larry to shout, "Build that wall!" Larry didn't want to do it, but Jeff got him to try it in one take.

During editing, Larry took it out, but Jeff kept putting it in. It made it through the test screening and got a medium-size laugh but nothing special. After the screening, it was decision time.

Larry was firm. "I want to lose that line."

Jeff was thinking to himself, "There's another fight coming down the pike for a much bigger joke I like." So, Jeff's strategy was to put his foot down and defend the wall line: "It doesn't hurt anything, it only helps. I don't understand taking it out when it's a nice punctuation to the run."

Larry responded, "It seems like we're already doing this joke."

"It's just one more thing, why not have it?"

Finally, Larry acquiesced. "All right, I see you really want this one. We'll do it."

Twenty minutes later into the show there's a moment where Cheryl goes down on Larry, and she has an allergic reaction to the talcum powder on Larry's groin. Cut to: The doors of the hospital burst open and a paramedic asks, "What happened?"

Larry says, "She had an allergic reaction to talcum powder."

The paramedic asks, "Did she ingest anything else?"

"Well, that's personal." And then Cheryl is wheeled past and Larry goes, "Sorry, sorry!"

Larry wanted to cut, "Well, that's personal." He argued, "It's beneath us, I don't want to keep it."

Jeff said, "Without it, the moment is empty."

Larry looked intractable. "I can't keep this. It drives me crazy. I don't like it."

Jeff continued to push. "This line is why we're doing the story. If we take it out, this part of the scene is dead, it's flat. There's nothing to replace it." So now Jeff had also put his foot down.

Larry sensed an opportunity; now he had Jeff in a trap, and he said, "Well, you can have one or the other."

Jeff considered and then solemnly and "reluctantly" made his choice. "I want this one."

"Build the wall" went away. Jeff gave in so he could get the one he really wanted. He knows he has to be a master tactician in the editing room; he'll do anything it takes to get the jokes he truly wants. After relating this story to me, Jeff added for the future Larry reading this, "By the way, Larry, I'm sorry. I'm so sorry."

The future Larry read it, laughed, and said, "That won't happen again. Not this season." Great comedy sometimes comes out of a never-ending arms race.

Getting Ahead of the Audience

A big part of the test screening is to test the efficacy of joke setups. A setup is an explanation of a premise. When you do a good job of making a setup clear before a comedy beat, a viewer does not have to think while the funny stuff happens. The problem with setups that are verbose or clumsy is that the intellectual part of the brain will over-ride the humor side if it is trying to put the pieces together, struggling to catch up, too far behind the storyline. If the setup is laid on too thick, if viewers are too far ahead of the story, it will eliminate the surprise as they predict what is going to happen next and get bored. You want the audience fully caught up, just a beat behind, and not ahead of the story. It's a delicate balance.

An opening scene in *Curb Your Enthusiasm* might have people talking, seemingly randomly, but within that first conversation they're carefully laying down five clues. Viewers are following three storylines they have no reason to believe will intersect. But when they do it's funny. Larry wants to trigger the audience at the ideal moment. He disguises the evidence enough so that the premise is clear, but the outcome is still a surprise at the end.

Steven Rasch has spent years studying how Larry structures episodes. "Most of us have to screen it with three different audiences and recut it to get that timing right. Larry can do it on the first pass. That's his brilliance. A lot of comedy relies on put-down comedy, people berating each other, being mean. We have that in *Curb Your Enthusiasm*. But the structure is more important. We will cut all the jokes if we have to, in order to keep the structure. It's because the structure is funny. The insults are ornamentation on existing funny situations."

Jokes are expendable, but story points are not. David Mandel witnessed this protocol on *Seinfeld*. "Decent jokes went out the window in the name of getting the cut shorter, so that you can keep the fact that Jerry has to tell Elaine, 'I'll pick you up at nine.' If you somehow try and get rid of, 'I'll pick you up at nine,' the whole story falls apart."

The Fresh-Joke Fallacy

David Mandel never does test screenings. When I asked him why, he replied, "I'm the test. I don't want to hear that they don't like a joke. I don't fucking care. If I like a joke, I like a joke." David Mandel rarely changes his mind after making a choice. However, there was one person who had to agree with David's choices on *Veep*: Julia Louis-Dreyfus. Luckily, she and David were pretty much always on the same page. She said, "Sometimes it takes a minute because you want to see various alternatives. But once I arrive at a decision, I'm pretty sanguine about it. I'm not a hand-wringer. The key goes in, the lock turns, you feel it. That's what it's like."

David Mandel did admit he has five friends from high school who he feels like he's writing for. He always checks in with them to see if they laughed at an episode. At home he will screen episodes for his wife, Becky. "I like to watch her and see if she is getting confused anywhere. It's more about length. When we get to that thirty-five-minute mark, I'm not really even looking at the screen. I'm taking note of what Becky's laughing at, and where is she checking out? Is she getting tired? And I go, 'Oh, god, there's still another four minutes of show.'"

If a producer considers cutting a joke that I think is one of the funniest in an episode, I will warn of the comedy error we are about to make. But that's as far as I will go in defending a joke. You can't get precious about anything. David Mandel is well aware of the fresh-joke fallacy, so he does take my warnings seriously. Sometimes an inferior joke seems better when we go through the footage because we have become desensitized to the first choice. You have to remember your first impression, long after the effect has worn off.

The way Jon Corn screens dailies is to rate the moments that make him laugh. Four stars (the best; must use it) to one star (not the best but still funny; might be useful in some iteration of the scene). It provides him with a record of what made him laugh right out of the gate. This method came in handy when Jon and Larry David were cutting the Seder scene in "The Survivor" (season four, episode nine). "We worked on that scene more than any other in the series, and after four days we thought, 'Is this still funny?' I was able to dig into my notes and supply a list of what made me laugh instinctually and see if it made the cut. Not something to use as a rule, but helpful when one is in the weeds."

Julian Doyle will also defend jokes he believes in. In *Monty Python and the Holy Grail*, the scene where the Black Knight's arms and legs are hacked off was cut out of the film by the producer, who said, "It's too bloody. It's killing the comedy." Even though the scene was out, Julian kept putting it back, until it finally stayed in. As it's arguably the most memorable scene in the entire film, it's hard to believe it almost didn't survive the editing process.

King Arthur facing a disarmed Black Knight in *Monty Python and the Holy Grail*.

Alec Berg feels that test screenings can be helpful, but they are a luxury there often isn't time for, so you have to train yourself to use your best judgment. "What's fascinating about showing a cut to people who have not seen it is that it doesn't even matter what their reaction is. You can watch your work ten times and feel it's perfect, but then watching *with* somebody forces you to see it in a more critical way. Similarly, with writing, even when the script is done, it's still not done. The process of getting it ready to shoot teaches you about what's working or not working. There are things you can't write until you are shooting it or preparing to shoot it, and then answers become clearer."

Alec also acknowledged that he can miss important things that don't become apparent until he is watching the show with five or six people who've never seen it. For example, in the *Barry* episode "Know Your Truth" (season one, episode eight), there's a shot where Barry (Bill Hader) is walking through the woods while Detective Moss (Paula Newsome) has a gun on him. A camera pulls back to reveal a gun hanging on a tree that Barry has stashed there. The problem that emerged was that both the gun and the tree were the same color. "One of our sound mixers said, 'I didn't even notice the gun until you pointed it out.' That was a problem. So, it's always good to get fresh eyes on your work, because we had to digitally change the color of the gun to chrome."

Scientific Comedy Testing

Sacha Baron Cohen is especially sensitive to the winnowing process once he gets in the editing room. While he is shooting, he is not certain which ideas are going to work. Part of Sacha's process on *Who Is America?* (2018) or *Borat: Cultural Learnings of America for Make Benefit Glorious Nation of Kazakhstan* (2006) was to overshoot. Sacha's method for evaluating his comedy is to screen, re-screen, test, get opinions, get more opinions, and tweak until he's out of time. Sacha wants to be as certain as possible that his choices are absolutely the funniest possible. "In my comedy, I want the audience to laugh as often and as hard as they can. But we also need the story to work, otherwise, the audience is going to get bored after they've stopped laughing. We need the audience to care about the characters and what they're trying to achieve. So, we hire two types of editors: editors who are great on story and editors who are specialists at making that scene as funny as possible."

During shooting we rarely see Sacha, because he is on location. But when he comes in to edit, it's all him toward the end. He prefers to do his first viewing of an editor's cut alone and make notes. In the final stretch, everybody gets involved, Sacha, the directors, the writers, the producers, all trying to find the funniest version. Sacha's preference is to let takes play out, so the audience can see the natural awkwardness when real people are presented with insane moments. Multiple test screenings are scheduled, first with family and friends, then with recruited audiences in Los Angeles and London, or in Germany, or in Sydney.

Sacha scribbles notes and ideas in his ever-present notebook. He is like a joke scientist, studying the testing data: "One of the reasons I record the laughter is I and the writers and the producer-director will fight for certain jokes. They remember the audience reaction through their own lens. They'll say 'That joke killed.' Then we pull out the [recording of the] joke and we find out, actually it hadn't gotten a smattering of laughter."

When I asked Sacha how he formulated this approach, he credited the Marx Brothers, who would take their show on the road and have somebody sit in the back row and mark which jokes worked and which didn't. By the time they finished the tour, the show was entirely killer jokes. And then they would film it.

Editing Improvised Scenes

When Sacha is filming undercover, there's no director who can shout, "Cut!" Or, "Let's do that again." So, he is trying to make sure he's getting enough pieces while shooting. Psychologically, Sacha starts with his subjects at a "normal" level of reality and escalates things to an absurd level, gradually moving the line as their interactions progress. Sacha keeps pushing things further and further, to see how far people will go. "They are essentially playing the straight man," said Sacha, "and I am the fish out of water." He often has a clipboard and marks when he feels he laid out the setup and got a funny response from the subject when they respond seriously. Then he looks for a killer line from himself plus another funny response as an escalation, and then another comeback. Also, he's fishing for funny looks to cut in as reactions. "Then internally, if I'm aware that we have enough for the edit, I move on to the next bit."

When things reach a point where Sacha gets a sense that people cannot be pushed any more, he backs off. But then he slowly builds things back up and again pushes the line further. Occasionally somebody figures out what is going on and gets angry. To get to a point where subjects are compliant, Sacha first spends an hour or two with them, getting them used to following commands. For example, Sacha's Erran Morad character in *Who Is America?* teaches self-defense. In the "Quinceanera" segment (episode three), Erran first spent an hour demonstrating actual self-defense techniques. "I try to make my character real and believable enough so that the person in the room will trust me. To do that I create a comprehensive backstory and a full knowledge of everything I've done that day, and that week. So the person can ask me any question and I'll be able to answer without pause." As the session progresses, Sacha makes more and more absurd requests, until a Georgia State congressman arrives at a point, where in that moment, he believes pulling his pants down and chasing Sacha with his ass out while screaming "USA!" is normal (episode two).

Author's collection.

Sacha Baron Cohen as Erran Morad, demonstrating defense training, from *Who Is America?*

It is not my job as the editor to make a value judgment on the people or the sketches. My goal is to find the funniest version of the footage. Sacha never forced any of his marks to do anything. It's uncanny how Sacha can get people to do such wild things, but if you put people in a room with somebody who presents as an authority figure, human nature is such that they fall in line. Sacha Baron Cohen understands human nature. He is giving us a comedy demonstration of the obedience principle. As funny as his comedy is, it is also a teaching moment. We should question what we are told. We should ask for evidence. There is an important lesson underneath the comedy.

Sacha's test-screening process is about finding the comedy sweet spots, and it is vastly different from the kind of testing a film studio does, where they are trying to get the overall favorables up as high as possible. One problem with the pursuit of ever higher numbers is that it leads to cutting out anything audiences respond negatively toward. It runs the risk of being forgettable. It is often those "objectionable" moments that we most remember and tell our friends about. Could you imagine *Curb Your Enthusiasm* without awkward moments? David Mandel's indictment of studio testing is harsh. "All group think does is round out sharp edges and so everything gets duller and duller as you smooth it down to a pointless nub. And the beautiful thing about a sharp edge is, yeah you can get hurt. It's viciously sharp. That's what's great about it."

CHAPTER THREE

The Editor's Philosophy

*You Can Be an Editor of Films, but It's Better
to Be a Filmmaker Who Edits*

*F**ind the funny.* That has become my mantra. As a filmmaker and
editor, my job is to find the best version of a scene, episode, or feature
film. Sometimes it comes from a sense of timing. Sometimes it means
trusting my instinct. Sometimes it's about knowing when to cut to
the monkey. What darn monkey? Where is this monkey?

Cut to the Monkey

Not every scene has a failsafe cutaway, like a reaction shot, a television, a computer screen, a cell phone, a clock, a burning fuse, the
dark crystal, or something to save you when you're stuck. One way
of ensuring you don't get boxed in is to have a reliable option to
cut to at any time. Like a monkey! Because any time you look at a
monkey, they are *always* doing something interesting. Or the monkey equivalent: dogs, cats, babies, aliens, or any wild animal will do.
I'm not the first to notice this principle. In *Anchorman: The Legend
of Ron Burgundy* (2004), there is a scene where Veronica Corning-
stone (Christina Applegate) falls into a bear pit. The DreamWorks
Pictures executives didn't get it. Judd Apatow recalled how director
Adam McKay had to meet to try to convince them. He talked about

the history of bears in comedy and why people find bears funny. They didn't understand what he was talking about but eventually relented because he was so passionate.

I asked Judd why animals are funny and his explanation was: "A wild animal, bear, monkey, or even a baby, they're not going to follow society's rules and do what you expect. So, at any moment, something unexpected could happen. It's an uncontrollable element. Adam McKay loves to throw a wild animal into things. In *Talladega Nights: The Ballad of Ricky Bobby* (2006), Will and Adam have to deal with an out-of-control cougar in the car. There's no denying an unpredictable, potentially dangerous animal is usually funny. It raises the stakes."

Grady Cooper directed a music video of the Squirrel Nut Zippers' song "The Suits Are Picking up the Bill." There was a capuchin monkey in the video that stole the show. "It was hilarious every time we cut to him," said Grady. "Monkeys are funny because their expressions are constantly changing. And yet they look surprised all the time. In general, we are all monkeys. We just try to hide it."

I talked with Sacha Baron Cohen for this book while he was in the middle of working on *Borat Subsequent Moviefilm: Delivery of Prodigious Bribe to American Regime for Make Benefit Once Glorious Nation of Kazakhstan* (2020). I had worked on the film for three weeks at the start, during a window between my *Curb Your Enthusiasm* and *The Comedy Store* schedules. Sacha said, "I hope you're right [about the monkey]. Because I'm working in a monkey joke at the moment."

Ivan Ladizinsky is also a cut-to-the-monkey adherent, describing it this way: "Monkeys are like silly, mischievous little children. If you don't know monkeys are funny, you should just go work at a bank." Finding the comedy is a big part of editing reality shows. The *Survivor* editors were like-minded about monkeys; the monkey cutaway became their favorite motif. Whenever they didn't have a good reaction, or when one of the contestants asked a dumb question or did something goofy, finding footage of a monkey with a quizzical look to cut to paid off.

Ivan gave another erudite example of this principle. "Two [*Survivor*] contestants in season three are walking through Africa and someone looks to the side. What is this person looking at? We don't know. It's nothing. But I cut to footage of an antelope taking a dump. Person looks—animal poops—person looks back—they keep walking. No one says anything about it."

Ivan's executive producer saw the editor's cut and complained, "That is disgusting. I don't like that. It has to go."

Ivan responded, "Yes, it's poo-poo humor. It's cheap toilet humor. But it's funny. The kids are gonna laugh." It was a fight, but, ultimately, they left it in.

The morning after the episode aired, the executive producer came back all charged up about the antelope poo scene. "A friend of mine from Illinois called and said that was *really* disgusting. We didn't need to see that. Why did we do that?"

Another editor, Jim Smith, overheard them and commented, "My two little girls fell off the couch laughing their asses off. They thought it was the funniest thing they had ever seen!"

Ivan wrapped up his case. "It was for them. It wasn't for your thirty-three-year-old friend in Illinois." Not everyone laughs at poo-poo humor. But Ivan knew who did.

The Most Important Person

Who are the most important persons on a feature film or television series? The studio or the network will say it's the stars. And they are right. At least, with respect to marketing. But I believe the three persons most important to the creative success of a project are:

1. **The writer**. Everything flows from the screenplay. There is nothing without a script. Writers are enormously underappreciated.
2. **The director (on a film) or the showrunner (on a television series)**. This person is in charge of all the creative decisions in every department.
3. **The editor**. Let's talk about why.

Sacha Baron Cohen calls editing "the most precise craft that affects the success or failure of your jokes."

Larry David revealed, "When I think about doing another season of *Curb Your Enthusiasm*, it's not the writing that's daunting, it's the editing."

David Mandel echoed Larry's sentiment. "The writing process is so horrible and shooting is so horrible and it seems like editing should now be the vacation. But the hard work is just beginning. It's like our job is bending metal, it's really hard to do, but we keep trying to do it."

Choosing badly in any of these three positions, writer, director/showrunner, or editor, can result in disaster for the project. Of these three, the editor is the most overlooked. Some producers view editors as interchangeable, often waiting until the last minute: "Get who's available!" However, the editor should be chosen with as much care as a writer. Nobody says, "Get whichever writer happens to be available." One reason editors are crucial is because they are also writers on a project—as a rewriter of the material. You can judge a screenwriter by the quality of sample scripts; does the story make you feel something? But how do you evaluate an editor? When you go to a car mechanic, you assume they're all good. But there are great mechanics and terrible ones. How do you know which is which? You look at their reviews. But editors aren't listed on Yelp.

When I asked Julia Louis-Dreyfus how she knows who to hire, she said, "Word of mouth, baby." Check references. In a meeting, if somebody asks me if I'm good, I say, "Call anybody I've worked with and ask them who's the best editor they've ever worked with." When I suggest that they laugh. And sometimes they call. Who an editor has worked with is more important than a reel.

Is there a way to determine a great editor by looking at the work? I would argue it is easier to evaluate a cinematographer's work. Are the images pretty and in focus? Yes or no? Did the editor pick the right takes? That's harder to answer, until you examine and compare all the choices, all the infinite possible combinations. So, what ways are there to evaluate the elusive art of editing? Read on. If you haven't gotten it by the end, hit me up for a refund.

The Editor Is a Truth Teller

Here's the first sign of a good editor: The editor must tell a producer or director the truth. Everybody else may be dancing around it throughout production. But editing is where reality is faced. When Julian Doyle would run a film for studio buyers, the executives would be trying to guess who the audience is for it. "Oh, Sean Connery's in it, but he's only in it for a little while." Instead, they should be watching and asking, "Do I enjoy it?" One of Julian's favorite moments in Orson Welles's *Citizen Kane* (1941) is when the camera lifts up past Kane's second wife (played by Dorothy Comingore) as she is singing, up and up to see two stagehands in the rafters. One turns to the other and holds his nose, indicating "she's rubbish."

The editor is the one who has to tell the directors what they really have, so together they can fix it. Producers hire me not because I know how to use an Avid keyboard, they hire me because I provide solutions. There are basic philosophies that underlie every choice editors make.

Hide the Edits

Steven Rasch's basic philosophy is hide the edits. "In a scripted world, you want to draw people in. Not chase them away. We're here to hide the flaws. You hide the man behind the curtain, unless you want to push the viewer's head back a little, like in an action sequence, or with a shocking cut, or some sort of jump cut, or when editing a montage." Edits disappear from the viewer's perception when cutting follows a natural flow of events. A cut at the wrong time calls attention to itself and interrupts the flow.

The Footage Tells You What to Do

Ivan Ladizinsky said his most basic rule is: The footage tells you what to do. The script was a goal. The footage is the reality. Once you are editing, the hopes and dreams of the writer and director are in the rearview mirror. In many cases, the cut mirrors the script exactly. But in others, the best version of the footage may only vaguely resemble the original goal.

Get Out of the Way

Another editorial principle is similar to the physician's Hippocratic Oath, *primum non nocere*, "first, do no harm." If it's funny, get out of the way.

I have sometimes hastily or accidentally thrown together an editorial moment that worked great. Then it got less funny the more I tried to improve it. You are tempted to think, "It can't be this easy." But sometimes it is. Your first instinct always knows how funny something is.

Alec Berg said that in the writer's room there is something called "first blurt." Somebody will pitch a joke, everybody laughs, and then they spend twenty minutes trying to improve it. But when it gets worse, or flatter, or if it's all lateral movement, somebody will finally say, "first blurt." There is something about the first version of some things that is pure and doesn't need to be changed or overthought.

The 80 Percent Objective

Good editing is primarily about choosing the right takes. Two different editors with the same footage will arrive at two different outcomes. I've found that a successful editor needs to hit an 80 percent or better success rate in picking the best takes. If producers have to change more than 20 percent of the takes, they get frustrated. A showrunner, producer, or director doesn't want to sit in the edit bay any longer than they have to. They have other things to do. Larry David expects an editor to have a similar sense of humor, to be able to at least get the cut into the right neighborhood: "I'm expecting the editor to be compatible, to share my sensibilities to some degree, choose the funniest takes, and give me a cut the way that I would want it put together."

I'm the hero when I make Larry David laugh and get him out of the editing room early and onto the golf course. If your sense of humor is similar to the creative voice behind a project, you will like the same jokes and more often than not choose the right takes. This is why editors often gravitate toward the kinds of shows they themselves enjoy. Jeff Schaffer finds an editor's comedic sensibility crucial. "If you don't know what you're looking for, you're not going to find it. If they make choices that are non-comedic, I wonder, 'Why is that in here?'" Jeff said he's watched a cut and asked the editor, "Where's all the other stuff we shot?"

"Oh, I didn't use any of that."

"Why? That's the funny stuff!" Jeff said editors who can actively select the best funny things are rare in editing.

When I was editing Mike Binder's HBO series *The Mind of the Married Man* (2001–2002), they hired a third editor from a successful sitcom to help with an accelerated post-production schedule. When he turned in his editor's cut, Mike was despondent, fearing this episode would have to be reshot. Mike had already reshot most of a prior episode because Mike was not happy with his script. With a second episode facing a reshoot, I asked Mike to let me take a crack at recutting the existing footage before they reshot it. I reedited all the scenes from scratch and then showed this cut to Mike. He exhaled, relieved, and said, "Oh, it's fine." For some reason, my sensibility was more in line with what Mike wanted for that show, and it came through in my choices. The third editor's chair was removed and we finished the season as we began, with the two original editors.

Editors Edit Like Their Personalities

Editors have different styles, attitudes, opinions, and approaches. Editors are people, not machines; we don't just push buttons, we bring a lifetime of emotions and thoughts and experiences to every edit. Just like writers and stand-up comedians have different voices, an editor's stamp will go on a show, but it's harder to define what that is. Showrunners get a sense of whose shows come together better and whose take more work. If you want a wild, outrageous, edgier, comedy editing style, you might try looking for an editor whose personality embodies those attitudes. If you want a more somber, brooding, laidback editing style, you might consider an editor who treads pensively and contemplates life's deepest meanings. Maybe you'll find one person who exemplifies both approaches. But what is crucial for comedy is that editors laugh in the right places. It also helps to smell nice and be a pleasant person to be around a lot.

"An editor is somebody that you have to spend an enormous amount of time with," Alec Berg said. "Comedy writing is the same. A lot of what you get hired for is: Do I want to spend hours and hours with this person?"

I asked, "If an editor gets comedy, will you overlook his bad choice in shoes?"

Alec nodded sagely. "Yes."

According to Steven Rasch, "Who you are is all important, because if you don't finesse the director, producers, or writers who come into your edit bay, you won't be able to survive. Plus, the back of your head has to look good, because that's all they see."

In Praise of the Introvert

Most of us are an ambivert to some extent, sometimes needing to be alone and other times needing to interact socially. But extroverts do not fare well alone in a room for long hours, for weeks at a time. Introverts excel at focusing.

Julian Doyle loves editing "because it presents you with an enjoyable puzzle so that you can forget about your impending doom." While on a project, Julian will find his brain embracing his inner introvert even when in public. "I may be at the bar and I'm having a drink and people are talking and I become absentminded and not quite listening to what they're saying because my brain is working out these problems in the background." He gets addicted to the problem-solving process, and when a long feature project is finally over, he experiences withdrawal. His solution to having lost his daily purpose is, "As soon as the film finishes, I go on holiday so that I know what I'm supposed to be doing: I'm supposed to be on holiday."

Jon Corn said he loves that there are moments of complete autonomy. "You are in your room, on your own, picking your next edit point. Anguishing over each cut. But right when I'm getting tired of that, it becomes collaborative."

Ivan Ladizinsky also loves the independence. "When I was on sets, I was a boom man, I was a second-unit director, but there's something great about being in an editing room by yourself. You have complete control for a few days, but then you have to let the other kids come in and play. And you have to be good with that." You have to be able to tolerate people sitting behind you, watching your every move, driving you crazy.

Temperament Is Crucial

Included in an editor's skill set is being able to get along with people. Jon Corn looks at it this way: "You are not going to be inspiring anybody if they want to get away from you. I've known a lot of skilled editors who have unappealing personality quirks and they never made it because they couldn't work well in the room. You have to perceive what role they want you to play. Some want you to opine, and some want you to just push the buttons. One is more fun than the other." Alec Berg said, "Nobody wants a chatty editor. It's not a cocktail party. You're there to work." Embrace this editorial doctrine: "I will shut the fuck up."

Julia Louis-Dreyfus considers personality an important factor in working with any member of the creative team, whether actor, director, director of photography, or editor. "You don't have to be best friends, but if you're not getting along from a personality point of view, it's not going to work."

Editing *Veep* (2012–2019) was probably the hardest job I've ever had. There was an unspoken mandate for perfection from David

Mandel—the highest caliber of work was demanded from everybody. David spared no one. That kind of atmosphere is not for everybody. I asked David why he is so hard on everybody, and he explained, "Because I'm going to hate stuff before I love it. I don't hate the editor, but I'm going to hate the thing I'm looking at. I'm going to hate myself. I'm going to hate my actors. I'm going to hate everything and be hateful until I am happy. My anger is simply always at myself. How did I get us into this mess? It's not editing together well because somewhere along the way I missed something. I didn't give a note to an actor and now I'm trapped. Or I wrote it incorrectly and now I'm scrambling to solve it. I need somebody who's not taking their editing personally, because it's not about them whatsoever. The scene is just not working until it is working."

And once you finally get to the place where it works, David transforms from an angry lion into a happy pussycat. I am evenly dispositioned enough, such that when a showrunner runs hot and cold it doesn't materially affect me. Or as David described me, as I'm working on solutions, "You just kind of ignore me to some extent."

Brad Hall recounted an experience he had working with David Mandel. Brad said he was directing a scene that wasn't working. Julia remembered it immediately: "That was in that bedroom?"

Brad nodded. "Yeah. The color drained from David's face. He was dying. I said, 'Okay. Let's rehearse it again.' And he goes, 'No, no. It'll never work. It'll never work.' It was like a death on the set for him. So, he went into the writers' room. And it was like a funeral in there. We had to get through the process of David hating everybody. Hating me. Two and a half hours later, still no script."

Julia recalled, "That was a rough time. He had to get through the grief."

"Right," said Brad. "He had to realize, 'This space in the show will work. We'll figure it out.' And sure enough, in the end it worked. It's not the greatest scene ever shot—"

David Mandel on the set of *Veep*, with executive producer Morgan Sackett. Also visible, second assistant director Ismael Jimenez and executive producer Peter Huyck.

Julia nodded. "But it worked."

It's even worse when you can't reshoot, and an editor has to find a way through with only the existing, flawed pieces. You have to stay calm, with producers watching, and keep trying solutions. When I asked Larry David what he likes about me as an editor, he said, "You never get ruffled. Never get rattled. You have a great disposition. You have great instincts. Your work is a reflection of your personality. You take care of everything so quickly and smoothly. I've never had a complaint."

"What's my flaw?"

"You're too easygoing. I'm jealous of your insouciance." That made me laugh. My "lack of any fucks left to give" has carried me through many a potentially catastrophic moment. To the editor, it's always going to feel like it's your fault. An important quality is to be able to glide through withering criticism like a fish through water.

Judd Apatow likens hiring an editor to "finding someone to get married to. Because you have to have matching temperaments. You have to enjoy each other's company. Some editors don't really want you in the room. They're annoyed by your presence. You're constantly making them change everything. You're constantly criticizing them. So, it requires someone who's grounded and centered and confident."

Bad Editors

What do bad editors do? It's kind of like asking what does a bad watchmaker do? Well, it looks like a watch, all the pieces are there, but the time is wrong. When I asked Ivan Ladizinsky, he said, "Editing takes time. If you think you're going to do a nine-to-five, I haven't seen many editors do that very well. Their work shows it; they get a lot of notes. Partly it's because they gave some of the work to their assistant to cut. I've always encouraged my assistants to cut after they have all of their work done, and I am happy to give feedback. But if you haven't looked at the footage, you don't know the material, and that's going to look bad."

Steven Rasch agreed a common mistake editors make is not to look at everything. "They start based on script notes. They use the circled takes and slam it together." On the set the director asks the script supervisor to "circle" favorite takes for the editor to use. Even on circled-take shows, Steven looks at everything. "And then if there was a good reason to vary from it, you explain later—but often they don't notice. There are certain showrunners who would look at a cut and ask, 'Is that the one I circled on set?' If I would say, 'No,' they wouldn't discuss it, they would just say, 'Take out yours, put in mine.' They didn't like me thinking too much. That was uncomfortable and boring. But you have to learn the rules, which are different on every project."

A hard part of the job, particularly when family responsibilities call, is being always available. When I'm done editing, that's when I relax, take a vacation, enjoy the time I've earned. But on some jobs, if the producer needs to work Saturday night at 8 p.m., I'm there. When Jeff Schaffer staggers editors so there's always somebody editing on a weekend, I make my schedule work. I'm there when they need me. My willingness to edit gets me invited back.

Alec Berg's analysis of bad editing is: "Editors sometimes misunderstand what a scene is about, or what the core idea of a scene is. What is the joke here? Or whose perspective is this from? If I'm shooting and I get a call from the editor asking, 'Hey, I'm cutting the scene, there are two ways I could go here. What do you think?' I'm always open to that. I would rather be asked than come into an edit and go, 'Whoa, this is not at all what I was thinking.'"

Judd Apatow said that a bad editor might not know when the argument needs to end. Or would not be open to exploring new ideas. "A bad editor would make you feel a lack of confidence in what you're doing. You need the editor to buck you up a bit. And I'm sure if you're making a terrible movie, that's difficult for an editor. Artists have precarious self-esteem, and some of an editor's role is leading the charge from a positive place."

Good Editors

A good editor is up for anything. Krista Vernoff said the best editors get excited by a good note. "They love trying different things with the existing footage. They're willing to try two hundred different songs to find the right one." Sometimes after I finished a nice, smooth, working version of a scene on *Veep*, David Mandel would decide to cut four lines, saying, "I want to go from point A to point F." My first thought was, "But what about B, C, D, and E? They are walking from one room to a completely different room! There's no way to do it without a jump that's going to throw the audience. It can't be done!" I would never take on such an impossible challenge myself. But somehow David thinks it might be feasible, so even if I think he's delusional, I have to give it my best shot. I would dig in, look at every take, try every variation. And it was often a complete shock when I'd find that the last take has an angle that briefly bridges the continuity gap. And then I'd have to admit, "Wow, that actually worked." I never would have gotten there without someone pushing me to do better. David is a fan of the collaboration: "That's why there is you and there is me working together. That's why it's not just you and it's also why it's not just me with a person who can press buttons, because we wouldn't solve it alone." As you become more experienced as an editor, your confidence to take big leaps grows. You get a sense of what you can accomplish and what you can get away with.

Judd Apatow said, "You always have to stay open, because when you worked so hard on something, it feels done, and when someone has a new idea, you want to punch them in the face. It's hard when you say to the editor, 'Did we miss anything? Let's take two hours and watch every take again.' But every time you rewatch the material, you find something."

Never say, "It can't be done," or, "That shot doesn't exist." No matter how good your memory is, you do not remember every moment. It probably does exist. There may be a take that fell through the cracks and didn't make it into your bin. You may have missed a phrase. You might have blinked. Something is there.

Banish Defensiveness

Never defend your editorial choices—unless asked. The editor's cut was your opportunity to make a pitch for the best choices. Now you have to synthesize new solutions. Many of your decisions will be overturned. The editor's goal is to get the person on the couch out of the room as quickly as possible. You can't get precious about any choices. Nobody cares why you did something that is not working for them. Krista Vernoff said she needs the editor to be able to pivot. "Nothing makes me crazier than an editor who is so attached to their own idea of the scene that when I give big notes, they take them in minuscule ways, trying to protect their initial instincts or vision."

"A bad editor spends a lot of energy editorializing why something works when it doesn't," according to Jon Corn. If asked why he cut something a particular way, Jon explains his decisions simply: "I did it that way because I thought it was funny." In the collaborative process, you often find that another solution is better than what you tried.

But Jon said that sometimes they would build twenty versions of a scene on *Curb Your Enthusiasm*, and then they would describe something and say, "Do you remember that great version? Where is that?"

And then Jon would say, "Oh, you mean the version in the editor's cut?" Those are moments where he thought, "Yes! I won that one." It's like when the USA beat the Russians in hockey in the 1980 Olympics. It's such a big victory because of who you're playing against.

When a producer asks you to try something, never offer resistance. Remember the collaborative rule of improv comedy: "yes, and. . . ." Saying "no" is a dead end. No matter what, the answer is, "Okay, let's try that." Always explore the idea. First make sure you fully understand what is being asked, what exactly is not working in the producer's mind, what is bumping up against them.

Producers want to try new variations as quickly as possible. You may end up right back where you started. Often you will be proven right, but sometimes they have to see for themselves how you invented the wheel. Get them out of the room faster by giving them what they want. Take what they hand you and go with it. Doing anything else is stalling the process.

From Alec Berg's perspective, when working with any creative person, he wants to make sure they feel like their creativity is appreciated. "I've seen it happen so many times where, if somebody has a bad bedside manner toward a cinematographer or toward an editor or toward a wardrobe supervisor, eventually that person goes, 'All right, fine. Just tell me what you want.' Then you're no longer getting creative input from that person because they're tired of getting shit on. I would imagine the flip side is true. From the editor's standpoint, you have to be smart about how you present ideas. So that it doesn't feel like you're bullying them."

The Person on the Couch

Steven Rasch once said to me, "Whoever is on the couch behind you is the boss." Once you finish your editor's cut, it's not yours anymore. If you think it's still your baby, you're going to get fired or pushed out. As much as you might have led on the work, you have to change your hat and let the person on the couch take the lead. Steven added, "But you want them to be smart. Ideally, smarter than you."

A hard-to-navigate situation is when there's a different person on the couch every day and they're not always communicating with each other. "Treat each one like they are calling the shots" was Steven's advice. "The projects with multiple bosses are the ones I try to avoid. That's what I try to find out before I take the job: Who's in the room? Who can come in and mess with me? How many layers? Television pilots are difficult because there are often conflicting power structures, and they're all vying for control." When considering a job, Steven talks to editors who have worked with those producers. "If I know anyone on that crew I'll ask, 'What are their work habits? What do they like?' I'll gauge that against what I like to do. If it's a good fit, I'll wing it. There's no one way to handle everybody. You will gather experience with different types of people."

Notes come from the director, writers, producers, and network executives, and they often conflict with each other. Not everybody can handle that environment. You have arrived when you've mastered the ability to offer a genuine opinion without taking sides. Good luck! A nice strategy after receiving instructions for an editorial change, or after a discussion in the room about what to change next, is to briefly paraphrase the task you are about to undertake. Offering a short summary of what you heard, before you launch into the change, puts you in charge. And it sets everybody at ease knowing you understand what they have been trying to communicate (often badly), and it prevents frustration and delay if you misunderstand the task at hand.

Perception Varies

A producer's perception of an edit (and their satisfaction with you) can be influenced by mood, which may be dependent upon prior events that day that have nothing to do with you and are out of your control. But some things are within your control, like managing a producer's blood-sugar level. There was a "hungry judge" study done where the judges started the day by granting parole to 65 percent of prisoners. But that ratio dropped to near zero by the end of the morning session. Then it bounced back to 65 percent right after lunch or a snack break.[1] The lesson? Keep plenty of whatever your couch people like to eat (gourmet cookies, muffins, healthy snacks) available in the edit bay, because every edit you make is being judged by brains and stomachs. A producer with a happy stomach is a better producer.

84

And now a note to producers on the subject of an editor's lunch. It's smart to pay for the editor's lunch. You want an editor's brain to be happy, focused, and creatively engaged in improving your project. The first half of the day, an editor is looking forward to a good lunch. The second half of the day is fueled by that lunch. If the editor has to spend creative energy making lunch, logistically arranging for food, leaving to eat, or picking up food, that's less time and creative energy spent on the project. Productivity suffers if the order is wrong, the food is inadequate, or it just plain sucks. Feeding editors good food keeps them happy, at their desk, and delivering better quality work. An editor with a happy stomach is a better editor.

Editors Are Hired for Opinions

Your opinion is best expressed through your work. I asked David Mandel what he wants from an editor, and he said: "Make a choice. Even if it's not perfectly in line, you've got to have a take. You're hired to be the editor, so edit. I want you to build a scene that's funny. I lose patience with an editor who is not confident in their work. We don't always have to agree on how something is cut, but I want them to approach their cut with a sense of comedy, and approach it like there's an off chance I could watch the editor's cut and say, 'Great, let's put it on television.'"

Alec Berg was in sync with David Mandel. "Sometimes an editor will go, 'I took a run at something, it might be totally wrong, but I took a swing here.' Sometimes I watch it and say, 'I appreciate that you tried that. It doesn't work at all.' And sometimes I go, 'That's crazy. I never would've thought of that. That's awesome.' That's like the analogy of cooking where the chef says, 'I tried this without meat. What do you think?'"

There is a scene in *Barry* (season one, "Chapter Seven: Loud, Fast, and Keep Going") that Alec wrote and directed where Barry is having a mental breakdown. Alec shot the footage with specific intentions for how it should be used to demonstrate Barry's mental state: how when a person starts freaking out, things start to loop. Alec explained exactly what he had in mind to editor Jeff Buchanan. "But what Jeff delivered was not at all what I had envisioned. It was so much better than what I had in mind. We undid everything we tried to do to it after the editor's cut. It aired the way he cut it."

Judd Apatow said he wants editors who have "clear, strong opinions, and at the same time are flexible, to help me with my vision of the film. I want to know what they would do if I did not exist, and then I want them to help me when I want to explore something different." Judd sees editing as having "a great conversation about the movie that lasts for nine months."

Judd recounted how it's easy to get lazy and not get the best out of your material. "A lot of times scenes are good, but they're not amazing. You could stop with good, or you could stop with very good, but hopefully you've given yourself enough time to go, 'I like this scene, but I don't love it. Let's disassemble it and start from scratch.' There is a line in *The King of Staten Island* (2020) where Pete Davidson is talking to his friend Igor (Moises Arias) and they're smoking pot.

Pete says, "Do you guys even really get high anymore? I don't think I get high anymore. I think I just kind of am myself."

Smoking pot continuously, Igor says, "I haven't been high in a while, man. But I still do it. I like the lifestyle."

This bit of dialogue wasn't in any of the prior cuts, and then Judd said, "Hey, can you recut this scene? I don't think it's fully working yet." They went back at it again, and in the next version a few things like that exchange turned up, making the scene stronger. "That's what you hope for," said Judd. "No direction. A great editor always reads my mind well." Krista Vernoff also finds that great editors begin to anticipate her notes: "After working together a few times, they learn a showrunner's sensibility and integrate it into the first cut so they can save us the one thing we are always short on, which is time."

Mike Binder said he likes to work with the same editor because there's a trust factor. "I'm not looking for a technician. I'm looking for somebody who is going to bring art to this. I'm looking for someone who's going to do it better than I can. Everybody wants to hire you once they know you can really help." Mike also considers a good editor to be another writer on the project. He has always asked me to read his scripts in advance for notes before shooting. He says it's because, "An editor has got to be able to see all the parts and fashion it in a way that makes it float above what's there. That's why I don't like to be in the editing room that much. You have to think of an editor a bit like an actor. You can't act for an actor. You can't give them line readings."

Be a Teacher

Another thing a good editor does is teach. I like to involve my assistants in the entire process. To the assistants who are eager to learn and move up, I will offer to do scene challenges, where we both separately cut a scene and then compare results. I'll critique my assistants' work, and they will critique mine. We both come up with ideas that occurred to neither of us. I'll incorporate the best ideas from both, and the scene gets better due to our collaboration. An assistant works a lot and their day is full. But if they really want to be an editor, they find time to cut scenes.

Be an Editor Who Makes Films

Orson Welles said that anybody could learn the technical jobs on a film in a few hours if they gave it their full attention. Learning how to create engaging stories is much harder. When Welles was asked if it is possible to be equally at home in the arts and the sciences, he said it is not just possible, it is necessary. "The wildest kind of lunacy is to go wandering up some single street. It's better not only for the individual but for society that our personal horizons should be as wide as possible."[2] In his 1886 speech to Harvard University undergraduate students, Supreme Court Justice Oliver Wendell Holmes Jr. said, "To be master of any branch of knowledge, you must master those which lie next to it; and thus to know anything you must know all."[3]

To be a good editor, expand your skills in every aspect that surrounds editing. David Mandel agreed. "I think you have to be well-rounded. It's necessary for a writer to understand editing, or that an editor understand writing, or for a director to look at both. Even if you're not a showrunner, you have to be able to do all these things." Editing is the showrunner's third bite at the apple, to fix what isn't working. With a perfect script and ideal casting, the editor is simply trimming and polishing. With problem scripts, the editor experiments with radically changing scene order, or creating new intent that wasn't there, or adding off-camera lines, all to solve problems where the writer or actor or director came up short.

Great editors need to be filmmakers. As an independent filmmaker, I learned to do multiple tasks, sometimes taking on every job on an indie film set. It helps to have been a production assistant, a camera operator, a writer, a sound mixer, a producer. All of these abilities contribute and cross-pollinate. I was making films from an early age and at some point, people finally started to notice my work and my editing—the rhythm, the beats, the choices, and, most important, the laughs.

Make That Film—I Mean It!

There was an editor who was an assistant on *Veep* who was eager to move up. Gena Fridman studied economics and photography at the University of California San Diego. After graduation he landed a mutual-fund trading job. He described those five years as "fun at first, then it became increasingly tedious and depressing, because you are picking up a phone and placing trade orders for somebody else, which reminds you of how much money they have and you don't." With no chance for growth, he became restless. While dating Rebekah Parmer (soon to become Mrs. Rebekah Fridman), who was an editor, Gena began watching her work, and he found that spending an hour in an editing room brought him more joy than any comparable moment in finance. In 2012 he quit his job and enrolled in a one-year vocational program to study editing, where he learned how to use Avid Media Composer and Adobe After Effects. He landed his first job as a second-assistant editor on a low-budget, religious-themed feature called *Pass the Light* (2015), and his new career began. When Gena and I were chatting in the *Veep* offices one day, I was surprised to discover he had never made his own films, nothing more elaborate than family home movies. And when I referenced classic films such as *Jeremiah Johnson* (1972), or *The Wild Bunch* (1969), or *Bringing up Baby* (1938), he shrugged, embarrassed, and said he'd never heard of them. He admitted the television series *Full House* (1987–1995) and *Family Matters* (1989–1998) were his formative influences.

Some editors come up through the system, beginning as interns, moving up to assistant editors, finally sharing co-edit credits, then building enough credits to hang up their own shingle. Others learn filmmaking overall, prior to focusing on editing as a specialty. I believe the best way to excel as an editor is to be a filmmaker first and then find your specialty, whether it is as production designer, wardrobe supervisor, writer, producer, camera person, sound designer, editor—take your pick, but *be a filmmaker first*. You have to master the language of film, which exists in the service of story. You are investing in yourself, and like any good investment, you must diversify.

Because basic editing software is now available on all computers, anybody can learn the technical side of editing. Julian Doyle started out making and cutting his own films. He recommended that novice editors try doing editing exercises: "I was watching the Clarke Gable–Norma Shearer film *Idiot's Delight* (1939), and because it's old, the lengths of the shots are longer than we would allow now. Take an old film like that and see if you can improve the editing."

Gena Fridman started watching some of the classic movies I gave him on a list, and then we would discuss his thoughts on each. He began researching the filmmakers, studying cinema as more than simply entertainment. After I suggested he make his own short film, he took my advice and wrote and directed a short called *Bread Pudding* (2019). He said, "It was stressful, because it cost fifteen thousand dollars, but the experience made me feel like I could actually be a real filmmaker." His film won an Award of Excellence at the Best Shorts Competition in San Diego, and now he had the bug. He has continued on this path, directing more shorts and music videos. When I asked him what he learned, he said, "I relooked at my first film and realized there's so much air in there. I just hadn't seen it. I had watched how you meticulously zoom in on each cut and remove any extra frames. And now, as an editor, my cuts are so much tighter." And having been a director of his own work, he said it gives him an outside perspective as an editor, a dimension that was missing from his prior work. "I'm not as critical of directors now. I spend less time complaining and more time looking for the solutions. Directing makes me a better editor, and editing makes me a better director." Gena's enthusiasm as an assistant, his willingness to cut scenes on his own time and then compare notes, his exuberance to challenge himself, it earned him a co-editing credit on a *Veep* episode called "Chicklet" (season six, episode five), on which we shared an Emmy nomination.

What Should a Filmmaker Study?

Mike Binder skipped college and jumped right into stand-up comedy and scriptwriting, but he has since changed his mind about that strategy. "I should have been a lot more educated than I am. I probably would have done a lot better. I wouldn't study show business, that's for sure." Mike said his preferred curriculum would be a diverse study of liberal arts. "It gives you more to write about, more sources for jokes and references than I had as a young guy. I could've used some curing. It's not a bad thing to learn about the world." *Curb Your Enthusiasm* editor Grady Cooper started out majoring in mechanical engineering, then switched to architecture, but ended up with an English major. "It's not that I couldn't decide, I just liked learning several different things, an early Renaissance man in progress."

Ten Crucial Areas of Study for the Filmmaker-Editor

1. Liberal Arts

When I asked Julia Louis-Dreyfus what a future filmmaker should study in college, she suggested English, literature, philosophy, and history—a liberal arts education. Do not learn only a trade, embrace a career. Do not overspecialize. Increase your broad spectrum of world knowledge. Learn from every discipline. You need to have an informed opinion, a thoughtful point of view supported by knowledge from every discipline.

Although they are all a part of liberal arts, I am separating literature, writing, psychology, science, art, and music for special emphasis, because each is so important.

2. Literature

My biggest regret is I did not study more literature and theater in college. I am still playing catch-up and will be until the day they stop publishing books. One of the most important skills you need, whether as an editor, director, or writer, is a thorough understanding of storytelling. You can read about it, but you can't absorb it until you practice it. Never stop reading books. Study the classics. Read about history. Read everything else: drama, science fiction, detective, romance, graphic novels, comic books, and nonfiction. Movies are made from all these sources. Judd Apatow had a down year after his television shows were canceled, and he and his wife had a baby, so he decided to spend that year reading such writers as Andre Dubus, and his son, Andre Dubus III, and Frederick Exley. When I asked what book inspired him the most, he said Dave Eggers's *A Heartbreaking Work of Staggering Genius* (2000). "I remember thinking that there was a much deeper way to look at characters than I had realized. Eggers got so specific and did not hold back from exploring all of the character's feelings and emotions. It's a dark, terror-fantasy of everything he's afraid of. . . . It made me realize I needed to go further in my creative work."

3. Writing

When I asked editor Ivan Ladizinsky what a young filmmaker should study, he said: "Anyone can learn to operate a machine. But what is telling a story? It's writing. And if you're telling the story with images, it's photography. It's editing. Study the language of film, writing stories with pictures."

See chapters 4 and 5 for a deeper look at writing for editors.

4. Psychology

Brad Hall emphasized how important it is to understand why people treat each other the way they do. It is crucial to have an understanding of how humans behave, think, and feel. Filmmakers and writers need to know what motivations underlie the choices each of their characters make.

According to Ivan Ladizinsky, you also have to know how to be supportive, like a psychologist. "The director comes back from the shoot, saying, 'I didn't get what I wanted. I screwed up. I'm a failure. I want to kill myself.' And you've got to help. You're there on all kinds of levels. Not just putting a movie together, but keeping the director together, keeping the producers happy—making them feel safe, making them feel like this is going to be a good thing."

5. Science

All the hard sciences, such as astronomy, biology, chemistry, and physics, describe the laws of the universe, which affect sound, optics, lighting, special effects, everything that impacts how you can capture and edit a scene. I would also include computers, data processing, and statistics. The social sciences, such as anthropology, sociology, economics, and political science, describe how societies work. Filmmakers need to have an understanding of the mechanics of the world within which they live. Reading blog rants and internet tirades about politics or culture won't provide the actual data you need to get there.

If a writer has never studied physics or astronomy but decides to set a story in space, it's disappointing when that movie is engaging but violates the laws of physics. If viewers are presented with a moment that makes them think, "that's not what would happen," the logic flaw takes them out of the story, and the viewing experience suffers. The movie *Gravity* (2013) is exciting and well made, but one science-defying moment after another mars the story. For example, Ryan Stone (Sandra Bullock) and Matt Kowalski (George Clooney) are repairing the Hubble Space Telescope. After their space shuttle is destroyed, they travel by jetpack to the International Space Station. However, these two installations are in very different locations over the Earth, and vastly dissimilar orbits (Hubble at 347 miles high and 17,150 miles per hour, and the ISS at 263 miles high and 17,130 miles per hour). A journey between them with a jetpack is impossible. To travel from one to the other and match velocities would take much more energy than a jetpack has available. Another scientific flaw is that Kowalski didn't have to die when they were both hanging on to a rope, because they were both stationary, meaning there was no force pulling Kowalski away. A tiny tug on his rope would have brought them together. If you write about something you are not familiar with, do exhaustive research.

6. Art

Go to museums. Look at how painters use light. The same ideas are applied in cinematography. Julian Doyle learned how to film his own projects. "In the past, to be a cameraman you started as a clapper loader (2nd assistant camera), then were promoted to focus puller (1st assistant camera), then to an upper echelon, and then to operating a camera. They really had nothing to do with each other. The best cameraperson I know, Terry Bedford (*Monty Python and the Holy Grail* [1975], *Jabberwocky* [1977]), trained in art school, which is much more valuable training than clapper loader."

7. Music

It helps to know how to communicate with composers. Instead of fumbling around with statements like, "This part is too short," you can be specific. "Let's make this cue two measures longer, and at the end give it an extra-long sustain on that last note."

When *Survivor* editor Ivan Ladizinsky was young, he collected movie scores. He was listening to Jerry Goldsmith and John Williams

A mind-bending moment from *Altered States*.

while everyone else was listening to Boston and Electric Light Orchestra. I remember doing the same thing, collecting scores I loved, such as *The Exorcist* (1973), *Alien* (1979), and *The Shining* (1980), studying them, using clips to use in my parodies. When I saw the wildly edited visuals in Ken Russell's film *Altered States* (1980), the accompanying musical score by John Corigliano blew me away. I was baffled, wondering, "What are those sounds? How is this musical magic accomplished? I didn't know you could do that!"

It was a moment similar to when I first heard such revolutionary works as Jeff Beck's *Blow by Blow* (1975), or Stanley Clarke's *School Days* (1976), or Van Halen's debut *Van Halen* (1978). Eddie Van Halen was an artist who colored outside of the lines. He said he never took formal guitar lessons. "Ninety percent of the things that I do on guitar, if I had taken lessons and learned by the book, I would not play at all the way I do. Because of the things that I created, technique-wise, and the way I play, they had to reinvent a whole new way to write music. Because they could not explain with regular notes what I was doing." That system, which indicates instrument fingering rather than

95

notes and was common during the Renaissance and Baroque eras, is called tablature. Eddie Van Halen also credited his father for this advice, "If you make a mistake, try to do it twice. And smile. That way, people will think you meant it."[4]

I ran out the same night I saw *Altered States* and bought John Corigliano's score and played it over and over. Corigliano had never been offered a feature film job, so he approached scoring like nobody before. When director Ken Russell was at the Los Angeles Philharmonic and heard "Concerto for Clarinet and Orchestra" by John Corigliano, he said, "That's the composer I want for my movie."[5] *Altered States* was overlooked at the 1981 Academy Awards, probably because it's so wonderfully weird, but the score and sound mix were nominated.

8. Comedy

Don't take comedy for granted. Study it. The word originates from the Greek word *kōmos*, meaning "to revel," from a ritualistic drunken procession performed by revelers. Take an improv class, an acting class, and a speech class. Find out what it's like to perform. Look for a course in the English literature department that examines theories of comedy. Learn the differences between humor, wit, satire, irony, burlesque, farce, and parody. Absorb and study classic comedy works such as Aristophanes's *Lysistrata* (411 BC), Shakespeare's *Twelfth Night* (1602), Molière's *Tartuffe* (1664), Mark Twain's *A Connecticut Yankee in King Arthur's Court* (1889), Jerome K. Jerome's *Three Men in a Boat* (1889), Woody Allen's *Getting Even* (1966), Jean Shepherd's *In God We Trust: All Others Pay Cash* (1966), Hunter S. Thompson's *Fear and Loathing in Las Vegas* (1971), Douglas Adams's *The Hitchhiker's Guide to the Galaxy* (1979), Charles Portis's *The Dog of the South* (1979), John Kennedy Toole's *A Confederacy of Dunces* (1980), and David Sedaris's *Naked* (1997). That's for starters. Reading these books is not a chore. You will laugh your way through the list.

9. Film—Production

Okay, fine, study film too. A primary endeavor in film schools is to teach students how to use image and sound equipment. You need to learn about f-stops, wardrobe, makeup, production scheduling, and the rest. Some of the best things that come out of film school, aside from the specific knowledge and practice you get from hands-on production, are the friendships and connections you will make. Many creative teams begin in college and last a lifetime.

10. Film—Aesthetics

Get esoteric. Ask what is cinema? Watching all the best movies and talking about them—that is what you do in film school. Find at least one class someplace where a wild-haired professor talks about montage, symbolism, and mise-en-scène.

These last two disciplines are a given. It's the other eight that get overlooked or receive inadequate attention. Are there any areas that are too esoteric and would be wasted effort for a filmmaker? Maybe meteorology, genetics, geography, journalism, or contract law? No! Let's call those numbers 11, 12, 13, 14, and 15. You will absorb valuable information from any area of study. For example, in a meteorology class you would learn how the sun heats the earth, causing air to rise, which causes condensation as air expands and the pressure drops, which leads to precipitation. This will give you some awareness for when your location shoot is going to be rained out. Did you know that most weather in the United States comes from the west? The sun heats the equator more than the poles, and, combined with the rotation of the earth, this creates the jet stream and the prevailing winds, which carries rain from west to east. On a set, recognizing weather patterns is crucial to the filmmaker who needs to get the shot before the deluge. In short, there is no area of study that is not helpful to a well-rounded understanding of a filmmaker's world.

Don't feel bad if you can't cover all these topics. It seems like a lot. But learn about as many as you can. And nobody says you can't continue learning after graduation. Keep reading.

And for fuck's sake, learn another language.

The Editor Is a Gatekeeper

The thing I love most about editing is watching a project come to life. The editing room is where all the elements come together. I get to choose my favorite versions of what the writers and actors have presented. It is where I get to laugh every day. An audience watches what *I* like; they see what makes *me* laugh. If you love a show I'm cutting, you are watching what I chose. When showrunners come in to work, they may change things up, switch out punch lines, and cut it down, but it starts with my twisted, quirky, personal preferences.

Please Yourself First—Early and Often

Alec Berg worries that someday we will understand social media to be profoundly damaging to society and to the human condition. "I'll get tweeted at every once in a while, and it's always like: 'You messed that up. That wasn't as good as this other thing.' There's an expectation that they want me to acknowledge that I made a mistake. I'll always reply, 'Sorry you didn't like it. I stand by my choice.' Then they're like, 'No! I'm the audience! Your job is to please the audience. And if I'm not pleased, you failed.' I say, 'That's not my job.

My job is to make something that I believe in and put it out there.' And as long as it makes me happy, and continues to make a large enough number of people happy, then I'll continue to have a career. As soon as it doesn't, I won't."

I make my movies for me and for me only. I trust that because I found a topic or a premise to be interesting, an audience will as well. But I don't try to guess what will please an audience. The same is true of me as the editor. As long as I pick the takes that make me (and Larry David) laugh, I will still have a job. If I don't, I could try mutual-fund trading.

CHAPTER FOUR

Editors Are Writers

Something May Start Out as Bad Writing, but If It Makes It Past Your Scissors, It's Bad Editing

Scott Conrad, the Oscar-winning editor (along with Richard Halsey) of *Rocky* (1976), has said, "Editing is the final rewrite."[1] Editor Jon Corn sees the editor as another step in the writing of the story, taking what was intended on the page, as filtered through the director, and through the actors, and assembling the result in a three-dimensional way. "It's important to let go of any preconceived notions that were in the script and move on to what you have in front of you and work with that." When filmmakers say, "We want what the script says," Jon's reaction sometimes is, "That's not what we have, but we've got something good here. You're not going to get there if you're trying to back into something you wished for, instead of moving forward with what you actually have."

According to Krista Vernoff, "I think it's as important for an editor to understand story structure as it is for a writer and a director. The best editors are deep inside the story right along with you." Alec Berg believes everybody on a crew should understand what the story is, because then they can be far more helpful to the process. "If you're a cinematographer and you understand this scene is about a guy seeing something carved on a tree, then you can start to think about how to best shoot it." Even if you fancy yourself the ultrainnovator who will come up with all new rules, you still have to learn the fundamentals before you go off into unknown zones.

If you are presented with a well-written script that is perfect, you don't have to know much about story structure because the story will take care of itself—if you don't damage it too much. But the perfect script is a rarity. Often pieces are missing, not shot, not covered well, or numerous other problems have to be addressed and fixed. The editor has to puzzle it out and come up with options, such as breaking scenes in half, rewriting lines, or suggesting what's needed for reshoots. This chapter provides a basic foundation in writing principles that every editor should know.

There Is No Substitute for Writing

How can you, the editor, become an expert on story structure? First step: start writing. Steven Rasch agreed: "It's good training, no matter how bad you are at it. Spend a semester in a writing class." Where? Anywhere, as long as it gets you writing. Jeff Schaffer also said, study whatever else you desire, but write. "Writing for television is not an art, it's a skill. It's like building a barrel. If you gave me a bunch of wood and said build a barrel, I would build a bad barrel the first time. If I built a hundred barrels, I'd probably build terrible barrels, but they would get better."

Absorb All the Great Films

I have been shocked to see blank stares from young editors when I referenced such movies as *The Philadelphia Story* (1940), *Sergeant York* (1941), *Unfaithfully Yours* (1948), *Seven Samurai* (1954), *Once Upon a Time in the West* (1968), *Phantasm* (1979), *Terms of Endearment* (1983), *Evil Dead II* (1987), *A Chinese Ghost Story* (1987), *Raising Arizona*

(1987), *The Killer* (1989), *Delicatessen* (1991), *Strictly Ballroom* (1992), or *Fresh* (1994). These movies are dramatic, romantic, suspenseful, and sometimes gory, but they all have supremely funny moments, and all are well edited. When you watch *Fresh*, notice the efficiency of Dorian Harris's editing, nothing goes on past the point; everything that remains supports the story. Watch how the occasional use of flash cuts and dissolves support the narrative.

The opening credits sequence in Sergio Leone's *Once Upon a Time in the West* (1968) is thirteen minutes long. It is about three men, Snaky (Jack Elam), Stony (Woody Strode), and Knuckles (Al Mulock), and a fly, simply waiting for a train carrying a man called Harmonica (Charles Bronson). There are barely four lines of dialogue in the first twelve minutes. And yet the scene is riveting. Why? It is a masterpiece of framing, music (only at the very end), sound design, and editing. And it's funny. The scene climaxes with a shoot-out, prefaced by this humorous exchange.

> Harmonica, ". . . Frank?"
>
> Snaky says, "Frank sent us."
>
> "You bring a horse for me?"
>
> Snaky laughs. "Looks like we're shy one horse."
>
> Harmonica shakes his head. "You brought two too many."

Author's collection.

Three outlaws versus Charles Bronson in *Once Upon a Time in the West*.

Why *must* you watch hilarious classic movies, such as: *Duck Soup* (1933), *His Girl Friday* (1940), *It's a Mad, Mad, Mad, Mad World* (1963), *They Call Me Trinity* (1970), *What's Up, Doc?* (1972), *This Is Spinal Tap* (1984), or *Roger and Me* (1989)? If you don't see these movies, you will be at a disadvantage compared to your competition, not just in television and feature films, but also for commercials, documentaries, and reality shows. You need to know what other editors know. Devour movies, new *and* classic films. Because there's an almost limitless supply in the history of movies, take in as many as possible.

Absorb the language of filmmaking and comedy construction. Immerse yourself in good storytelling. A would-be filmmaker and editor must be familiar with such directors as Frank Capra, Howard Hawks, Billy Wilder, Stanley Donen, Blake Edwards, and Alfred Hitchcock. Hitchcock once said, "For me, suspense doesn't have any value unless it's balanced by humor."[2] Hitchcock's droll, wry sense of humor shows in his framing and editing. Watch for Hitchcock's brief cameos in his movies, a clue that it's all a joke. Such as his appearance in a newspaper ad for a weight-loss product called "Reduco" in *Lifeboat* (1944).

Also seek out the best films coming out of other thriving film industries, such as Hong Kong, South Korea, India, Italy, Australia, and others. Don't ignore quirky B movies in your cinema diet either, such as Peter Jackson's inventive, low-budget horror-comedy *Braindead* (1992, a.k.a. *Dead Alive*). Suffer through bad storytelling as well. There is much to be learned from others' mistakes.

Study movies all the way back to the silent era. You must know who Harold Lloyd, Charlie Chaplin, and Buster Keaton were. Jackie Chan is a modern version of these comedians. Watch for silent-film-gag homages in the Jackie Chan movies *Project A* (1983), *Police Story* (1985), and *Armour of God* (1986). "I wanted to be like a Chaplin or Buster Keaton," Chan said, "but all the martial arts directors I worked with wanted me to copy Bruce Lee. So, after I got famous, I started to

Alfred Hitchcock's cameo appearance is in a newspaper ad in *Lifeboat*.

change a lot of things. . . . When Bruce Lee yowled, I'd punch doing a funny face like it hurt. Whatever Bruce Lee did, I'd do the opposite."[3] Chan's films are amazing acrobatic exhibitions, but much of the humor is built in the editing. Chan knows a reaction shot is just as important as the shot showing the incredible stunt. In *Project A: Part II* (1987), Chan re-created the building-collapse stunt from Buster Keaton's *Steamboat Bill, Jr.* (1928). And as the wall is falling, Chan cuts to the shocked reactions from his pursuers.

Do not ignore early television series and comedy shorts such as the *Our Gang* films, also known as *The Little Rascals* (1922–1944). Learn who Ernie Kovacs and Sid Caesar were. Most every plot you enjoy on your favorite sitcom today probably has a precursor in an episode of *The Dick Van Dyke Show* (1961–1966), and that storyline also probably made a stop in many other places, before you enjoyed it again recently on last year's sitcom episode. Study the source.

Of course, nobody has time to watch every movie and television series in history. This is a sampling of ideas to consider. But seek out as many as you can. If you watch only the current offerings on your favorite streaming platforms, you will miss out on an immense number of possibilities. Jon Corn realized one day as he was editing *Curb Your Enthusiasm*: "Being able to contribute to one of the greatest shows in television history, to have the trust and acceptance of this group of people, it makes me think all that time I spent as a kid watching comedy movies and television wasn't a waste of time. It was actually part of a process of getting here."

Watch Actively

When you see something that moves you, write it down. Look for the plot point that turns each act. Story structure is: problem, complication, resolution. Try writing out the story beats of your favorite movie. This will sharpen your awareness of story structure and how similarly it gets laid out in newer movies.

Whenever you see something you love, make a note: a camera angle, a plot twist, a character quirk, a line of dialogue, anything that strikes you as impactful. While watching *The Lady Eve* (1941), I noted the dialogue as Henry Fonda falls over a couch when he can't take his eyes off Barbara Stanwyck. Fonda's father, played by Charles Coburn, yells, "That couch has been there fifteen years and nobody ever fell over it before!" It occurred to me that great laugh-line might have landed even stronger if director Preston Sturges's editor had trimmed it to, "That couch has been there for fifteen years!" Instead, it goes on past the punch line, and the clause "and nobody ever fell over it before" explains the joke. If you find a character explaining a punch line, something probably misfired.

Write It and Rewrite It

Novice writers start out thinking their first draft is done. But their work is just beginning. Ernest Hemingway once said to his Key West deckhand, "The first draft of anything is shit."[4] In Hemingway's (posthumous) memoir he wrote, "It often took me a full morning of work to write a paragraph."[5]

When American journalist George Plimpton interviewed Hemingway for *The Paris Review* in 1958, Hemingway said, "I rewrote the ending of *A Farewell to Arms*, the last page of it, thirty-nine times before I was satisfied."

Plimpton asked, "Was there some technical problem there? What was it that had stumped you?"

Hemingway said, "Getting the words right."[6]

How many testimonials on rewriting from Hemingway do you need? The first draft is a starting point. Mike Binder rewrote *Coup de Ville* (1990) forty times to satisfy first himself, then producer Larry Brezner, and then director Joe Roth. I asked Mike, "Why did you work so hard and rewrite it so many times?"

Mike said, "That's not a lot. I've done that many drafts on everything I've ever made. You're supposed to do that many drafts on good movies and TV shows. I look at it like an hour of stand-up comedy. You don't get an hour's worth of great jokes all at once, you find them one at a time. A great story is a bunch of pieces that come together in moments; emotions that fit together as pieces of a puzzle that connect in all the different drafts."

I got to know Mike Binder when I started at my first job in Hollywood, working for manager-producers Larry Brezner and Buddy Morra. Eager to get his first film made, Mike came into the office every few weeks to discuss script notes with Larry Brezner. I remember how the young Mike was always ready to do whatever it took, happy to rewrite, no matter how disheartening it might feel to start over. He said, "I never saw it as abuse because I never thought, 'Okay, this thing's done.' Larry Brezner was producing *Good Morning, Vietnam*, another great comedy, and yet he was willing to spend hours on my script. I thought, 'If Larry Brezner is willing to play ball, I'll keep batting it back and forth.' That's why producers say, 'I need to go on to another writer,' because writers get burned out too soon. Larry didn't think I was burned out because, I'd go, 'Okay, let me try and come up with something.'"

Of *Curb Your Enthusiasm*, Larry David said, "The editing is where we really create the show." Jeff Schaffer said they write the show three times. "First we write the outline. The outline is everything. If the stories aren't good, it doesn't matter. The second time it gets written is on set, where every scene is a live rewrite. You are finding all the magic, all the great digressions. The third time it gets written is in the editing room."

Less Is More

The core of rewriting is cutting. If a line or a scene does not affect the story or move it forward, remove it. According to legend, when they asked Michelangelo how he made his statue of David, he said, "You chip away the stone that doesn't look like David." The way Mike Binder updated this notion is, "Chip away everything that's in the way of telling the story the right way." This is the essence of editing: Trim away everything that is not related to the story. Whether writing or editing, give every act, scene, or line the value test: Does it build character, increase interest, cause problems, add suspense, or move the story forward? If not, is it at least funny? If it does not do at least one of these things, it has to go.

What Is Story Structure?

There are countless books on writing. Thousands of pages dissect, analyze, and explain story structure. Syd Field was the first, in his 1979 book *Screenplay*, to examine three-act structure in movies. He explained how plot points are incidents that turn the action in a new direction, the most crucial being the inciting incident, which launches the story—and that one needs to happen very early. Robert McKee further developed screenplay-structure analysis in his 1997 writing manual *Story*, focusing on how every scene and every act must alternate in polarity. He also made central the importance of conflict and how no story moves forward without it.

Nearly all successful movies follow similar rules. Multi-act structure begins with a setup of a situation, followed by rising action in a second act (or multiple acts) that adds complications, with a final act that rushes toward a climax and a resolution. Hollywood didn't invent story structure. This formula for the way human beings like to have stories told to them has been around for as long as humans have been telling stories. Aristotle was the first to outline this format in 330 BC in his playwriting manual *Poetics*, where he suggested every story must have a beginning, middle, and end (*prologue, parados, episode, stasimon*, and *exodos*).

A Protagonist Changes

In the 1949 book *The Hero with a Thousand Faces*, Joseph Campbell pointed out that most hero myths have a common pattern: A hero goes on an adventure beyond his (or her) normal world, and in a decisive crisis versus extraordinary forces, he wins a victory, and then he comes home changed or transformed for the better. The stories of

Buddha, Moses, and Christ follow this pattern, as well as those of Jane Eyre, Luke Skywalker, and Harry Potter.

The protagonist (or co-protagonists when there's a group) in a movie is the one who changes the most by learning the lesson posed by the story's theme. This is called character arcing. Good guys accept change and see it as a positive force. Bad guys refuse to change (they can change, it's just not necessary). The antagonist represents the other side of the theme's argument. Change is good because it represents rebirth, the promise of a fresh start. A good story should be so important, so life-changing that it affects everybody involved (even the audience).

If you are not sure who your protagonist is, it's the most active person. A hero cannot be passively caught up in events. Ideally, the hero causes every plot point to happen and has the most conflict, the longest emotional journey, and the most primal goal.

Audiences Must Care about the Hero

Even in the silliest jokefest, such as *Airplane!* (1980), the audience gets invested in whether Ted Striker (Robert Hays) is going to succeed. When Judd Apatow made *Walk Hard* (2007), he realized that the crowd really cared about John C. Reilly's relationship with his father (played by Raymond J. Barry), who was so mean to him. Even if it was ridiculous, they had to resolve that storyline in a way that was satisfying. If you can make people care about the characters, then you can do all the comedy you want. Judd found that people were emotionally connected to Adam Sandler's character in *You Don't Mess with the Zohan* (2008), because at the center is a love story.

Julia Louis-Dreyfus does not believe characters have to necessarily be *likable* for the audience to care about them and root for them. In *Veep*, the word likable would not be at the top of the list describing

Selina Meyer. But she is strong. Like Selina, Tony Soprano, Jamie Lannister, Don Draper, and Dexter Morgan are all strong, captivating anti-heroes. Even with actual villains such as Anakin Skywalker in the *Star Wars* films or Elphaba Thropp in *Wicked*, Judd Apatow pointed out, "You may not want them to take the road they are on, but if you're tracking them with a personal, emotional, rooting interest, you do care; you feel for them."

A Story Begins with a Theme

A plot begins when a dramatic question is posed, such as: Will the hero defeat the evil threat? Will the protagonist win over the love interest? Will the investigator solve the crime? Will the family get to safety? This question is answered at the end, after a climax.

A character must state a theme at some point, early in the setup. What themes interest you as a writer? Perhaps: Evil should be punished. Or: Love will triumph. Maybe: The universe is an absurd joke. When young, our themes parrot our parents' beliefs. Then our friends. Then our teachers. And then the bloggers and lunatics we read on the internet. As we mature, our opinions coalesce as we form our own philosophies about life, our point of view of society, and our grievances. Your themes are notions that you will wrestle with and work through in your writing. Writing and filmmaking begin with theme, a case you want to make to the world. A plot lays out an argument in favor of that theme.

When editing a movie that is not working, one approach is to deconstruct the story and examine its foundation. Look for what is missing and then rebuild. You may discover that a thematic question was never clearly asked. Billy Wilder once said, "Everything you build up in act one comes back to haunt you in act three. If you do something for which you don't have payoffs in the third act, then you've failed."[7] Jeff Schaffer, David Mandel, and Alec Berg had a saying: "If it's too long in the middle, you pay an invisible bill at the end." As an editor, if you can recognize when story structure has been violated, and if you can offer solutions in the editing room, you will be the savior.

Different Genres Exist for a Reason

In my film *Suckers* (2001), my co-writer Joe Yannetty and I took a chance in attempting a genre shift from the second to the third act. The protagonist's stakes increase from overcoming real-world difficulties in the car sales world, to surviving a life-and-death encounter with drug dealers and loan sharks. Audiences are not used to changing genre midstream within a movie—they find it disconcerting. (Ironically, I'm doing a bit of a genre shift in this book, spilling so much ink about writing in a book about editing. But I promise they are fundamentally linked.) Quentin Tarantino and Robert Rodriguez attempted a genre shift in *From Dusk Till Dawn* (1996). It starts out as a crime-caper/road-chase and then shifts to a supernatural, monster movie.

Judd Apatow upended expectations in *Funny People* (2009), which switches halfway through from Adam Sandler as a dying comedian deciding to mentor a younger comic played by Seth Rogen, to a love story about Sandler trying to win back an ex-girlfriend, played by Leslie Mann. Even though some viewers complained that it became two movies, to Judd, the fact that it switches gears completely was what intrigued him. "I liked that it confounded expectations. [The second half of the movie is] almost like a second episode of a TV series. And yet, the propulsion of the story is still in that structure: obstacles getting worse and worse and then a third act with a resolution to the larger problem."

It may be tempting to try to invent a new genre, to write something that's never been written, to break all the rules, but if you do, be aware that audiences are resistant. If you don't stick to a clear genre, or if you write a structureless character piece, without a strong theme, without an opening question, you're taking a big chance. If you give an audience a story told in a way that they don't want to receive it, they'll turn the channel. Or you should just admit you're making an art film. European films are refreshing because they violate the rules, but they also remind us why the rules exist. But don't expect to make a living as a writer of art films. There are a lot of starving artists out there. If you're going to build a house, you are better off following well-known architectural fundamentals instead of trying to invent a whole new foundational framework your first time out. You can get creative with how you use those fundamentals. Your real challenge is to invent a new cosmetic look for that established structural framework.

Begin the Story as Soon as Possible

Present the inciting incident right away—on page one if possible, or by page ten, but absolutely no later than the end of act one. Start with a murder, a violent event, a breakup, an infraction, an infection, a violation, something that actively puts people in conflict and launches a story by asking a dramatic question. If you keep viewers waiting for the inciting incident until thirty-five minutes in, you risk losing them. Many of the best movies and television episodes give you a dead body in the first scene. As Billy Wilder once said of his openings, "You grab them by the throat, their heart is beating, and you never let go."[8]

Every Scene Must Have Conflict

There is no story without conflict. If you are editing a scene that is not working, ask yourself, "What is the conflict?" Conflict does not necessarily mean arguing or physical fighting. Any form of opposition, any barrier between a protagonist and a goal is conflict. Opposition can be verbal, physical, emotional, mental, environmental, societal, extraterrestrial, subatomic, or . . . use your imagination.

Alec Berg warns, "There's nothing deadlier than a conversation between people who all know the same thing and agree." *Silicon Valley* (2014–2019) was a show about people doing something uncinematic: They sit at computers and type all day. Alec Berg likes to arrange forces to be on opposing sides, which naturally fosters arguments. One of my favorite dramas is an Iranian film called *A Separation* (2011). The film begins with an argument in a divorce court and the heated arguments continue nonstop to the end of the movie. The film is captivating.

When I asked Julia Louis-Dreyfus how important conflict is in a scene, she replied without hesitation: "Crucial. It must be there. There always has to be something for me to push against. It can be as simple as a banana."

Julia described a scene in *Veep* (season four, episode three, "Data") where Selina tells Gary, "I need an energy bar. No, apple. No, fuck it, cheese."

Gary says, "Ma'am, cheese is on its way. Here's an interim banana."

Selina tries but can't open the banana so she gives it back to Gary, saying, "This doesn't even work."

"It's very small," said Julia. "It's almost nothing. But it's important."

Brad Hall agreed, laughing at Julia's reliving of the scene. "It's a perfect example because it has nothing to do with the scene, but it has everything to do with it, because you're so frustrated that you can't open a banana."

Also laughing, I added, "A child can open a banana."

Brad nodded. "A monkey can open a banana. Quite literally." But Selina can't open the banana in that moment. And that is very funny.

Selina versus a banana, and the banana wins, in *Veep*.

David Mandel elaborated on how obstacles create comedy. "In a scene where two people want something different, or if they want the same thing but they're on opposing sides, it raises the level of what the comedy can be. Any time in *Veep* that Selina and Jonah did a scene together, you'd get much more, because they're antagonistic. It's why so many of the Selina–Tom James scenes are so good, because while they're both attracted to each other, they're also trying to kill each other."

Alec Berg explained how there are two main types of plots in *Curb Your Enthusiasm*, stories where Larry is the asshole and stories where Larry runs into the asshole, all of which leads to tons of arguing. "Sometimes he's a crusader for the rights of all of us. And sometimes he's the guy that you go, 'Oh, my God, you're never gonna believe the asshole that I ran into.'" But, in every scene there is something for Larry to rail against.

Much of Larry David's humor comes from engaging with those who violate social mores, thus inconveniencing others. Larry goes over the line in every show. But how far over that line can he go and it's still funny? Jeff Schaffer calls Larry's on-screen persona "Our Guy." "We have to protect Our Guy and make sure he is sympathetic." The audience has to be with Larry as he is defending society against perceived social injustices: the guy abusing the carpool lane, or the person who cuts in line and does a "chat and cut," or the person taking too many free samples of ice cream. How many flavors should you be allowed to taste before you are violating society's unwritten rules of sampling? All the jokes flow out of the setup of these humorous situations. In "The Ida Funkhouser Roadside Memorial" (season six, episode three), Larry walks into an ice-cream shop. Once we clearly and quickly established that Larry is annoyed while a woman (actress Robin Bartlett) is tasting flavors, then how many flavors she chose determined the length of the scene.

The flavor-tasting woman says, "Could I try the tiramisu?"

Behind her, Larry scoffs, "That's a good one, get that."

She turns on Larry. "I think I will. Thank you." Back to the server. "And I think I'd like to try the banana, please."

"Banana! Whoa! It might taste like, let me guess, a banana!"

She tries to ignore Larry. "And some chocolate."

Larry is getting even more frustrated. "This is so rude. You are a sample abuser!"

She turns back to Larry. "What's the matter with you?"

"You are abusing your sampling privileges. One sample, two samples at the most. You can't just go on sampling."

"Yes, yes I can." Back to the server. "You know what, I'm going to have just a plain vanilla, please. Thank you."

"Oh, a decision's been made. Enjoy."

Snidely, "Thank you." She walks out.

Now it's Larry's turn. "Vanilla. She winds up with vanilla? You've got to be kidding me." (Pause.) "How is the vanilla?"

Once a conflict-laden situation is conceived, an actor is cast who will push back against Larry David's attempt to chastise them. Success in a well-written improv scene depends upon casting. Larry needs somebody who will give it right back. Good arguing is good comedy—and good story.

Conflict Can Be Emotional

Judd Apatow's movies are about someone facing an obstacle, and then the obstacles get more complicated until there's a turning point where everything falls apart, which launches a third act and a resolution. Judd said one of his inspirations was playwright John Guare, author of the 1971 play *The House of Blue Leaves*. Guare said of writing: "Paint yourself into a corner, and say, 'How do I get out of this one?' Sometimes you get out of it. Sometimes you think you're getting out of it, but the audience doesn't. The idea is to push yourself, to not start repeating yourself."[9]

Judd's favorite source of conflict is an emotional block. His guiding principle is: ruin someone's life and see what they do. Not dissimilar to the biblical story of Job. Great writers are mean to their characters, they make them suffer. They make them less and less happy as the story progresses. In William Foster-Harris's book *The Basic Patterns of Plot* (1959), his advice is, "Make the problem worse and worse and worse! Make it as bad as you possibly can and then add some more! . . . Then inevitably, through reversal, you will arrive suddenly at unexpected *solution* and light."[10] Doom your hero. Characters need to struggle. Give your hero a fatal flaw, a weakness that impedes their ability to attain their goal, a failing that must eventually be overcome.

If you look at Judd's film *Bridesmaids* (2011), it's about a person whose life is falling apart: She's gone bankrupt, she's in a terrible relationship, and her friend is enjoying a wonderful, new engagement. It forces her to deal with who she is and why things aren't going better. In *The Big Sick* (2017), a guy falls in love with a woman in a coma and has to face why he can't commit. *The 40-Year-Old Virgin* (2005) is about a man who missed out on having sex and thinks no one could ever love him. Judd acts like a psychologist as much as a writer. He learned from Garry Shandling, when he was writing for *The Larry Sanders Show* (1992–1998), to look for characters' obstacles on the road back to emotional health. "When I work with people, I'll ask, 'What do you think it would take for you to move past your emotional blocks?' It's a self-exploration. 'What are your struggles? Where is your ego out of control? If you can drop your fears and your ego, would you be happier? Would you become a more giving, healthy, loving person?' It's fun to watch people be a mess and try to evolve."

When editing powerful, dramatic scenes in *Grey's Anatomy*, I learned one of Krista Vernoff's methods for making emotional scenes stronger is to bring characters right to the edge of crying, without letting them actually shed the tears. If you let them tiptoe right up to the line, but don't let the dam burst, the emotion plays much stronger than if the actors begin crying.

Life Is a Struggle

Most situations in life experienced between people are a power struggle of some kind, a continual renegotiation for more or less control or freedom, between spouses, siblings, parent and child, employer and employee. We are constantly engaging in cost-benefit analyses of relationships, of compromising or holding firm, of sticking around or leaving. If you were to list all of your favorite movies, probably every one of them is a fight.

There can be conflict between:

1. man versus man (or woman)
2. man versus himself
3. man versus society
4. man versus nature
5. man versus technology
6. man versus supernatural
7. man versus god (or alien)

Combining these layers of conflict can provide even stronger stories. If there is no "versus" in a story, you probably do not have a strong plot yet. Sometimes the movie industry likes to come right out and tell you who is fighting; they put "vs." in the title, such as *King Kong vs. Godzilla* (1963), *Kramer vs. Kramer* (1979), *Batman v Superman: Dawn of Justice* (2016).

The Plots

There are debates about how many basic plots exist. There are different ways to dissect exactly what a story is. William Foster-Harris wrote in his book *The Basic Patterns of Plot*, "Just as a good fiction story is always a parable, so a correct fictional plot, the map of the story, must contain a problem, the solution, and the answer." Foster-Harris separates plots into a happy ending or an unhappy ending—depending on whether the hero chooses the right or the wrong action at the decision point. "The 'wrong' choice will seem to be the safe, sane, and sensible one, the 'right' [choice will seem to be] ruinous." But that difficult choice, which Foster-Harris calls passing through the "dark moment," leads to a reversal. The virtuous hero will make the right choice, which requires a personal sacrifice, for the sake of others, which leads to a greater good and a positive ending. Even if protagonists making the right choice die, they die the right way. The selfish protagonist gives way to the wrong emotion, makes the wrong choice, the easier choice, then passes through the reversal, and ends up with nothing. Even if this protagonist lives, it is a miserable, regretful existence. If Ebenezer Scrooge had kept all his riches at the end of Charles Dickens's *A Christmas Carol* (1843), even though it would have been the safe choice, it would have led to a life of more personal misery. By sacrificing his own financial safety and giving his money away, he passes through a reversal, with a happier ending for all.[11]

Almost every movie follows one of six master trajectories:

1. Fall, then a rise—*North by Northwest* (1959), *Die Hard* (1988), *The Bourne Identity* (2002)
2. Rise—*Forest Gump* (1994), *Slumdog Millionaire* (2008)
3. Fall—*Romeo and Juliet* (1595), *Titanic* (1997)
4. Rise, then fall—*Icarus* (30 BC), *Scarface* (1932)
5. Rise, fall, then rise—*Cinderella, or The Little Glass Slipper* (1697), *Charlie and the Chocolate Factory* (1964)
6. Fall, rise, then fall—*Oedipus Rex* (430 BC), *The Jerk* (1979)

Story arc number one, a fall then a rise, is the most often-used plot. It is the core structure of an innocent hero experiencing a sudden event leading to a life-or-death fight. It is also known as "man in a hole." The other five arcs are found less often.

In his Jungian-influenced book, *The Seven Basic Plots: Why We Tell Stories* (2004), Christopher Booker contends there are seven primary story frameworks:

1. Overcoming the monster—*Beowulf* (1815), *Frankenstein* (1818)
2. Rags to riches—*Jane Eyre* (1846), *David Copperfield* (1850)
3. The quest—*Treasure Island* (1883), *The Lord of the Rings* (1954)

4. Voyage and return—*The Time Machine* (1895), *The Martian* (2014)
5. Comedy—*A Midsummer Night's Dream* (1600), *The Importance of Being Earnest* (1895)
6. Tragedy—*Madame Bovary* (1857), *Anna Karenina* (1878)
7. Rebirth—*Beauty and the Beast* (1740), *Spirited Away* (2001)

There are many others that can be used as well. They can be combined and often overlap. But do not overcomplicate things. Do not overload a story with too many conceits. You are only allowed one coincidence per story, and it is usually the inciting incident. Your hero should have only one superpower, or one piece of magic, or one core motivation.

Here is a baker's dozen of other solid plot motivations:

1. Revenge—*Death Wish* (1974), *Blue Ruin* (2013)
2. Coming of age—*Stand by Me* (1986), *Y Tu Mamá También* (2001)
3. Redemption—*It's a Wonderful Life* (1946), *Gran Torino* (2008)
4. Solving a mystery—*The Big Sleep* (1946), *The Girl with the Dragon Tattoo* (2011)
5. Self-sacrifice—*Star Trek II: The Wrath of Kahn* (1982), *The Iron Giant* (1999)
6. Fight the power—*One Flew Over the Cuckoo's Nest* (1975), *V for Vendetta* (2005)
7. Life-or-death crisis—*12 Monkeys* (1995), *Into the Wild* (2007)
8. Supernatural—*Ghost Busters* (1984), *Hereditary* (2018)
9. Superhero—*Superman* (1978), *Chronicle* (2012)
10. The fool wins—*The Pink Panther* (1963), *National Lampoon's Animal House* (1978)
11. The chase—*Gone in 60 Seconds* (1974), *The French Connection* (1971)
12. The rescue—*Escape from New York* (1981), *Aliens* (1986)
13. The escape—*Midnight Express* (1978), *The Shawshank Redemption* (1994)

The most used plot of all is *boy meets girl, boy loses girl, boy wins girl back* (and any variation such as girl meets boy, boy meets boy, girl meets girl, kid meets dog, alien meets human, alien meets alien, Porsche 911 meets Chevrolet Corvette, etc.). All romantic movies follow this plan. Most of the other plots listed above probably also have an X-meets-Y plotline as well. As an editor analyzing a story, it helps to recognize which plot is which. You need to know exactly what kind of machine you are building, or, what kind of being you are helping to bring to life.

Beware *the idiot plot*, where there would be no story if your protagonist stopped making stupid decisions. A stronger story is when protagonists believe they are making the right choices, and they still get in trouble. It may be nerve-racking to watch a tightly drawn idiot plot, but it is ultimately not as satisfying. *Uncut Gems* (2019) is an example where there is nonstop arguing and conflict, but every decision Howard Ratner makes is a dumb one. If Ratner stopped making foolish decisions, the movie would be over. It is frustrating for a viewer to watch a protagonist, the person whose shoes they are putting themselves in, make bad decisions. Some crime films fall into this category where they put the audience into the position of having to follow the story of foolish criminals they don't like. And then it's a relief when the movie ends.

The Premise

What are you writing about? What is your premise? What is the theme? The fewer words needed to describe your idea the better. If you can get it down to three to five words, that's going to be easy to pitch (and easy for executives to remember). The simple thematic premise of *The Terminator* (1984) is "man fights technology."

The premise is the most important element a scene or an episode needs. What is the show about? Larry David explained his approach to writing premises: "It can't be just, 'My friend is staying in the house and he's stealing from me.' Or, 'My friend is flirting with my girlfriend.' That's such a common, typical idea. It's not original. There's nothing to it. We don't even consider that an idea. The premise has to be inherently funny on its own. If I tell you an idea for any of our episodes you should laugh or smile from what I'm saying."

I asked, "Like the doll premise?" (Season two, episode seven.)

"Right. 'A little girl asks you to give her doll a haircut.' If I tell somebody that, they're going to laugh. That's one of my all-time favorites."

I had to know. "Is that from your own life?"

"Yes. From staring at my child's doll. Wanting to give it a haircut. I'm wondering how she'd react if I cut that doll's hair, because I thought it would look better with shorter hair."

Curb Your Enthusiasm added a layer of joy to Larry's life because experiences that may have been upsetting became great premises. Larry admitted, "Ordinarily I don't like to go out of the house. But I found it's good to leave, because I come up with more stuff. It justifies me doing something I don't really want to do. Going to a wedding, a dinner, or particularly a funeral."

The writing on *Curb Your Enthusiasm* starts with Larry David's collection of premises, often things he has personally experienced during the past year, and then he writes a situation to put the potential comedy of this premise to the test. "If you have a funny premise, you'll have a funny scene." Some days Larry will walk into the editing room talking about an incident that just happened that could be an idea for next season. The best premises are about something small, perhaps mundane, but laden with potential conflict, and then Larry examines it and pushes it to an extreme.

Write the Logline First

In the 2005 writing manual *Save the Cat!*, Blake Snyder analyzed premise in the form of a "logline." He emphasized how important it is, before writing a script, to compose a succinct, one- or two-sentence logline that gives a description of an entire story. A logline must have an active protagonist with a clear primal goal, plus a stronger antagonist in opposition to that goal. Both should be a familiar type and have a descriptive adjective. The protagonist's goal is linked to the incident that launches the story. The higher the stakes the better. The logline should set the tone, and possibly include a killer title within it. You have to be able to imagine an entire storyline from it.

Here's an example of a logline: A plucky farm boy joins a rebellion to save a beautiful princess and the galaxy from a powerful commander of a planet-destroying spaceship. One reason *Star Wars: Episode IV—A New Hope* (1977) works is because it can be simplified. A dash of irony also helps, such as this logline for the series *Dexter* (2006–2013): A serial killer vows to kill only other killers.

If you cannot describe a story succinctly, development executives' eyes will glaze over. If executives cannot quickly grasp the conflict and main characters in a couple of sentences, they will not be able to concisely pitch it to their bosses. Plus, the marketing department will struggle with how to sell it. One mistake novice pitch writers make is to become engrossed in details of setting. Producers don't buy settings, they buy stories. What matters is: Who is the hero, what is the goal, what are the obstacles, and who is the antagonist? Settings are easily changed.

Write an Outline

After you've come up with a great premise and logline, the next step is to write an outline with a solid, structural basis. Some writers prefer to avoid outlines. Sometimes that works and sometimes it doesn't. Douglas E. Richards, writer of science-fiction thrillers, prefers to let a story evolve as he writes it: "I never have any idea of what the finished plot might be, nor the ending, nor key twists and turns, until I'm at least halfway through it. It's like jumping off a cliff, having some vague sense that there's a deep pool of water out of sight below, and praying that I'll be able to spot the water before I splatter on the ground."[12]

Before *you* jump off a cliff, you best be certain there is water below. You may succeed with a looser structure in a novel, but you won't have that kind of leeway in a movie or television episode. Can you build a house without a blueprint? You might get away with it if you are building a shed. But not a skyscraper. Write the outline first. You can always deviate from it if you get a brainstorm. But if you write yourself into a cul-de-sac, it's hard to write your way out of it.

If you are looking at the footage of a project that doesn't seem to be working, chances are good that the problems are structural, possibly with other problems laid on top. Even if you improve the dialogue or add dozens of jokes, if the structure is bad, it's never going to rise to a higher level.

Valerie Flueger Veras, senior vice president of post-production at Legendary Pictures, analyzes a problematic horror or action film by removing all the horror moments and action set-pieces. Then the producers look at the bare-bones storyline to make sure it plays. She said she picked this wisdom up from producer Jason Blum, who has said, "If you take out all the scares, would [the film] work as a Sundance indie drama? That's what makes some of them really good. They work dramatically without being scary. And then the scares are even scarier."[13] The drama should work all by itself, without the ornamentation. Once you make sure it does, then add the horror and action pieces, like hanging decorations on a strong framework.

Story Can Not Be Improvised

In *Curb Your Enthusiasm* and *The League*, the dialogue is improvised, but these shows still follow the rules of story. A situation is fully written in advance. A script for *Curb Your Enthusiasm* will have a paragraph for each scene, which sets up the situation, the conflict, what's at stake, who is annoying whom, and maybe thrown in are a few suggestions for lines of dialogue. I've edited versions of scenes where they used none of the dialogue that was suggested, they went in a different direction once they got to the set. But story points rarely change.

Jeff Schaffer prefers to have a strong outline to guide him when writing dialogue on set. "You have the structure, you know the scene is funny, but then you're going to come up with something new. It's like this live, comedy, sporting event. If someone says something, I know how to say it right back. But if you're sitting in a room alone, no one's saying anything to you, and that's not nearly as fun."

The Outline Is More Important Than the Dialogue

Spend most of your energy building a fully working story outline. Once you have an outline that works, one that makes you excited to sit down and reread it, then move on to filling in the dialogue and the exposition. Almost anybody can hang a painting on the wall or choose granite, marble, or tile. But very few can design the geometrically synchronous framework of a beautiful building. Often new writers get over-anxious to begin and then never finish the script because they get stuck when they inevitably run into unsolved structure problems. Sitcom is short for situation-comedy. Part of writing and editing comedy is making sure a *situation* is itself funny or engaging. Comedy does not rely primarily on funny lines. A humorous situation must first stand on its own. Funny dialogue naturally follows when you place characters in funny situations.

Of *Curb Your Enthusiasm*, Alec Berg said, "We spent months honing those outlines to the point where any one of us could have taken an outline and written a script from it in a day. Ninety-five percent of the writing work is done. It just isn't put in the format of a script yet. The final layer of paint gets put on by all these brilliant actors on the day of the shoot." David Mandel agreed. "If I have an outline of a great story, I can write the script in a night and make a pretty damn funny episode because the hard part is the story." Jeff Schaffer maps out the story in the outline. "If the stories aren't good, it doesn't matter. Pick good funny stories that haven't been done before and then figure out the comedy geometry on a dry-erase board, and how they're going to end in a cool way."

David Mandel faults some episodes of *Seinfeld* that have great jokes but don't work. "If you were to isolate any scene or couple of jokes, they might be some of the best we ever did on *Seinfeld*. But if the story doesn't work, the episode doesn't work, therefore it's not one of the great ones. The jokes hang on the skeleton of a really good outline." Alec Berg agreed that jokes come later. "Once you know who's in the scene and what they want, the jokes are the easiest part. That's the layer that goes on last. But everything underneath it is what makes it actually work." Alec said he spends most of his time on character and the story beats. He asks, what is each show about? And what choice is the character forced to make and what does that reveal to us about who that person is? "The way Bill Hader and I write is, he will ask, 'What if something like this happened?' I'll say, 'Wait, how do we get to that?' I'm much more left brained than he is, more about laying the pipe for the story. Bill tends to work more in 'what ifs.'"

Writing the Shooting Script

Once your outline is solid, write that great script. Alec Berg thinks about the scriptwriting process like making a wish list, or a shopping list. "These are all the things I think I need to make a meal. The shooting process is like when you are finally at the grocery store and your list meets reality." You know what you want, but you don't have time to grab everything, so you prioritize and compromise. They are out of one item, but another is cheaper. You get what you can and then present those ingredients to the editor, your chef. Alec calls editing "the death of hope. Because that's where you go, 'Oh, we don't have it. What do we do?' And you just have to make it with what you have." If the editors have experience, and a few new ideas, plus a little panache, they make it work.

Make Each Character Unique

None of the dialogue should be interchangeable among characters. One way to add conflict is to give each character a different voice. To make sure your characters are in opposition, create a character wheel, where you place each character at the end of a spoke coming out from the center. Make sure there is a corresponding character with opposite personality traits on the other side of each spoke. With opposites, conflict flows naturally. Perhaps one character is a health nut and the other a hypochondriac. One sleeps late and the other rises with the sun. One is fastidious and the other is slovenly. That gives you Neil Simon's paradigm for *The Odd Couple* (1965). A potential list of opposite emotional, physical, or intellectual traits is endless.

1. lazy versus industrious
2. psychic versus skeptic
3. narcissistic versus insecure
4. young versus old
5. pious versus pervert
6. glutton versus nibbler
7. stoner versus bright-eyed
8. nerd versus jock
9. reckless versus risk averse

The Comedy Couple

During season fourteen of *Grey's Anatomy*, the producers wanted to shift back toward their roots, where stories were lighter and had more comedy. Showrunner Krista Vernoff's style is: "I like to keep you laughing until I make you cry." Krista likes to sometimes include a "comedy couple" B-story. The main couple's arc is dramatic and serious; people are dying and they're dealing with death and grief. To offset that, the younger interns have events in their relationships that are awkward and funny. Their romantic gyrations provide humorous relief among the life-and-death A-stories. Krista said this came from her background studying classical theater in college, particularly Shakespeare and Commedia dell'arte, which utilizes similar archetypes. "The First Lovers were melodramatic in their love. The Second Lovers were silly and messy and funny."

Author's collection.

Two interns work out amusing relationship issues on *Grey's Anatomy*.

Editing Comedy Dialogue

Jeff Schaffer described what's next after shooting an episode with improvised dialogue: "We dump it at the editor's doorstep like some sort of baby no one wanted and go, 'Clean it up. I'll see him when he graduates from college.'"

In the *Curb Your Enthusiasm* episode "Mister Softee" (season eight, episode nine), comedian Robert Smigel played a mechanic who is supposed to fix Larry's car. It was very difficult to edit their scenes because they were laughing so hard. They would begin, then laugh, stop, and back up. "Okay, say that again." They would get two lines further and then another big laugh would force them to back up again. The stop-and-start process makes editing difficult, but when actors make Larry laugh, we are onto something. Robert Smigel said Larry's laughing only made him go for it even harder. "It was like being in a fantasy baseball camp, showing up and getting to hit pitches from Tom Seaver. Or Mariano Rivera, for the kids." The kind of dialogue that comes out of these exchanges is something nobody could have written alone. Larry said it's rare that he goes home thinking, "I wish I had *written* that scene instead."

While cutting episodes of the HBO series *Crashing* (2017–2019), I could hear Judd Apatow in the background of the footage, throwing out a continual stream of alternative lines to actors, giving me a lot of choices as an editor. He also loves it when an actor improves upon his jokes or comes up with a better idea. "If you allow people to improvise, they reveal parts of themselves that are surprising. The amount of choices that Pete Davidson made during *The King of Staten Island* that I could never have anticipated is enormous. Every day he would do something that I was shocked by. And then sometimes I think, 'I like that line, but let's get a couple of options because there is a chance that we are caught up in the moment and it will not translate to the editing room.'"

After you've got takes the way the scene is scripted, if there's time, directors sometimes do a "one for fun" take, where the actors are encouraged to try it any way they want, with lots of ad-libbing. You may get a funny line or two out of it, so if you have time, it can bear fruit. Usually in those kinds of ad-libbed takes, there's very little new material, plot-wise, so we don't use a lot of it. Non-comedic actors mostly repeat story exposition, restating what they've read in the scene. Actors are not writers; it's not their strength. But on any show, actors do contribute to the writing process. During rehearsal they add stage business, try out different versions of lines, and come up with new ideas. Julia Louis-Dreyfus said, "As an actor, it's incumbent upon you to add layers to what's on the page. You're adding frosting to the cake. Your job isn't to say the words and get out. You have to bring it to life. It's exciting."

When Judd Apatow is filming, he'll try to imagine what he might need in the editing room to fix a scene if it doesn't work, or if it doesn't play at a test screening. "If this scene is too funny, then maybe I'll think it's lost its sense of importance in the story. I may need to do a version where I strip out the jokes. I'll say, 'Don't try to be funny, let's just play the reality this time.' And sometimes I do the opposite, 'That was a serious version, but let's see if we can get away with a joke right in the middle of this heavy moment.' Then in editing we are rewriting the entire movie. Sometimes it's like we've shot a documentary and we're finding the story in post. In some movies we sit closer to the script than others."

Ignore What I Just Said

Of course, you can break any of these rules. Many successful stories do, and somehow it still works—maybe even better. But the successful filmmakers who break the rules usually do so on purpose, after understanding the rules, and knowing why they are breaking them. But go ahead, experiment. Push the boundaries. That's how you find out where they are. And now that you are ready to write, what should you write about?

CHAPTER FIVE

The Source of Inspiration

Everybody Has At Least One Great Story Inside Them

An independent filmmaker has to be a writer because great screenplays are exceedingly rare. Nobody is going to hand you that amazing script for free. You might think, "I am not a writer. I don't have any ideas. I can't write anything." Are you sure about that?

Where do ideas come from? If your life has been a blank slate, of course you can't sit in a room and generate new ideas from nothing. Ideas come from experience. From life. From history. From research. From all that came before. The inspiration for that next editorial choice comes from the same place as the inspiration for that great story idea. You are not a blank slate. You have lived and witnessed a multitude of events. You can begin by writing a story based on your own life. Start there. Your story will be engaging if you are willing to rip open your soul. Write about the skeletons in the closet, the family secrets, the suppressed feelings; write about things that you wouldn't tell your shrink. That is the kind of writing that stands out. Ernest Hemingway said, to get started, "Write the truest sentence that you know." And then "go on from there."[1]

Still not sure where to start? Keep a journal. Try writing for ten minutes every morning when you wake up. In her book *The Artist's Way: A Spiritual Path to Higher Creativity* (1992), Julia Cameron calls them morning pages, stream of consciousness writing, expressing whatever passes through your mind. Through this method you will begin to uncover ideas you didn't even know you had.

Mike Binder's first screenplay, *Coup de Ville* (1990), was based on a family story. Mike's father and uncles told anecdotes around holiday dinners about the time they drove their father's classic Cadillac from Detroit to Florida. They smashed it up on the way, but like in the movie *Rashomon* (1950), they each told a different version of what happened.

Jeff Schaffer believes ideas are everywhere. As he is walking around, he is writing things down. Judd Apatow's mantra is: "Write what you want to see." It could be your passion for something silly, or it could be for something emotional, as long as you care about what you're doing. "Everything I've done," Judd said, "whether it's high-minded or silly, I've done because I'm obsessed with it. It's like with a band. You can tell if they're just crankin' out music because it's time to make a new album. And then with someone like Billie Eilish, or Kid Cudi, you realize they're opening up and sharing something personal. When I met Seth Rogen, the comedy fan in me thought: 'If this guy was in a movie, that would be cool.' And really that's all it is. 'Oh, if Amy Schumer had a movie, that would be cool.' And now I just try to make that movie, the one that I wish existed."

Author's collection.

Three brothers attempt to deliver their father's Cadillac, in *Coup de Ville*.

Who are you writing for? If it's a screenplay you're crafting, you're writing for the gatekeeper.

Get Past the Reader

Screenwriter Edward Neumeier began as a story analyst. He often dreaded his job because he hated reading bad writing. When it felt like everything he read was terrible, it put him in a bad mood. But he had to get through each script to summarize it so his bosses didn't have to read it. He said readers only read dialogue. Avoid long or detailed description; it's irrelevant until it's time to shoot. He warned, "Be a writer, not a director. Don't include how to shoot the film. Just tell the story and what the characters say. If you write the scene well enough, the camera is going to have to do what you want it to." Neumeier would speed-read the first thirty pages, skim the dialogue in the middle, jump to the end, write a list of characters, a quick summary, and move on.

As a writer, you've got to get past that person, the one who's disconsolate and has no patience. Neumeier's advice was, "Write for the person who has to read hundreds of scripts and has seen it all. Keep him or her excited, turning pages, reading to the end. When a great script suddenly came through, it would almost cause a heart attack. If you can win over that story analyst, they will become your best advocate and rave about the script."

Talent Is Discipline

While working on *Starship Troopers*, Edward Neumeier once commiserated to director Paul Verhoeven, "I wish I was more talented."

Verhoeven replied, "Yeah, we all do."

Neumeier came to realize that talent is discipline. "You cannot *not* write. It's easy to not write. You have to make yourself sit down and write. That's talent." Dedicate time to writing. When I'm on an editing job, I set aside one day on the weekend to deal with various disasters, and the other day is for writing. I have to get in my hours, usually two before lunch, and four after. Thinking of a whole project is overwhelming, so I set an achievable goal, like a draft of a first-act outline, or five pages. Many writers talk about achieving a certain number of words per day. Stephen King puts his goal at two thousand words.[2] Sometimes when I finish only one decent paragraph, it's a celebration. The point is to keep chipping away.

If you are still protesting, "I can't write!" what about the hundreds of texts, e-mails, and social media posts you wrote today? For a few hours, shift your focus away from those time-wasters. Open a document. Think about a character, or a person you have known. Now ask, what is their fatal flaw? Maybe: "My father can't let go of the past; he tries to control me with threats to stop paying my dorm rent." Or, "My sister acts like a jerk; she's in pain because she's been jealous since we were toddlers." Or maybe think of yourself: "I can't say 'I love you' to anybody because my emotions have been crushed so many times." Now describe that person's most embarrassing moment they've ever experienced. Sit there until you write at least one paragraph. It's okay to write it badly at first. Just get something on the page. Later you can revise it. That first paragraph, a description of a character with a problem, that is the beginning of a story. And an embarrassing incident comes with a built-in punch line, an automatic ending, just like when you would tell the anecdote to your friends.

When Edward Neumeier analyzed hundreds of scripts, he realized stories are all about survival: "We are pattern-seeking primates who came from the African savanna. We've been here a long time, but there have been a lot of people before us. And all they were trying to do was not get killed. Social survival is love stories. Physical survival is action adventure. Stories are an educational process for the audience: Here is how you survive this situation."

New Is Sometimes a New Combination

If you are still looking at that page thinking, "I don't have any ideas," one way to prime your creative pump is to take your favorite movies or television shows and combine them; mix them up into a new concoction and see what fresh thing pops out. It's common at studio pitches to say, "This is a combination of this and that." This helps the noncreative creative-executives better understand what sort of beast you are creating. There may be no new ideas under the sun, but there are an infinite number of new combinations. You can use a mash-up as an inspiration to create your own, new, unique expression. Consider examples of what has already come out of the mash-up machine.

+ George Bernard Shaw's 1913 play *Pygmalion* found inspiration in the Greek myth about a sculptor who falls in love with his statue as well as Charles Perrault's 1697 short story *Cinderella, or The Little Glass Slipper*. Other stories that share a similar plot arc that followed are *Pinocchio* (1940), *My Fair Lady* (1964), and *Pretty Woman* (1990).
+ The series *Lost* (2004–2010) is like a mixture of the novel *Robinson Crusoe* (1719) (and its modern version, *Cast Away* [2000]), the series *Gilligan's Island* (1964–1967), and the movies *Alive* (1993) and *Mysterious Island* (1961).
+ *The Purge* (2013) has elements that are an homage to an episode of *Star Trek* called "The Return of the Archons" (1967), and both have antecedents in the ancient Greek holiday Kronia and the ancient Roman festival of Saturnalia and the "Two Minutes Hate" from George Orwell's 1949 novel *Nineteen Eighty-Four*.

✦ *Get Out* (2017) is a combination of *In the Heat of the Night* (1967) plus *Guess Who's Coming to Dinner* (1967) with a dash of *The Step-ford Wives* (1975).

As you actively examine stories, you will see patterns and begin to notice where filmmakers found inspiration. If you want to analyze a few more famous examples, watch the following movies and compare their precursors. Decide for yourself who was inspired by what.

✦ Quentin Tarantino's *Reservoir Dogs* (1992) versus Ringo Lam's *City on Fire* (1987) versus Stanley Kubrick's *The Killing* (1956).

✦ George Lucas's *Star Wars: Episode IV—A New Hope* (1977) versus Akira Kurosawa's *The Hidden Fortress* (1958).

✦ James Cameron's *Avatar* (2009) versus science-fiction author Poul Anderson's novelette *Call Me Joe* (1957) and Kevin Costner's *Dances with Wolves* (1990) and the animated movie *FernGully: The Last Rainforest* (1992).

✦ Walt Disney Pictures's animated *The Lion King* (1994 and 2019) versus Osamu Tezuka's Japanese-anime television-series *Jungle Emperor, a.k.a. Kimba the White Lion* (1965–1967) versus William Shakespeare's *The Tragedy of Hamlet, Prince of Denmark* (1600).

The Lion King isn't the only work to borrow from *Hamlet*. John Milton's poem *Paradise Lost* (1667), Henry Fielding's novel *Tom Jones* (1749), Charles Dickens's novel *Great Expectations* (1861), and many other works have been inspired by or reference *Hamlet*. Before you decide to give Shakespeare all the credit, Shakespeare's *Hamlet* is based on sixteen books compiling the Norse legend, *History of the Danes* (originally published in 1200), by Saxo Grammaticus.

In the late 1980s, after I moved to Los Angeles, I took a seminar at the American Film Institute. Each week they invited a different director, who would show a clip and talk about their movies. One week, director James Cameron showed the climactic ending of his incredible sequel *Aliens* (1986) where Ellen Ripley (Sigourney Weaver) fights the alien queen while wearing an exosuit. Cameron said that the studio executives were having a hard time understanding the scene when he first pitched it so he told them, "Imagine this fight being like a scene from *Rocky.*" That's how Cameron saw his movie, the scenes were like scenes from somewhere else, yet reworked with his own unique vision.

When the question-and-answer session arrived, I asked Cameron, "Have you ever seen the movie *Cyborg 2087*?" I was genuinely curious about his writing influences as a filmmaker. *Cyborg 2087* is a 1966 low-budget science-fiction film about a "good" cyborg sent from the future being chased by "bad" cyborgs. The good cyborg's mission is to prevent a scientist from revealing his new discovery, which will cause future tyranny. *The Terminator* (1991) is about a future war where machines send a "bad" cyborg back in time to kill the mother of the leader of the human resistance, and the humans send a soldier back to protect her.

Cameron's pause before answering my question was brief. "Isn't that the film that stars Michael Rennie? That was kind of a bad movie, wasn't it?" He had seen *Cyborg 2087*, and he knew it was similar enough to feel he should point out that his film was superior, which it certainly was.

Over the years, Cameron has defended himself against lawsuits, one side effect of success. If you do pay homage to prior works, or intentionally bring an influence forward into your work, you need to be aware of the rules of copyright. I'm not an attorney and this book is not a source of bona fide legal advice. To get legal advice before you write any story with material that might be protected, consult a competent, licensed copyright attorney to learn your rights.

For the most part, all works published in the United States before 1923 are in the U.S. public domain. You can lift anything you want from Chaucer, Shakespeare, Bram Stoker, or Edgar Allan

Poe. Some works copyrighted between 1923 and 1964 are also in the public domain, due to copyright owners neglecting to do a required renewal. Each year more works enter the public domain. In 2021 copyrighted works from before 1925 also entered the public domain, such as F. Scott Fitzgerald's *The Great Gatsby* and Ernest Hemingway's *In Our Time*. But keep in mind that even though an adapted work like a film might be in the public domain, an underlying work that it is based upon might not be. If you want to be certain, do the research. Works copyrighted after 1977 are all off limits (for several more decades at a minimum).

Here's an example of a very talented writer possibly being inspired and creating a unique, new idea out of an old one. There's a 1960 *Twilight Zone* episode called "Elegy" (season one, episode twenty) that could have been the seed of inspiration for Michael Crichton's movie *Westworld* (1973). In *The Twilight Zone* episode, a humanlike robot is in charge of Happy Glades, a mortuary built on an asteroid, which is designed "to re-create the exact conditions under which the dear departed would be most happy." The robotic caretaker asks three stranded astronauts which fantasy-based section they would prefer to be placed in, the Medieval Period, the Roman, the Egyptian, the Wild Western section, or some other time period of their choosing. Crichton's characters, dialogue, setting, and plot were all different. His movie takes a germ of an idea to a new level by making a space mortuary into a theme park, an idea he further reworked in *Jurassic Park* (1993).

Stephen King may have also grown up watching *The Twilight Zone* episodes. King's 1980 novel *Firestarter* has a similar conceit to *The Twilight Zone* episode called "The Prime Mover" (1961, season two, episode twenty-one), written by Charles Beaumont, in which a character (played by Buddy Ebsen) has telekinetic powers that give him headaches. King's version may or may not be inspired by this classic television episode, but his story vastly expands on

A man uses his telekinetic powers for gambling, in an episode of *The Twilight Zone.*

a kernel of an idea presented in that episode. Anybody can write about characters with psychic abilities. There are scores of books and movies about telekinesis.

An example where somebody tried to prove the writers went too far is *The Waterboy* (1998). Tim Herlihy and Adam Sandler based the script on one of Sandler's *Saturday Night Live* characters. But Harold Lloyd's granddaughter filed a lawsuit against Buena Vista Pictures, claiming the film was an unofficial remake of Harold Lloyd's silent film *The Freshman* (1925). Ultimately the court denied her a victory. Ironically, Harold Lloyd had also been sued for *The Freshman* by author H. C. Witwer, who claimed that Lloyd's film was a copy of his 1915 satirical short story "The Emancipation of Rodney." Witwer also lost. It is very difficult to successfully prove theft of a protected work.

Ideas Are Not Copyrightable

Why is it possible to rework older ideas? Because *ideas* are not protected. The "marketplace of ideas" concept has emerged as the dominant public policy in laws protecting free speech. Only a particular expression of an idea that is fixed in a tangible medium can be copyrighted and owned; at that point it becomes an intellectual property, or an IP. You may be able to trademark something, which distinguishes commercial goods, but you cannot copyright a title, phrase, or slogan. Hundreds of works are titled "I Love You." To prevent marketing confusion arising from duplicate movie titles, the motion picture studios have an agreement among themselves where they self-regulate their use of titles.

You may pitch the greatest idea, but you can't copyright it until you have written it down (or recorded it in some fixed way). Once you do write that great script, don't bother registering it at the Writers Guild of America (WGA) because registration is not as strong as copyright. WGA registration expires after five years (it is renewable, if you don't forget, for another five years, during a six-month window, for another payment). Registering a work with the U.S. Copyright Office is a more permanent record (author's life plus seventy years). You can open an account and upload your work via their website.

Don't Steal, Be Inspired

There was once a successful writer who worked frequently, bought a nice house, got married, and then got divorced. He had a mortgage to keep up, plus alimony and child support. He reached a point where he felt like he was out of ideas, but he had bills to pay so he had to keep coming up with ideas in order to keep getting television writing jobs. He scoured books, movies, and other scripts, appropriating ideas to feed a voracious pipeline. When he steered close to what he feared might be too similar to outright copying, he hoped no one would notice. He lived in fear of being caught, until that ball of fear metastasized into a cancer that killed him.

When you immerse yourself in a universe of stories, use them as seasoning to your own creativity. Make them your muse, to stimulate your own writing. But don't copy from other works.

Two Case Studies

When is it inspiration, or homage, or parallel idea generation, and when is it stealing? Ideas are free, but copyrighted works are properties that belong to somebody else. You need to fully understand the difference because there is a potential legal downside to "borrowing" prior works. I will outline two case studies from my own experience to present examples of how either situation can come about.

The *Amistad* Project

In 1993 a writer and comedian named Steven Carey Lassoff pitched me a story of an amazing historical incident about a slave ship mutiny and how ex-president John Quincy Adams argued the former captives' case for freedom to the Supreme Court—and won. We wrote a pitch about the Amistad story and attached producer Mike Flint, who set a pitch meeting at HBO.

At the meeting, we pitched the story and left a treatment entitled *Voyage to Justice: The Trial of the Amistad*. They said they were intrigued but HBO could not proceed based solely upon a treatment. Mike Flint asked if we could submit the screenplay when finished, and they said yes. Over the next eighteen months we did further research, wrote a screenplay, and registered it at the copyright office in November of 1994. Mike called HBO, and they said to send over the script. Not long after, they responded to say they would be returning the screenplay because HBO had already begun developing an Amistad project. Bob Cooper (HBO senior vice president) was in charge of the project. They were apologetic but maintained that it was simply a mistake. When Mike suggested that HBO buy out the original co-writers (us!) who had been there with the pitch first, the development executive quickly got off the phone.

We were disheartened. Did they develop our idea or was there a parallel pitch that came in after us? There was no way to know without initiating a lawsuit and getting to the discovery phase. When faced with a situation like this you say, "That's showbiz!" and then move on. Parallel idea generation happens a lot, and ideas are not protectable. If you feel like you have a valid claim, you can look for an attorney who specializes in copyright. If you initiate legal action, be prepared to spend a lot of money. Good lawyers don't take jobs on commission. We met with attorney Mark Kalmansohn to get an opinion. Kalmansohn had represented Harve Bennett when he sued Paramount for his net profits on the *Star Trek* films. He was also a former U.S. Department of Justice prosecutor, known for hunting down Lucian Ludwig Kozminski, a Jewish oberkapo (an SS-appointed enforcer), who was convicted in 1982 of swindling fellow Holocaust survivors.

There Are No Damages Until a Work Is Released

Mark Kalmansohn explained that there was not much we could do unless and until HBO made a movie. Anybody can hire somebody to write a screenplay based on anything they want. There are no damages until a film is actually released. Another aspect weakening our case was that our story was based on a historical incident, over which nobody can claim ownership. So, we moved on.

Two years later, in 1997, it was announced in *Variety* that Bob Cooper and DreamWorks Pictures would be combining efforts to produce an Amistad film.[3,4] Now that a production was public and imminent, and because we had a strong paper trail for our meeting and submission, Kalmansohn advised sending a letter, putting HBO on notice that we believed we had a claim, to see if they would offer a preemptive settlement. A letter would cost only an hour of our lawyer's time. In the letter Kalmansohn summarized the history of our submission; he cited legal precedent and asked for credit and compensation totaling $1 million for lost salaries. Kalmansohn finished with a personal touch: "One theme of the Amistad story is that, in 1840 the American legal system could and did work to protect the little guy. We believe a jury will agree the American legal system can still do that today."

HBO business affairs responded with their version of a you-have-no-case letter, insisting that the HBO Amistad project was developed independent of our Amistad pitch. But they didn't dispute the fact that we were there first. It was depressing that months later they said yes to somebody else. Once again, do you let it go? Or do you start spending real money paying an attorney? Mike and I decided we were not interested in going to court. But Steven Carey Lassoff had found the story, and he was less inclined to let it go. None of us wanted to spend thousands of dollars on a lawsuit. I suggested Mark Kalmansohn call HBO and have one more conversation.

The Final Round

Kalmansohn spoke to HBO business affairs in New York and said, "One of the three parties has a desire to follow this through, and it will be out of my hands at that point. Right now, I have a degree of client control, but the loose cannon's next attorney would likely go on a fishing expedition at HBO and DreamWorks."

HBO's lawyer responded, "HBO would like to dispose of this Amistad claim without any action being filed." Mark's final call brought them off their intractable position. I am unable to discuss whether there was a settlement, or a dollar amount, only that the matter has been fully resolved.

According to Box Office Mojo, Steven Spielberg's *Amistad* was released by DreamWorks Distribution in December of 1997 and returned $44 million on a $36 million budget. I watched the movie in a theater with Mike Flint. I really wanted to enjoy the film because I loved the historical story so much, but it landed with a dramatic thud. Spielberg took an exciting story in American history and told a politically correct version, minus the excitement of many of the actual events. But, of course I would say that I liked our script better.

The credited author of the DreamWorks Pictures' *Amistad* screenplay ended up having his own legal issues, resulting from the author of a book about the same historical event feeling that her work had been used as a basis for that script.[5] Never assume that you can directly appropriate material in a book simply because it is about a historical event. Some material and characters may be unique and created by the author and could be protected. Do your own research. Use multiple sources. Go back to original accounts.

Suckers

Live by the sword, die by the sword. The next year I found myself playing defense when my film *Suckers* began production. Anybody can write a story about car salesmen. But as soon as Joe Yannetty and I wrote a specific script called *Suckers*, about Joe's life as a car salesman, that specific written account became our intellectual property. We registered our screenplay with the U.S. Copyright Office. Then one day, in 1998, while we were casting the film, a man named Steven Estrella walked into the lobby of Neo Motion Pictures and demanded to speak to the producers. He claimed that we had stolen his idea from a screenplay he had written called *The Deskman*, and he demanded payment. He initially refused to leave despite polite requests but eventually walked out vowing loudly that he would sue.

Steve Estrella found an attorney, who was willing to write the usual threatening letter. Nancy Sorel, an actress and Estrella's producer, was accused by Estrella of conspiring with Neo Motion Pictures to defraud him. Sorel had worked with actor Michael Chiklis on *The Commish* in 1992. She gave Chiklis a copy of *The Deskman* around the time we were casting *Suckers* in 1998. Chiklis was one of many actors who came in to read for the lead in *Suckers* and he told Sorel about our film, who then told Estrella. That led to Estrella losing a gasket in the Neo Motion Pictures lobby.

Sorel called and spoke with Neo Motion Pictures' producer Joel Soisson while I happened to be there. Sorel said that she was confused by Estella's threatening letter because she had never had any contact with anybody at Neo Motion Pictures. And we had never heard of this guy or seen his *Deskman* script. I asked her why she thought Estrella would go nuts over this, and she said, "Because it's the guy's only script, he's desperate, he's waiting tables, and he doesn't want to do that anymore." Miserable people will try to steal your joy, thinking it will make them feel better. Joe Yannetty and I were both upset at being accused of stealing somebody else's work.

I suggested we call Mark Kalmansohn, and Neo Motion Pictures hired him to respond formally. He wrote a letter to Estrella's lawyer saying "your client's claims are illusory and unpersuasive, and your characterization of the legal principles at issue inaccurate. We therefore remain hopeful that this response will prompt your reconsideration of these contentions and resolve the matter without any litigation."

The Copyright Tests

For a successful copyright infringement claim to prevail, it is not enough to have similarities, there has to be a finding of "substantial similarity." First there needs to be a quantifiable evaluation called an "extrinsic test," a complex analysis by qualified observers who consider the "total concept and feel" in *all eight* of the following categories: theme, plot, sequence of events, mood, setting, pace, characters, and dialogue. And there also is an "intrinsic test," where they consider if in the judgment of an ordinary person there is substantial similarity.

Another aspect that is considered is *scenes à faire*, a French term that translates to "scene that must be done." It is a concept that holds that certain stock or generic elements customary to a particular genre are not protectable and must be excluded. For example, stories that are created independently about gladiators, plumbers, or police officers are bound to have natural similarities that are inherent to their genre. Any car-salesmen scripts would have salesmen, pressure to sell faster, lying, disgruntled customers, sales dialogue, or other similar elements.

We were relieved when Mark Kalmansohn's letter scared off this attorney who was gambling on a quick payoff. The game was over. For a while.

The Second Round

Steve Estrella found another lawyer who sent a second letter. Producer W. K. Border sent back a succinct response: "After conferring with our counsel and in response to your correspondence dated June 23, 1998, which provided no new information, our position has not changed." That was the end of it again. This time for a year and a half.

In October of 1999, after a premiere screening of *Suckers* at the AFI Film Festival, a man walked up to producer Michael Leahy outside the theater. He leaned in close and said, "Do you remember me?" Michael didn't at first, and then it clicked.

Steve Estrella said, "I'm not done with you. I'll be coming back." Then he stalked off. For about five minutes he watched from afar. Then he walked back up to Michael and said, "You can tell Heckle and Jeckle inside that I'm coming back." Finally, he skulked away. But only for another year.

A Lawsuit Is Filed

In September of 2000, Estrella dug up a third attorney, Elliott L. Aheroni, who went beyond sending threatening letters and filed a lawsuit for $1.5 million, plus $1.5 million in punitive damages. Once there is a legal filing, everything becomes public record.

You must reply to a legal complaint. If you ignore it, you automatically lose and owe the money. There are two ways to respond. The simplest is to file an "answer," which Mark Kalmansohn could write in a few hours—meaning it would cost only a few hundred dollars. Producer Joel Soisson liked that idea. But an answer would not have any chance of dispensing with Estrella's Complaint. It is simply a response to the allegations.

Another way to respond is to file a "motion to dismiss" to get rid of the entire lawsuit based on defects in the Complaint. The advantage to a more aggressive filing is that even though it is a long shot, it might get Estrella's Complaint thrown out before the beginning of a summary judgment phase or a trial.

Mark Kalmansohn discovered that Estrella didn't copyright his screenplay *The Deskman* until May 17, 1999, three years after our screenplay was copyrighted, and long after he had access to our script. Since the entity being sued was the production company, the decision on how to proceed was up to the producers, and they took the aggressive stance. Filing all these motions so far cost in the neighborhood of ten thousand dollars, mainly due to the hours of work involved.

The Ruling

In January of 2001, our motion to dismiss was granted by Judge Carlos R. Moreno of the U.S. District Court for the Central District of California. Estrella's federal Complaint was thrown out—not on the merits of our motion, but due to their motion for continuance (extension of his deadline to respond) being filed late, making it invalid.

It was a technical win, and the game was not over. Judge Moreno granted our motions, but "with a leave to amend," which allowed Estrella's lawyer to refile again within 180 days, which he did. The particular judge you happen to draw can have a big impact on the trajectory of a case, because they are all individuals with different perspectives.

We were forced to have Kalmansohn rack up more billable hours filing another reply. Soon after, Judge Moreno ruled again, this time on the merits of our motions, dismissing three of Estrella's claims (based only on facial defects in the Complaint, as no evidence had yet been presented), leaving only the most minor "pendent" state law claim of conversion, which left the lawsuit alive, if on life support. An example of conversion would be if you were left in charge of somebody's cattle and you sold one and kept the money.

150

Mark Kalmansohn filed a motion with the Court to reconsider. He cited several examples, such as a suit over the script for the movie *Daylight* (1996), which showed how conversion does not apply with respect to a screenplay. Conversion only applies with respect to tangible property and its lack of return to its proper owner. In the case of a screenplay, the ideas contained within are not *tangible* property, only the paper script itself is, and Estrella had never asked for his script back, much less proved that we ever had access to it.

The Next Round

Estrella's attorney, Elliott L. Aheroni, filed an Amended Complaint (attempting to fix the prior facial defects in his Complaint) for copyright infringement, breach of contract, conversion, and fraud. So, we had to submit another motion to dismiss. And then Aheroni filed another opposition, late once again. The judge has discretion to allow late filings. By this point it was becoming abundantly clear why studios settle claims. These filings can go through many rounds, racking up thousands in an attorney's billable hours.

The next ruling was disappointing. The judge dismissed the breach of contract claim, but he took the narrowest approach toward the conversion, fraud, and copyright claims and allowed them to go forward. At this point the Neo Motion Pictures producers wanted the nightmare with no end in sight to go away. W. K. Border complained that the legal costs had now reached $25,000 and he would have done things differently and gone straight to trial. I asked him where he was getting his legal guidance and he said, "From my own layman's knowledge." I said, "You might want to get another opinion." He finally accepted that we were in this fight to the end—unless we offered settlement money. But nobody felt like rewarding this guy's legal harassment.

Is It Better to Go Directly to Trial?

Strategically and financially, going directly to trial is the last thing you want to do. It is better to do everything you can to have a case tossed out before a trial because discovery and the trial itself are the truly expensive parts. Aheroni knew this and was trying to push the case into this phase so we would be motivated to pay them off a dollar amount that would be less than the cost of going forward.

The discovery phase precedes a trial. It includes requests for production of documents, interrogatories (a list of questions), requests for admission (admit or deny the truth of statements under oath), and depositions (sworn testimony recorded outside of court). The whole idea of discovery is to set the case up for a summary judgment hearing. The price tag of discovery is in the neighborhood of $75,000 or more. The attorney's fees and court reporter fees for a deposition could easily exceed $10,000 per day. What's the price tag of a trial itself? Unknown. Maybe $200,000 or much more. The upside is that you may collect that in sanctions and costs from the losing party—if they have the money. If you skip the discovery phase and decide to appear in court for a summary judgment hearing unprepared, with nothing but your indignation, the judge will rip you to shreds for not distilling the case down to the relevant points.

The goal of the motion phase is to strip away as much of the plaintiff's case as possible. We had succeeded in knocking out only one of Estrella's four claims: the breach of contract claim.

Script Similarity Analysis

Mark Kalmansohn proposed a way of shortcutting the process by eliminating any document requests, depositions, and other discovery. Instead, we would go for the jugular in a narrow summary judgment approach by eliciting an "expert's" side-by-side comparison of Estrella's script and the *Suckers* film by an impartial, accredited expert (cost of $2,000 to $7,500, or more). If this direct attack on the federal copyright infringement claim succeeded, the two "pendent" claims under state law for conversion and fraud also would go down the tubes along with the federal copyright claim.

Mark Kalmansohn hired Linda Seger (script "doctor," screenwriting teacher, and author of the 1990 book *Creating Unforgettable Characters*), and her analysis found virtually no similarity of protectable elements. Both had a main character with a pregnant wife who has to sell a lot of cars within a prescribed period of time, and they both sometimes gamble. But that's where the similarities ended.

Elliott Aheroni filed a pleading claiming they had also secured the services of their own expert and anticipated that "evidence in opposition to Defendants' motion will be disclosed, indicating striking similarities in the script, both in mood and delivery. . . ." Aheroni appeared to be out of his depth, as "delivery" is not part of the extrinsic test.

The Final Ruling

In July of 2001, eleven months after Elliott Aheroni first filed suit, we had our day in court for a summary judgment hearing. When Aheroni had his moment at the podium, he said all he wanted to do was get into discovery. Mark Kalmansohn pointed out there were various preexisting common elements in both works while also stressing there was no overlap of protectable elements. Judge Carlos R. Moreno appeared visibly angry. He said that he had spent eight hours comparing the two works and found no protectable similarity, writing, "In copyright cases, it is not highly favored to grant summary judgment; however, a finding that two competing works are not substantially similar is sufficient for granting summary judgment."

Courtesy of Blink, Inc.

Suckers, starring Daniel Benzali, Lori Loughlin, and Louis Mandylor.

Judge Moreno also awarded attorneys' fees. Mark Kalmansohn's billings totaled $60,500. A judge ordinarily selects a sum (often a percentage between 50 and 80 percent) based on billing records. Estrella was obligated to pay our costs or he would be in contempt. A lien could be placed on any property he owns. We could also garnish his wages until the debt was satisfied. The next step was to get the Order, which was good for ten years, and attach Estrella's assets. An investigator turned up a guy in a rent-controlled apartment with less than $1,000 in the bank and a federal tax lien against him for $2,357. There would be no money to be squeezed out of this sad case. It was time to move on.

Where Are They Now?

Suckers was acquired by HBO and premiered as an HBO original movie, and it has gone on to achieve a cult following.

Attorney Elliott Leonard Aheroni was disbarred by the State Bar of California in 2002 for misappropriation of client funds and "engaging in acts of moral turpitude."[6]

154

Mark Kalmansohn is continuing to represent a select group of clients at his entertainment and intellectual property law practice, Kalmansohn and Andersen, LLP.

Mike Flint is still developing historical epics, working on a story about his father, Mitchell Flint, a U.S. Navy fighter pilot who was one of the first dozen volunteers who created the Israeli Air Force in 1948 at the start of the Arab-Israeli War.

After twenty-five years and fifty movies, NEO Motion Pictures (a.k.a. Neo Art and Logic) closed their doors in 2016. W. K. Border retired. Joel Soisson says he considers himself "kind of like the Eagles. I unretire every few months so I can have another reunion tour with myself and occasionally make another movie." Michael Leahy says he is "continuing to produce movies with finesse."

Stay Out of Court

If you made it through all the pleadings and complaints above, congratulations. It is a confusing, costly, and frustrating process. One thing we learned is that there is a typical nuisance sum a studio is willing to pay to settle a case to avoid the process of filings and pleadings. If somebody insists on more than a nuisance amount, a studio will conclude they may as well spend that money on defense instead. But if you do file a lawsuit, it will certainly cost you and your attorney a lot of time and money. And you may lose and end up owing far more than you expected. The real lesson is that life is better when you avoid courtrooms.

I also learned that you can't stake your career on one idea. I have had many projects in the works, only to see somebody else with a similar concept get over the finish line first. I have gotten there first sometimes too. Keep writing and keep creating. If you persist you will eventually win a race. And on the way there, don't let anybody steal your joy.

CHAPTER SIX

The Bag of Tricks

Speed Is a Function of Making Fewer Wrong Choices

Every editor has super-special secret techniques honed over time. In this chapter I will reveal the crucial skills I have developed, especially the tricks I use when footage needs to achieve maximum hilarity.

Working Fast

An editor needs to work quickly. If you can't instantly try new variations, it rapidly gets frustrating for the director or producers in the room. You have to be able to make a change and then restore it if it doesn't work. Brad Hall said he appreciates when an editor is technically proficient. "There's a flow that you get into. And if that stops, like when the computer crashes, that's like, 'Oh, no. . . .' You have to ramp it up again."

Before hiring me for *Grey's Anatomy*, Krista Vernoff asked, "Can you work quickly?" A showrunner's time is spread thinly; every minute is valuable. The last thing they want to do is wait for changes. Krista said, "I don't have much patience. It's my biggest personal character defect. I am always working to cultivate more patience, but I work fast and I work best with other artists who work fast." My answer to her question was that there are many people who can push buttons faster than me, but nobody will choose the right takes faster.

Three Minutes Per Day

Before starting on *Curb Your Enthusiasm*, I asked to observe both edi-tors, Jon Corn (who I was replacing) and Steven Rasch, so I could learn their approaches. Because transcripts lagged several days behind shooting, they would write notes by hand, paraphrasing good lines and jotting down the timecode (the numerical location every piece of footage has). I picked up on their process, though I later formulated my own system where I wouldn't need the transcripts (see chapter 9), until later, when the producers came in and wanted to search for a line or a phrase.

Steven Rasch's goal on a single-camera half-hour show is to com-plete a solid three minutes of finished screen time per day, with mixed audio and sound effects, which is approximately one, typical, large scene. Then he feels like he's done his duty. On *Grey's Anatomy*, I had to move even faster if I endeavored to "cut to camera" (completing all the scenes that had been shot the day before), which was around five or six minutes of screen time. For a multi-camera show (shot in front of a live audience), Steven Rasch said he needed to cut seven to ten minutes per day because they moved even quicker. That was possible "because the timing was baked in after many rehearsals, and that makes it easier, which is why multi-cam comedy editors are not as respected." On a feature film, if they have money, the pace is slower because more care is taken and you have to work through more foot-age for each scene. But if it's a low-budget feature, the speed is closer to the television pace; three to six minutes per day of cut material.

Reduce the Click Count

One way to work efficiently is to streamline your process by devising a work pattern that requires the fewest clicks to achieve the same result. Learn the shortcut keys. Program most-used shortcuts to the function keys. Get off the mouse and onto the keyboard as much as you can. You can hit a key faster than you can move the mouse.

Keep It New

Steven Rasch cautions editors to carefully read the script "before you waste time in an earlier scene doing things that don't relate downstream. Approaching a project holistically informs you as to pace and how much to dwell on certain reactions." Sometimes I prefer not to read a script for a television episode in advance, because I can better gauge the comedy of a scene as each line hits me fresh. The compromise, for me, is to read the script once, then try to forget specifics, so that I can respond to the footage on its own terms. After I finish my best cut of a scene, then I will carefully read the scene to see if I missed anything.

Make as Few Edits as Possible

Good editors know when *not* to cut, when to stay on something and let it breathe. If something is working in a performance, I don't cut at all. Normally I'm forced to make a lot of cuts to improve pacing and fix dialogue. Therefore, I want to avoid making cuts anywhere I can. Overcutting, or cutting just to cut, is an attempt to inject energy, a sign of desperation, a loss of control of a scene.

Cut to Where You Would Want to Look Next

When deciding which angle to choose, I consider the god's-eye view. I think of myself as a curious, omniscient entity observing the action. From that perspective, I ask, "Where would I like to be looking next?" Then I cut to what I would want to see at any given moment during a scene.

Find the Honesty

A great performance is one that elicits an emotional response. "Whether it's comedy or drama or reality," said Ivan Ladizinsky, "I'm looking into the performers' eyes to see if they're lying or if there's honesty." When humans communicate, we look primarily to the face. Psychologists have estimated that, depending on context, 60 percent of our communication is nonverbal.[1,2] Psychological masks hide true feelings. Drama often mines the contrast between what is presented by a person's public mask and the truth.

Create Emotional Reactions

Whether I am cutting a movie, a documentary, a commercial, or a sitcom, I want an emotional reaction: laughter, tears, or anger—or all three. Movies that win awards are stories that make people cry. Academy voters give awards because they *felt* something, not because they have intimately studied what it takes to achieve good editing, good acting, good makeup, or good wardrobe supervision. If you want an award, work on a project that presents a strong emotional story told well.

Match Energies

Alec Berg noticed how actors' styles are diverse and peak differently. "Theater actors make a choice about what level they're going to play something and they stay at that level throughout the take. On *Barry*, we have actors who, if they do four takes of something, you end up using almost all of one take. And it's not always the first or the last take. An actor will find a certain level and they'll play everything at that level." And then there are actors who are all over the place, they give you a scattergun of choices to build a performance from different takes. Depending on what take you're using from one actor, you need a level from the other actor that matches. You see a demonstration of this effect in a scene from *Barry* (season one, "Chapter Seven: Loud, Fast and Keep Going") when Sally (Sarah Goldberg) is bombing onstage in front of her agent, until Barry appears and delivers his one line. At that moment, Barry is in the middle of an emotional breakdown. The devastation in Barry's delivery is real. Sally responds to Barry's level of genuine sadness, and it propels her soliloquy above her usual mediocre acting to an outstanding emotional performance. Bill Hader won an Emmy Award for his performance in this episode.

In Mike Binder's *Black or White* (2014), Paula Newsome played the judge in the courtroom climax. Her choices ranged all over the place. It was frustrating to build a performance from such disparate performances; however, it wasn't a bad thing. It was a lot of work to break everything down, even words and syllables, and start building. But all the pieces were there; in fact, her process provided such a wide variety of choices that what you see in the final product is one of the best performances in the film.

When I was working on *The Mind of the Married Man* (2001–2002), I noticed that actor Doug Williams had this habit that was costing him screen time. I invited him into the editing room and showed him one of his performances, where he was adding long pauses within sentences. When actors get dramatic, they like to pause and marinate in it.

I said to Doug, "I think you want more screen time. I want to give you more screen time. If you were to deliver each sentence without stopping, I could stay on your face without having to go to a reaction of somebody else to pull up the pause." He had no idea this was affecting his performance in the edit, and his ensuing performances were much tighter. Actors who haven't studied their own dailies objectively are usually not aware of their peccadillos. They will look at the final product and go, "Wow, I'm pretty good!" while having no idea how many pauses, ums, you knows, and mispronunciations have been fixed. A good lesson for actors is to write, shoot, and edit your own scene sometime. You will learn about yourself and improve your technique. It's a very different thing from looking at playback on set in video village. Actors also need to exercise their writing muscle as well as their acting muscle. They have to bring ideas, backstories, dialogue ideas, and stage business—this is all creative writing.

Remove Everything Inessential

Humans are pattern seekers. We look to the sky and impose a framing of organized constellations on a random scattering of stars. Disarray causes anxiety. Patterns are pleasing. We prefer to edit our world, to line things up, to attempt to control the chaos around us. Editing is finding the most concise and effective organization of a chaotic myriad of pieces. Julian Doyle began as a photographer before settling on editing. His rule of framing was: "Lose the rubbish. When the frame is tight, the story is tight. If the frame is loose in the wrong way, you lose the tension."

Versions of the saying, "in writing, you must kill all your darlings," have been attributed to Allen Ginsberg, William Faulkner, Oscar Wilde, Anton Chekov, Stephen King, and others. The earliest version is probably by writer Arthur Quiller-Couch in 1916. "Whenever you feel an impulse to perpetrate a piece of exceptionally fine writing, obey it—wholeheartedly—and delete it before sending your manuscript to press. Murder your darlings."[3] They are all telling you not to get attached to beloved ideas. If something is getting in the way of the story, it has to go. Alec Berg maintained that, "with almost no exceptions, the shortest version of every show I've ever worked on was the best version."

If a scene doesn't work, but it is necessary, Julian Doyle will chop it down as short as possible so it doesn't lose the audience. "Like the three-headed knight in *Monty Python and the Holy Grail*. I cut that down to the minimum because the suit didn't work, but we really needed it for a gag that followed later in the film."

Steven Rasch thinks of editing like proofreading a college paper. "Take out all the typos and bad grammar and it improves, even if it isn't stellar. If you take out all the things in a scene that are not great, it gets better. You might have a terrific ensemble with one bad actor you have to minimize." How do you know when it's bad acting? Steven puts it this way: "Cut whatever reveals that it is *actors* talking, not *characters* talking." Actors look at marks, they look in the lens, they fumble for their lines. Remove these mistakes.

Cut the Walks

Cutting the walks is also called cutting shoe leather. The walk from here to there is not interesting. When I was editing my first short film, *Warped*, I asked director Howard Storm (director of *Fernwood Tonight* [1977] and *Mork & Mindy* [1978–1982]) about a dilemma I was facing. I had a shot of a woman driving up to a house, shutting off the car, opening the door, getting out, and walking to the front door. It took a long time for her to do all those things. Howard suggested keeping the shot of the car pulling up, to set the location, but then use the action and sound of the car door slamming to jump cut her already out of the car and moving toward the house. The audience

163

understands she turned off the car and opened the door. We don't need to see it. Slamming the door and exiting the frame took much less time. Most of the shoe leather was removed. I've used this trick constantly ever since.

If somebody exits a scene and then enters another scene in a new location, we understand they had to walk or drive from one place to another. Keeping anything between the end of one scene and the start of the next will test the audience's patience. Always cover the walks, stage waits, or crossing to grab a prop with a good line. Waiting for an actor to walk across a room in order to get to the next story beat is death. I sometimes tell directors not to waste time shooting elaborate crane shots unless they put important dialogue on the shot, otherwise we will most likely cut it for time.

Exceptions to this rule can be seen in *Breaking Bad* (2008–2013). They often luxuriate in shoe leather, spending entire scenes on the process of getting from one place to another. They earn their credit for this two ways. They present these scenes in visually arresting ways that hold attention. They have also trained the viewer to know that at any moment a seemingly mundane walk from here to there could erupt into violence. Their use of shoe leather has become foreplay to carnage. But if a walk is not contributing to the story, it has to go.

The "Oner" Has a Target on It

A long tracking shot is another kind of shoe leather. Sometimes a shot is called a "oner" if they cover the entire scene with it. The difficulty is that you can't adjust the timing within the tracking shot, you are unable to cut between takes to improve performance. What happened on set is irrelevant. I don't care how much sweat and money went into that incredible shot. I would sooner use a simple reaction shot than the costly tracking shot if the cheaper shot has a stronger impact. Alec Berg pointed out how filmmakers have to get past the sunk-cost fallacy. "We worked so hard on that that we need to leave it in." If it isn't absolutely essential, if you can tell the story without it, you have to cut it, or cut it down.

In the Preston Sturges comedy *The Miracle of Morgan's Creek* (1944), there are several long tracking shots. If you watch for the cut points, you will notice that Sturges got into the editing room and discovered he needed to edit between takes, but because he shot oners, he didn't have any way to hide an edit. So Sturges created an optical blowup on Trudy Kockenlocker (Betty Hutton) as she and Norval Jones (Eddie Bracken) walk along, manufacturing a close-up so Sturges could briefly cut in to her and then return wide to continue with a different take. I bet Sturges wished he had put a monkey in the scene.

When Julian Doyle was editing *Brazil* (1985), he came across a shot that dollied all the way down the Ministry of Information office and then back again. The purpose of the shot was to show multitudes of drab office workers scurrying about. The problem was that it was at the end of this track that the audience finally meets the protagonist, Sam Lowry (Jonathan Pryce), and it's already ten minutes into the film. So, Julian trimmed the shot.

Terry Gilliam saw the cut and said, "You can't cut that. It took us all morning to do that track."

A tracking two-shot from *The Miracle of Morgan's Creek*.

A close-up created via optical blowup.

Julian replied, "It's holding up the film, we haven't even got to the lead character."

Terry Gilliam said, "No, no, it's got to go back."

Julian had to find a way of putting it back, despite the fact that the length was harming the film. His solution was to add a song to it. "The audience will be enjoying the music as we track around and hopefully that'll carry us and they won't feel that the whole thing is a holdup."

When Julian ran that version, Terry Gilliam was sitting in front and his hand went up as he shouted, "Great, great, you've solved it!" Julian chose a song called "Brazil," which is what triggered Gilliam to call the film *Brazil*.

Once in a while, the all-in-one shot works, but it's a cross between a risky gamble and a specialized skill. When Mandel, Schaffer, and Berg were working on revising *How the Grinch Stole Christmas* (2000), during an opening sequence Ron Howard had rolled the dice and shot much of it in one take, but it wasn't working. David Mandel said, "We were able to steal close-ups of a cash register from another scene and intercut it. That allowed us to speed up the shot, so something that wasn't working was now working better."

Author's collection.

The scores of workers who inhabit the Ministry of Information in *Brazil*.

166

Setups Are Primary

There is no comedy without punch lines, but the setup is equally as important. A messy setup leads to an unclear payoff. If Sacha Baron Cohen believes a joke is funny, yet the punch line is not working, before he gives up on it, he will analyze the setup: "The setup is like math. If you don't have the building blocks, you can never be good at math. It's the same with comedy. The blocks have to be crystal clear. What does this person think? What does the other person think? Particularly if you have a scene which is farcical. You have to make the progression absolutely clear."

On *Curb Your Enthusiasm*, we spent more time working on fixing setups than improving punch lines. A setup must be concise, well-annunciated, and clear, or the punch line is not going to land. If you closely watch an episode of *Curb Your Enthusiasm*, you will notice many lines are delivered over the back of Larry David's head, or under reaction shots, because lines have been re-voiced to fix or improve a setup. If they had said the information on camera, we would have shown their faces. Sometimes actors have forgotten to emphasize an important setup in the moment while improvising dialogue. Or if an entire scene gets cut, a line may be needed to fill in the crucial story information that's now missing. The dialogue magic that comes out of improvising is worth the possibility of missing some exposition during shooting. This is another place where editor becomes writer, as you add missing lines or adjust existing setups. Larry said he couldn't imagine doing *Curb Your Enthusiasm* if ADR had not been invented. "It's unthinkable. When we did *Seinfeld*, I don't even remember doing any ADR. We just had the script, so it was much different."

Jeff Schaffer is always focused on getting solid setups because you don't want people to be thinking when they should be laughing. "The audience has to clearly know what the game is: 'Larry is lying to the hotel clerk because he wants the coffee beans.' Once everybody understands the situation, then you can run the scene and do the jokes." Often, they will drop the same information in a few different locations, because they are not sure which location is going to work better. And then later they decide where to take out duplicative setups.

Debbie Allen, one of the executive producers of *Grey's Anatomy*, said they like to hammer home story points and sometimes repeat them. They imagine their audience is somebody doing their ironing in Indianapolis while watching the show. Are they going to follow this story while they're a little bit distracted? In that case, there are multiple opportunities to pick up the information and stay involved.

Feature Every Frame of the Punch Line

Jokes are not as funny delivered off camera. Never cut away from the speaker before they *completely* finish saying a punch line. I learned this from Mike Binder while cutting *The Mind of the Married Man*, when I made the mistake of cutting away five frames too soon. I was trying to match continuity. But continuity is secondary to comedy.

Similarly, when I see a funny line delivered in a wide shot, or a side angle, I look for it in a closer angle, and a front angle. Punch lines are funnier on the face. A wide angle or side angle is okay for a setup, but get on the face for the punch line (and the reaction to the joke).

Never Go Out on a Blink

Director David Mackay once recommended an editor to me with his highest praise: "He's very good, he never goes out on a blink." Mackay was right. When you cut while an actor's eyes are still open it's less distracting. Also, cut before their eyes start to shift, or before they begin some kind of unfinished movement. Some actors are especially blinky or shifty. Editors love actors who don't blink. Sometimes blinking messes up the preferred timing of a cut. Going out on a blink on purpose will make an audience feel unsettled and distracted. Storytelling requires an audience to be invested for the maximum impact, not distracted from it. Occasionally a blink is the lesser of evils, when you have to wait for the end of a punch line. Otherwise, blink avoidance is the rule.

The Four-Frame Delay

When editing a conversation, I will sometimes delay cutting back and forth to each consecutive speaker by several frames—blinks and continuity issues permitting. It generally feels more natural to a viewer when you delay visual edits, because if you're watching two people speak, when you're looking back and forth, you're missing the first fraction of a second. It takes a beat to shift your glance from one person to the other. It's the natural way we perceive people speaking. This type of edit is also called an asymmetric edit, or a pre-lap, when the audio comes before the video, because you delayed the picture by a few frames.

Look for Comedy in Wide Shots

Close-ups are for dramatic moments, to feel more emotion. Performances are funnier in wider shots because you see more body language. You can't see how awkwardly somebody is standing if you are seeing them only from the shoulders up.

The Rule of Three

The strongest geometric figure is a triangle. Similarly, the strongest multipart joke has three sections, or three examples, or three beats. It's always three people who walk into a bar; not two or four. Goldilocks meets three bears. There are three wishes. Storytelling works best with three-act structure. In cutting a montage, showing three shots feels good. Two feels inadequate and four begins to verge on overindulgence.

Avoid Flashbacks and Voice-Overs

Flashbacks and voice-overs are crutches used to prop up a weak narrative. Flashbacks are often a gimmick to try to inject energy into a slow first act. Voice-overs are sometimes added to explain information that filmmakers failed to impart or to help a confusing plot. Try to make the story stand on its own before adding these Band-Aids.

Find the Sweet Spot

Comedy gets funnier as it speeds up. Until it starts to get less funny. There is a comedy sweet spot. You have to find that natural balance, to get to the funniest number of edits for a scene. Alec Berg describes finding the sweet spot like two people standing at a piano playing different notes, going, "No, no, no. Wait, hold on. That sounds interesting. What's that?" You're not sitting down with a pad of paper and writing notes out of thin air. You're listening to it and reacting. "Wait, take another frame off there." Or asking, "What if we were in the wide shot instead of a tight shot?" It's just tuning, until you find the spot.

Reverse Your Perspective

An editor is expected to bring a fresh perspective to a story, a scene, or a line of dialogue. Art helps others to see slices of the world from a new perspective, the way the artist saw it. Whether I'm creating a shot list, directing actors, or editing a scene, if something is not working, I will consider the exact opposite of my original idea. If I started a scene with a high, wide landscape, I instead will try a low-angle, extreme close-up, and see if the scene launches better from a radically different perspective. When you find the less obvious path it will surprise the audience. They like surprises.

Build Momentum

Jokes, scenes, acts, and stories have to continually increase in pace, magnitude, and energy. Running gags have to get bigger and go further each time. The climax must have more intensity than anything that preceded it. "Anti-climactic" is the label applied to a scene or an ending that violates this rule. Pacing is so important the next chapter takes a deep dive into this area.

CHAPTER SEVEN

Get the Rhythm

Faster Comedy Is Funnier Comedy

Because editing is rhythmic, the editor has to improve the beat. There is an infinite number of rhythmic, comedic choices. It takes finding the right drummer, er, editor, to create the best rhythm.

Curb Your Enthusiasm editor Steven Rasch loves to reference music as an editing metaphor. In Steven's analogy, he's like the drummer setting the pace for Larry David, the Miles Davis of comedy. A scene becomes less funny if Steven lets the performers get away from the beat, which is particularly important when they are improvising dialogue, like jazz musicians, always testing and trying ideas.

Comedies are about rhythm, which means timing and pace. Jeff Schaffer said, "Half the time I feel like I can edit with my eyes closed because I know when the next beat should be. It's almost musical, I know what the sound should be. I know when the next note should play." Brad Hall pointed out how it's a problem when an editor has a different rhythmic sense than the director or showrunner. Julia Louis-Dreyfus agreed. "It's very hard to communicate how to solve that: 'Can't you hear it? What do you mean you can't hear it?'"

Alec Berg was a drummer in junior high school and high school in the orchestra and in rock bands. To him, comedy is something that's played very much by ear. "Mike Judge is a musician. Bill Hader is an impressionist. They both have incredibly good ears for rhythm and tone. And so, a lot of it is playing different notes and seeing what sounds right." Judd Apatow also likens comedy to music, where a joke is like a song. "If the rhythm isn't right and the melody isn't working, it all crumbles." There are reasons Shakespeare's writing flows like poetry. Good writing has rhythm. Rhyme can be funnier. Alliteration or consonance can strengthen a line.

When possible, cut between sentences, between words, or between syllables, so you are cutting on the beat. Avoid cutting in the middle of a word, or a phrase, or a thought. Editing creates a flow of beats that feels right to viewers. If that seems like I'm stating the obvious, what's not so apparent is that the right pace is often vastly different from what felt right to the writer, the director, and the actors on the set.

Pacing

Pacing is deciding when to slow down and when to speed up. Pacing has to continually increase overall as a story progresses. The stakes have to keep rising. Keep the dangers coming faster and faster, accelerating until the climax. You can and should have multiple plots interwoven throughout a story, thematically tied, all developing concurrently, different characters each with their own goals and obstacles. In structuring an ending, make sure all the subplots resolve in order of importance, so that the A plot is the last to climax. An editor's job is to figure out which plot is which.

You get up to three minutes per scene to make a point. An audience gets restless if a scene lasts longer. A four-minute scene better have a damn good reason for outstaying its welcome. Sometimes, if an element within the scene changes, such as another person walks into the conversation and changes the composition of the characters, that gives the scene a reset. This is sometimes called a French scene. In this case, the dynamic has changed, so you can get away with extending the time.

Julian Doyle has an axiom that "if an audience doesn't want to know what's going to happen next, then cut fast. When they do want to know what's going to happen next, slow down." You have to know where the audience's anticipation level is at any particular time. If they are ahead of the story, you're in trouble. Move as fast as possible until the bomb is on the bus and it's about to explode. Then you can slow time down. Because the audience wants to know what's going to happen. Who's going to die? How are they going to get out of it?

Speed

An episode of *Veep* probably has more words per minute than any show on television, and within those sentences, we'd try to fit as many laughs as possible. The joke-per-minute ratio (jpm) was high. Steven Rasch once observed, "Nobody breathes on *Veep*." Larry David also needs someone who cuts at a high jpm rate. The way I approached these shows was to increase the pacing as much as possible without affecting a viewer's ability to receive, perceive, and enjoy a joke. Certain jokes play better with a pause followed by a reaction. Other jokes are best when thrown away, or minimized; they are funnier in the background. If we slowed down and put them out front, they would not be as funny.

Julian Doyle warned not to cut fast simply because you have heard the dialogue a hundred times. You may know the line, but the audience may need air around it to absorb it. "You should know when the dialogue is important and when it isn't," said Julian. "I don't mind not hearing the dialogue at the beginning of *Alien*, when they've woken up and they're mumbling around the table, because it's not important dialogue." Julian also cautions comedians to be careful not to damage their work. Sometimes performers will strive to re-create in editing the exact timing that matches the way they delivered the lines originally.

In *Monty Python's Life of Brian* (1979), there is a scene where Brian is being chased and he stops to buy a fake beard. The beard salesman says, "It's twenty shekels."

Brian hurriedly replies, "All right, here's the twenty shekels."

The salesman is aghast. "No, no, you've got to haggle!" He won't sell the fake beard if Brian tries to skip over the negotiating step.

When they watched the raw takes of this scene in a hotel in Tunisia, the crew was laughing at everything when it was playing continuously in the two shot. When they watched the scene in the singles, they never laughed because they saw only half the scene. As a result, Eric Idle and Graham Chapman told Julian to stay in the two shot for the whole scene. When they got back to London and ran a cut of the film for a test audience, they didn't laugh much at the haggling scene that played in the unedited two shot. Julian had already prepared a second version of the haggling scene where he put in the close-ups, so he could adjust the timing, to speed everything up. When Julian showed that faster

Author's collection.

Graham Chapman and Eric Idle argue over haggling etiquette, in *Monty Python's Life of Brian*.

version they said, "Oh yeah, that seems to work much better." Although the two shot was funny on its own, when placed within the body of the film, in a chase scene, the natural pacing seemed too slow. The faster pacing of the intercut singles played funnier. Perception of time changes when a scene is intercut. You have to play with the timing to find the funniest pacing for that particular moment.

How Fast Is Too Fast?

Don't go fast just for the sake of speed. The idea is to speed things up until the pace feels appropriate to the material. *Veep* was a breakneck seventh-gear television show. There was sometimes debate about whether we were moving too fast. When David Mandel mentioned how much he loves Billy Wilder movies, I blurted out, "*One, Two, Three!*" David looked at me and said, "That's why we work together." Billy Wilder once said of his 1961 comedy *One, Two, Three*, "The general idea was, let's make the fastest picture in the world . . . we did not wait, for once, for the big laughs. We went *through* the big laughs."[1] Billy Wilder and I. A. L. Diamond's screenplay for *One, Two, Three* has an instruction at the beginning that reads: "This piece must be played molto furioso. Suggested speed: 110 miles an hour—on the curves—140 miles an hour on the straightaways."[2]

David Mandel likes how that sort of frenetic energy adds to the comedy. "When you're going that fast, it's like a great joke is sneaking up on you and whacking you from behind." David also believes in treating the audience like they are really smart people. "They'll figure it out. Don't treat them like dummies and slow it down and spoon-feed it. If I'm seeing something explained eighteen different times, or you artificially put in a flashback to underline something for the nineteenth time, I'm asleep."

David admitted, "I'm a fast talker in my life. That's how I speak to my friends. We talk quickly and wave our arms. And that's how I want my characters talking. Fast and furious."

"Selina is a lot like you," I noted.

"Yes, well. . . ."

"Has anyone told you that?"

"No."

"Let me be the first."

"Over the years I have given her my same history and life."

"When she said, 'I hate food,' I thought, 'That's David.'"

He launched right in. "I hate every food from every restaurant ever. That's what it was like ordering lunch at *Veep*. It was like, 'Do not show me a menu!'" We had used up every restaurant in a ten-mile radius. Lunch was a dreaded time at *Veep*—until somebody could uncover a new, acceptable location. For a while Palestinian chicken was the thing, until that flavor expired. Then Chinese dim sum was our savior, until dumplings lost their luster. We'd be adrift until we found a new, safe culinary harbor.

Quality and Quantity

Going for speed doesn't mean you trim and trim until you have a string of punch lines. Punch lines don't work without appropriately paced setups. It's the same as a thriller, where the anticipation and tension of a scene builds and builds. Alec Berg finds that building a laugh is similar to a scare in a horror movie. There is tension and release. In comedy, he said filmmakers sometimes make the mistake of trying to keep too many laughs. "There's a sense that more laughs means more comedy. But an A-plus laugh is logarithmic. It's not twice as good as a B-plus laugh. An A-plus laugh is *ten times* as good. If you create a film that has four or five massive laughs, it's a classic. If you make something that has one hundred B-plus laughs, it's not as memorable. Those big laughs are the ones that you have to curate. And sometimes that means not being funny for a stretch of time to build that tension. Those are genre-defining laughs."

The Dramatic Pause

There is a reason it is called a "dramatic pause." How long should a pause be? No longer than absolutely necessary to make a point. Any editor can lay down a dramatic pause. The good editor knows when to cut it off. If there are too many pauses throughout, the pause loses its meaning.

On *Grey's Anatomy* I had to slow my pacing down, particularly in heavier scenes, to allow moments for the audience to experience the emotion. *Grey's Anatomy* is a particularly challenging show to edit because not only is it a drama, it also has comedic scenes, plus it is an action show with fast-moving, bloody, medical sequences. Krista Vernoff said she prefers to remove a whole scene rather than take all the air out of a whole bunch of scenes. "I know showrunners who will lift the beautifully shot openings and closings of scenes in order to keep all of their dialogue intact, and I try not to do that. I try to let some of the director's vision stay in the show."

Awkward Pauses

When I was cutting *Crashing*, I had to slow down my pacing again. I had just come off of *Veep*, so my natural instinct was to put the pedal to the metal. But then I realized I needed to put pauses back in. On that show, the scenes needed to breathe, to emphasize awkward moments, so we could feel what Pete Holmes was feeling as he was starting out as a mediocre comedian surrounded by better comedians. A lot of the scenes were about not being prepared for opportunities.

When he was told, "We need you to be the warm-up guy on *Doctor Oz*," we feel his panic because he doesn't know how to do it.

Silicon Valley (2014–2019) marinates in the comedy of the awkward silence. When all the characters are socially awkward, it affects the rhythm and timing. Much of *The Office* (2005–2013) followed a rhythm where somebody speaks, followed by the awkward moment, or a look at the camera.

Julia Louis-Dreyfus had to sign off on the final cut of every *Veep* episode, and sometimes she felt the pacing went a little too fast. "There've been a couple moments when I said to David, 'Wait, we have to stretch this out a tad more. We need ten more frames at the tail. That's gonna feel more right.'"

Pauses Are Momentum Killers

Allow me to emphasize this: *The enemy of comedy is the unnecessary pause.* Jeff Schaffer agreed. "The only reason to pause is when the joke demands the pause. Otherwise keep going. Go to the next joke. Go to the next moment."

As we were trimming an episode of *Curb Your Enthusiasm*, Larry David asked me to remove a tiny pause between two lines, saying, "Some things I would have just let go before, but I can't accept pauses like that anymore."

Sometimes a bridge line is added to fill empty space; you never want to have a dead moment. Someone's got to be speaking at all times, unless that pause is deliberate.

The Intentional Pause

There is no pausing in comedy unless you *choose* to pause, for emphasis. Sometimes pauses are written into the script. In *Veep*, the scripted shorthand was to cut to Gary for specific reactions: "Gary gasps." "Gary doesn't like it." "Gary makes a noise."

Once you set a strong pace, it's fun to suddenly hit the brakes. Then, going slowly becomes the emphasis, like in the final episode of *Veep* (season seven, episode seven, "Veep") when everyone leaves the Oval Office and Selina stares silently into the abyss. Several seconds feels like several minutes compared to the pace of the rest of the show.

There is a *Veep* scene (season six, episode one, "Omaha") where the newly broke, ex-president Selina Meyer has been put on an allowance by Catherine (Sarah Sutherland), her emotionally fragile daughter. Selina realizes that to get more money she now has to go through Catherine's girlfriend, Marjorie (Clea DuVall), who is not easily bullied. In the footage, the scene careened forward to this point of realization and rocketed right past it. I thought it would be funny to stop everything and dwell on this moment, lingering on each of their faces as they acknowledge the other's presence, size each other up, and then go into battle. I created a moment that was not in the script or the actors' performances. This was possible because great actors don't simply wait until it's their turn to speak. Both Julia Louis-Dreyfus and Clea DuVall were fully connected to their characters and actively listening. According to Julia, "You can tell when people check out, or if they're thinking: 'What am I going to do to be funny?' You've got to be really present. It takes a tremendous amount of concentration. When I'm working, I sweat profusely—and I'm not a sweater. It's the concentration." The silent moment I was able to create as a result became an emphasis when surrounded by rapid-fire dialogue; the pause itself got a laugh. Producers love it when you add an unscripted laugh via editing.

Julian Doyle often played with pause lengths. "John Cleese has a natural pause in his performance. Somebody will be talking to him and say, 'Your mother is here.' Long natural pause, then, 'What?' I'd further stretch the pause and put it back. That's where you must have a sense of comedy, to find the funniest length. If you don't, you'll be messing up their timing."

Catherine informs her mother of a new financial arrangement, in a scene from *Veep*.

Marjorie reacts to the situation.

Selina sizes up her opponent.

Remove the Baggage

Actors add handles to their lines when they are not secure in their performance. They fumble, stumble, stutter, say words twice, swallow words, or add space, especially when they are reaching for lines. Even the best actors fatten up their performances with lots of "word baggage." I stitch together half sentences, dangling clauses, and stutters. I do anything I can to make the dialogue flow as elegantly as possible.

When you start to pay attention, it's shocking how many times people in everyday life say, "um," "uh," "you know," and countless other fillers. Occasionally they add an "alright," "okay," "so," "like," "besides," "yeah-no," or many other unnecessary expressions. These barnacles are everywhere and they have to be scraped off. Jeff Schaffer calls it "wiping away the word dust."

The word "literally" is almost always misused and has to be removed. "In any way, shape, or form" is triply redundant. Pick one. It's enough. News anchors like to say they "report out" the news. "Out" is redundant, because where else would it go? Are you going to report it in? They should simply report the news. This is probably an unwitting combining of "put out" and "report."

Writers and actors love to insert an announcement word at the beginning of a line. A common one is "look," or "listen." These expressions say, "Hey, I'm going to speak now!" You don't need to announce your presence. Just say what you have to say. It's better to begin speaking the line without preamble. I cut these announcements.

Also unnecessary is starting a sentence with "the fact is," or "again," or "frankly," or "to be honest." If you start a sentence with "frankly" or "honestly," it implies you have been lying all along. Beginning with "again" is an insult to the listeners, accusing them of not being able to understand you the first time. I'll remove it, unless the intent in dialogue is to be insulting.

"By and large" is meaningless and redundant. Unless the words are absolutely needed for meaning or context, I remove these linguistic freeloaders.

A sign of an amateur editor is when they leave a pause, or "um," or "you know" underneath a reaction shot. If we are seeing somebody other than the speaker, the editor has total control over the dialogue and should remove anything unnecessary. If the camera is stable enough, I have brazenly jump cut out an "um" while looking right at an actor who paused mid-sentence. If the jump cut is seamless, I keep it. And there is software to smooth together the pause-ectomy with a fluid morph. It is the latest go-to technology for making performances tighter. Editor Grady Cooper once even replaced somebody's entire head when he needed a better reaction within the frame.

The Air Pass

After finishing a respectable cut of a scene, I do an air pass. I remove all the pauses that I do not choose to have in the scene for emphasis. And then again, when the project is assembled, I will go through the entire episode and do another air pass, surprised at myself for having missed so many opportunities to remove unnecessary pauses in my last pass.

Once I took over an episode when another editor left a show. I went through the existing forty-minute producer's cut and removed three minutes of air and other baggage-laden momentum killers, without eliminating any lines. I don't cut out every single pause, only the ones that are harmful. I showed my revised version to Jeff Schaffer and asked him to let me know if any of the faster changes bumped him from his prior producer's cut. A handful of my speed-ups did feel rushed or didn't work, but we kept 95 percent. He said, "You sucked out air I didn't even know was there. It's tightened up where it needs to be, without making it seem like someone put it on fast-forward.

We'll always tell you if it feels too fast, or if I'm missing this moment, or I need to open it up to check in with somebody in a reaction shot."

Correct the Grammar

I am thrown off track when I hear somebody mispronounce words or use unintended bad grammar. Some commonly mispronounced or misused words are: arctic, nuclear, or hone in. You cannot hone in on something. You could *home in* on it. Or you could hone a plank of wood. Another of my pet peeves is when actors mispronounce "asterisk." There are two S's in asterisk. I'll find a "sk" sound somewhere in their performance and surgically replace the "x" to make it grammatically correct. Sometimes the transgressing actor will pronounce it correctly by accident in one take, and I'll steal just the word and "line stuff" it—a term for using the audio from a different take and putting it in an actor's mouth if the lip sync matches. I'll locate a consonant like a P, B, or M, where you can see the lips open in a single frame, and use that as a sync point to line up the words.

Feature the Punch Line

After I identify the setup and the punch line, I eliminate everything extraneous between these two things, to get to the punch line as quickly as possible. Distractions reduce the impact of humor. The unnecessary pause, bad grammar, imprecise annunciation, inelegant visuals, anything that takes you out of the moment or reminds you that you're watching a screen will interfere with the landing of a punch line.

When possible, put the funniest part of a line at the *end* of the sentence. Often you will find the biggest laugh is buried somewhere before the end. Put the biggest moment at the end of the sentence, and the end of the scene, and the end of the act. Don't go on after the best part. After the punch line, it's time for a new bit, or a new setup.

Another impediment to the punch line is something Sacha Baron Cohen calls the "double reveal," which is when there are multiple punch lines available and you try to pay off a setup twice with two punch lines. Sacha believes two payoffs are less potent than a single powerful payoff. Any diversion confuses the brain. Once you have a punch line that is sudden and clear, the laugh is bigger, and then you can build on that joke. In a set-piece, such as the naked fight in *Borat: Cultural Learnings of America for Make Benefit Glorious Nation of Kazakhstan* (2006), there is a simple premise. In this case, it is a physical fight like we've seen in many movies. This time, the difference is that the two actors are naked. When the audience buys into that premise, they're ready to laugh. *Then* you can finesse how to build and increase the laughter during that scene.

That's not to say you can never get away with paying off a joke twice, but it is an expert-level challenge. Punch lines are usually an either/or choice, because they are in response to a setup. But sometimes I'll try to jam two good punch lines in, one after another, just as an experiment, to see what happens. Most of the time it doesn't work. But it can be effective with insults, where one builds on top of another in a litany of put-downs.

Anti-Rhythms

Jump cuts call attention to the editing process, creating an anti-rhythm. They are best used to intentionally disrupt the tempo of a scene. Jump cutting can be an effective tool to indicate a character's disorientation or a fracturing of time: flash forwards, flash backwards, or subtracting frames.

186

Jump cutting is another advanced technique. It is difficult to do well. Steven Rasch warns against jump cutting in comedy. "To do jump cuts or to have obvious edits that your brain can't process as being continuous hurts comedy."

I got Mike Binder into experimenting with jump cutting on the series *The Mind of the Married Man*. I had done a lot of jump cutting in my film *Suckers*, and Mike noticed. He said, "I found it an easy short-hand to get past a lot of bullshit. You could just jump into another place. Sometimes you get away with it, sometimes you don't. Some editors can do it and some can't."

There is a scene in John Woo's *The Killer* (1989) with screen-direction jump cuts between the two main characters, assassin Ah Jong (Chow Yun-Fat) and Inspector Li Ying (Danny Lee), when they're sitting and talking after a shoot-out. Normally filmmakers draw a 180-degree line between two characters, and cameras stay on one side of the line. Woo wanted to show these two characters are different sides of the same person. By crossing the 180-degree line with every cut, they're positioned the same way, looking in the same screen direction in a matched cut. The intentional use of a normally jarring technique is used to make a subliminal point. One is a policeman and one is a contract killer. They're opposites. Yet they're the same.

Orson Welles fractured the chronological narrative in *Citizen Kane* (1941). The story jumps around in time as an investigative reporter interviews sources as he tries to piece together a portrait of a dead man. Tony Scott brought a strong visual sensibility to his first feature, *The Hunger* (1983). Drawing from his experience working in advertising, he created a tour-de-force of editing in the film's opening sequence, which featured Catherine Deneuve, David Bowie, and Ann Magnuson, underscored to Bauhaus's "Bella Lugosi's Dead." Scott uses flash cuts, freeze frames, flashbacks, flash forwards, extreme close-ups, sound interruptions, and cuts to caged monkeys (!), all combining to create disorientation and increased horror.

An establishing shot from *The Killer*, showing the geography of the actors.

Ah Jong (Chow Yun-Fat), looking to the right, the same screen direction as the master shot.

Inspector Li Ying (Danny Lee), also looking to the right, the opposite screen direction as the master shot.

Continuity Cutting

An editor strives to maintain consistent continuity from one edit to another. Hiding mismatches is a game that editors play, striving for an elegant flow. Doing 15 percent blowups in order to reframe and hide visual jumps is common. Another trick is to do a split screen to keep the performance you like on one side of the frame and replace a problem on the other side.

How important is continuity? For Jeff Schaffer, "If the joke needs the jump, we'll live with it. The script supervisor often says, 'The pen was in the wrong hand, so you can't use that take.' I just go, 'Uh huh. Yeah, we'll throw that whole take away with all that funny stuff because the pen was in the wrong hand. Let me go burn the footage.' Nobody cares about the pen if they are laughing." Plus, now you can digitally put the pen wherever you want it.

Once Judd Apatow notices something is a mismatch, he says it drives him crazy. "If someone has one hair changing place from shot to shot, I'm calling the CGI [computer-generated imagery] guy to fix it." But Judd allowed if you are totally into a scene, continuity gets overlooked. He recalled a moment in *One Flew Over the Cuckoo's Nest* (1975) where Randle McMurphy (Jack Nicholson) is strangling Nurse Ratched (Louise Fletcher) and he's wearing a hat. But in one shot there's no hat. Next shot, the hat is back again. No one notices the missing hat because the audience is so into the intensity of the scene.

Judd likes flexibility in the editing room, so sometimes he shoots the same scene twice with the actors in different wardrobe, because wardrobe continuity affects how much scenes can be moved around. In a few scenes in *The King of Staten Island*, Judd put Pete Davidson in a sweatshirt so those scenes could go anywhere in the movie.

I try not to jump the 180-degree line if possible. When I do make the jump, I try to stay on the other side from that point forward. Maintaining continuity is about removing jarring instances that remind viewers that they are watching a screen. As you gain more experience, you begin to subordinate continuity in favor of other priorities. There are indeed times when you can discount continuity. When a scene is moving slowly, jumps in continuity may stand out more than when you are speeding through a scene at a rapid pace. Also, if everybody is sitting around a conference table, or seated on an airplane, where the geography is rigidly set, the audience will not be confused if you jump around in your cutting pattern. Still, the priority is to cut for performance, for emotion, and if continuity gets in the way it may be sacrificed. But if you confuse the audience with a jump cut, or by crossing the line, and if that confusion harms the comedy, then stick with continuity.

It's Too Long

First cuts are always too long. Whenever someone asks me to look at a cut of their film I can say with confidence before I've seen it, "It's too long." We tend to leave in all these great things we love that are harming the overall impact.

Jeff Schaffer, Alec Berg, and David Mandel co-wrote *Eurotrip* (2004). When they tested it, audiences weren't laughing as much as they hoped they would at the end, and nobody could pinpoint why. David agonized over the problem. "A lot of times you do something in the middle of a movie that isn't directly connected to the end, except the end is now ten minutes later than it should be. And often that ten minutes is the difference. It's not that you've done anything wrong with your ending, you've just worn them out." It was a tough lesson for the filmmakers, because the audience never says, "It felt long in the middle, and that's why I didn't like the ending." The guys had to read the clues to solve the mystery.

Overall pacing needs to get faster as a film progresses, because an audience is getting tired. When HandMade Films produced *Monty*

Python Live at the Hollywood Bowl (1982), they had a sixty-minute version that wasn't working. George Harrison's business manager told the filmmakers, "We've got to make it a feature film to get it released." They were against expanding it—until he said, "All your money is tied up in it." Suddenly everybody was agreeable. So they asked Julian Doyle, "Can you go in and make it a feature length, at least seventy minutes, and make it work?"

The filmed show was a series of sketches onstage and about half-way through they had an intermission with John Cleese coming out dressed as an ice-cream vendor, yelling, "Albatross! Albatross!"

Julian reorganized the sketches, knowing that "it's all about expectation. I took the intermission and moved it to three-quarters of the way through the film, so that the audience thinks there's much more left. Then when the film finished at seventy minutes, it seemed to work."

Julian faced a similar problem with *Brazil* (1985). Like most films, the story is ultimately about a guy who is trying to win over the girl. About three-quarters of the way through, he actually gets the girl. "They jump in bed and there's a shot above, where the drapery turns and it becomes an iris and closes. That feels like an ending. The trouble was that there was another twenty minutes after that. You had to move quickly to a conclusion after that iris." Julian took out waking up in the morning and two scenes afterward. In his version, immediately after the iris closes a drill hole appears above and the police come down, before the audience has a chance to think it's the end. But Terry Gilliam restored the scenes, which slows down the rush to the ending, leaving the pacing of the ending flawed.

When to Take Your Time

In his films, Judd Apatow likes a longer first act where not much needs to happen. He is content to create a world, introduce the characters, and set up all the situations. "If those scenes are really interesting or funny, you don't care that the story's not starting. But once it does start, you want people to be invested in some goal the character has, or your hopes for the character. In *The King of Staten Island* (2020), Pete Davidson doesn't really have a goal, but we want him to be okay. So, it's a different type of propulsion." His story doesn't begin until his mother meets a new man at the end of act one, which forces Pete to examine his own emotional blocks.

A television pilot is different from a feature film. It's a lot to ask of a network to green-light a series based on a pilot that doesn't launch the story. In the pilot for *Crashing*, Judd Apatow and Pete Holmes began the story immediately with Pete Holmes catching his wife cheating, and it forces him to jump into the life of being a comedian. It's something he's always been afraid to commit to, but that changes in a moment of inspiration.

The Button

It's a well-known writing rule to enter every scene as late as possible and get out as early as you can. The ending of a scene is called the button. Stand-up comedians call it the blow-off, or blow for short. You need a strong moment to end a scene: the biggest punch line, a reversal, a question asked, a big dramatic moment. You want to get out on the strongest beat. Never dribble on after the strongest punch. If you hang around after the punch line, audiences get anxious to get on with it. You have to make sure you are cutting as soon as the point is made. Anything that comes after that's not supremely essential has to go.

Larry David sometimes relies on music to help end a scene. "If you don't have a great out, the music will tell you the scene is over and we're moving on." Music is a stand-in for a laugh track, cuing the laughs and the emotional reaction at the end of the scene.

In *Curb Your Enthusiasm* (season ten, episode seven, "The Ugly Section"), Larry David has a climactic moment of realization after the maître d' (Nick Kroll) seats him in the ugly section of a restaurant. Larry shouts to the sky, "How did I wind up here?!" In hindsight, Larry said he felt that improvised moment was his highlight of the season. "Because it was so true. I've always suspected I was ugly. That's what people are relating to. And if you went through it, chances are the audience has too. The truth is funny for sure." After that moment, there was still most of the scene that followed, which was funny in itself, but it was stronger to end that scene early. Larry admitted he didn't recognize that was the best ending for the scene until HBO executives Amy Gravitt and Ben Wasserstein suggested it in their network notes. Larry is good at appreciating when somebody else has a good idea. He's only interested in how to get to the best version.

Author's collection.

Jeff Garlin watches Larry David try to get out of the ugly section, but Nick Kroll disagrees, in *Curb Your Enthusiasm*.

The button for the *Veep* finale raised the question of how much is too much Tom Hanks? David Mandel explained why he ended the last episode, and the seven-season run of *Veep*, on an actor who was not even in the show. "I love it because I felt like no one else is going to do this. No one else is going to turn the last two minutes of their show into a guy reading the straightest dialogue about Tom Hanks's [future] death. I laugh every time Mike McLintock says, 'An American everyman comfortable in both comedy and drama.' It's not a joke. It's just the fact that the moment keeps going. You think maybe this is going to end, but no. The praise for Tom Hanks just keeps coming." Nobody saw that ending coming.

CHAPTER EIGHT

Sound Is King

Comedy Lives in the Soundtrack

A whole chapter dedicated to sound? What madness is this? What if I told you sound is the most important part of editing, especially for comedy? Film may be a visual medium, but comedy is in the performance, and performance lives in the sound. Of course, reaction shots, facial expressions, body language, sight gags, and visual comedy are important, but most of the plot is in what is being said and how it's being said. Orson Welles came from radio, where he had to deliver an entire story with sound. When he transitioned to film, he brought his elaborate sound stylings and added stunning visuals.

There is a long tradition of successful comedy albums. From Nichols and May to The Firesign Theater to Monty Python to Cheech and Chong; everything you need is in the soundtrack. Alec Berg credits comedy albums with teaching him how sound can be comedically independent because "with a comedy album I had to imagine what was happening." Alec said he plays recordings by comedians Bob Elliott and Ray Goulding in almost every writers' room. Any comedy writer would be wise to know who they are. Berg said, "It's stunning to me that people have never heard of these guys. If you listen to 'Slow Talkers of America' or 'Komodo Dragon' (collected on the album *A Night of Two Stars* [1984]), those are masterclasses in timing. And they're just as funny today."

Jeff Schaffer also believes comedy is in the sound. "You can say a line a million different ways but only a few of them are really funny. And that changes with every setup, in every context. That's why the sound mix is vital. You know how the words are supposed to sound. There's a funnier way. I want it to be: 'Oh I dunno,' not, 'I don't know.' I'm always listening for the right answer or the funniest sound."

My editorial bag of tricks has a special compartment just for the sound techniques, which help me wring the most out of a scene.

The Audio Tracks

I like to keep all the audio tracks that are recorded on location attached to the source footage and the grouped clips so that I can access the cleanest sound for any given character at any time. Usually a location mixer uses one or two boom microphones plus an isolated lavalier mic on each actor. A boom records the best quality, but the lavalier has a tighter, quieter pick-up pattern that improves quality in loud locations. I often ask my assistant to make a list of track assignments for any scene with many characters, so that I can quickly find a particular actor's line. Otherwise, I would have to click on each track and listen. Sometimes that's as many as fifteen clicks, plus listening time, to get the same answer that the track-assignment grid can show me in seconds. A good mixer puts the main actors on the same track every time; that continuity makes it easier to find the actor that you need.

1. Track one—the mix track (all tracks combined)
2. Track two—the boom (or booms)
3. Track three—the star actor
4. Track four and beyond—the other actors

In my timeline the first four tracks are dialogue. Five through eight are sound effects. And nine through twelve are music. To keep a timeline

SC #	Takes	Tk1	Tk2	Tk3	Tk4	Tk5	Tk6	Tk7	Tk8	Tk9	Tk10	Tk11	Tk12	Tk13	Tk14	15	16
1	OMITTED																
2	OMITTED																
3	OMITTED																
4	X704-1	MixL	MixR	Boom	N/G	Podium	Aux1	Aux2									
4	X704A-1	MixL	MixR	Boom	Blank	Blank	Podium	Wyoming	Aux1	Aux2							
5	ALL	MixL	MixR	Boom	Selina	Gary	Ben	Kent	Catherine	Marjorie	Keith	Aux1	Aux2				
6	FURLONG	MixL	MixR	Boom	N/G	Furlong	Podium	Aux1	Aux2								
6	MCCABE	MixL	MixR	Boom	Mike	Jane	N/G	Blank	Aux1	Aux2							
7	ALL	MixL	MixR	Boom	Selina	Gary	Ben	Kent	Catherine	Marjorie	Keith	Aux1	Aux2				
8	ALL	MixL	MixR	Boom	Selina	Gary	Devito	Ben	Kent	Keith	Aux1	Aux2					
9	ALL	MixL	MixR	Boom	Selina	Gary	Amy	Jonah	Ben	Kent	Buddy	Leon	Keith	See note	Booms	Aux	
10	ALL	MixL	MixR	Boom	Selina	Gary	Amy	Ben	Kent	Keith	Worker	Aux1	Aux2				
11	ALL	MixL	MixR	Boom	Dan	Jaeger	Richard	Mila	Aux1	Aux2							
12	ANCHOR	MixL	MixR	Boom	Lav	Aux	Blank										
12	ALL	MixL	MixR	Boom	Selina	Gary	Ben	Catherine	Marjorie	Aux1	Aux2						
13	ALL	MixL	MixR	Boom	Selina	Gary	Ben	Kent	Keith	Devito	Aux1	Aux2					
13	ANCHOR	MixL	MixR	Boom	Lav	Aux	Blank										
14	ALL	MixL	MixR	Boom	Selina	Gary	Aux1	Aux2									
15	ALL	MixL	MixR	Boom	Selina	Gary	Grimace	Aux1	Aux2								
16	ALL	MixL	MixR	Boom	Selina	Gary	Ben	Kent	Keith	Aux1	Aux2						
17	SC 15	MixL	MixR	Boom	Selina	Gary	Grimace	Aux1	Aux2								
17	SC 16	MixL	MixR	Boom	Selina	Gary	Ben	Kent	Keith	Aux1	Aux2						
17	SC 17	MixL	MixR	Boom	Selina	Gary	N/G	Aux1	Aux2								
18	ALL	MixL	MixR	Boom	Mike	Jane	N/G	Aux1	Aux2								

VEEP — 707 Track Assignments. *Note: Sc 9 Track 13 = Furlong & Kemi & Will!*

An audio track grid from an episode of *Veep*.

manageable, I work with the mix track until I need to clean things up. Having the isolated tracks (isos) available comes in handy for separating dialogue overlaps. While shooting coverage, a good director will remind actors to separate their lines from each other, so that editors can control the pacing and the timing later. We can always add overlaps. But actors caught up in the moment talk over each other, and the isolated tracks can save a performance from contamination.

If a scene is filmed in a loud location, like a busy street, I begin with the isos in place and then clean up every line. Some editors work only with the mix track and leave clean-up work to the sound designer's team. But that leaves cuts sounding dirty and clunky—and less funny. Clean audio is funnier audio.

I also ask my assistant to put the start-of-take locator just *before* the call of action on every take. That way, when I go to a locator, either for myself or for a producer, I'll hear "action" called. That way I am 100 percent certain I'm not missing anything. On a series, we standardize the locator colors among all the editors and assistants to make it easier to find things between episodes.

Editing for Sound

As I watch through the dailies, I *listen* for the best performances. The audio track is where structure is built. Proper framing, rich color, and beautiful camera moves are ornamentation that need a solid audio framework. Once I have heard and chosen all the best performances, then I switch my focus to making a scene flow visually.

Steven Rasch is also a sound-based editor. Unless he's building a montage or an action sequence, he cuts with sound as primary, picture secondary. "The timing is in the sound and the words, how they land. Not the pictures," Steven said. "Visual cutting is a different art. People read these books about editing and say, 'The guy cuts the whole scene with the sound off,' and I go, 'Well, he's not cutting comedy.'" Comedy showrunners are so writing-driven that they know if it's correct, even with their eyes closed. It's picture second in the comedy world. With writer-driven shows that don't emphasize visual elements, you have to make sure it doesn't become merely a radio play with pictures. One way to inject a cinematic feel is to design nice transitions. Directors should plan for a way to get from one scene to the next with a visually arresting style.

Polish the Sound

I attack my editor's cut like it's the final cut. If a scene is good, but the sound is rough, producers may feel like it's not working creatively.

198

They can't separate the two things. When you present the same scene with clean sound, the identical editorial choices are perceived as better choices. They don't attribute it to the sound mix. They perceive the performances to be better. I have watched scenes where the takes used were good but an editor skipped the polishing step, and the result was less effective.

To make my editor's cut sound as perfect as possible, I balance levels and add equalization or filtration where needed. Sometimes it helps to use the EQ tool to take off the very bottom, or the high end. If the scene is in a hallway with some echo, but I'm stealing a line from somewhere drier or more muted, a little reverb does wonders. I remove digital blips and imperfections. When there's a clunk or a bump on a line, I'll find another take where that word or phrase is clean and replace it.

Each actor's mic picks up a slightly different ambience. If it is markedly different, the ambience shift becomes obvious when intercutting. One solution is to delay the outgoing ambience, to post-lap it into the next shot, right up to the start of the next word; then the outgoing ambience is overpowered by the incoming dialogue. It can be a subtle thing, but when ambience is not snugged up, if it happens a lot, you hear bumps in ambience on every cut, and it's one more thing that takes you out of the story. If the difference is extreme, you may have to build an ambience loop and play it in the scene whenever you cut to the quieter mic, to balance the feel overall.

Diction and Clarity

After choosing the best takes, my focus shifts to enunciation, diction, and clarity. I look for the most concise, clearest version of an actor's performance. If you cannot clearly hear the words in a setup, the punch line isn't going to land.

I clear out verbal tics, overloud breaths, and incessant lip smacks—some actors smack their lips before every line, another subconscious way to announce they are about to speak.

If the writers thought something is funny enough to write it that way in the script, it probably is, so I look for a take where the actor performed the line as written. Occasionally an actor will stumble onto a better, shorter, or funnier version, but that is rare. However, when you are working with comedian-actors such as Jason Mantzoukas, or J. B. Smoove, or Sarah Silverman, you have to fasten your seatbelt and go with their comedic instincts; they often come up with gems that work better than what was written.

Word Blending

When trimming lines or combining takes, look for the spot where a blend would be seamless. Typically, editors cut between sentences, or even phrases. But you can also edit smaller pieces, down to syllables, by cutting seamlessly on consonants like T's, P's, and B's. Most often used are F's, S's, and Sh's. It is more difficult to cut seamlessly in the middle of a vowel. Adding a one-frame audio-dissolve softener helps.

When Ivan Ladizinsky watches footage, not only does he mark funny moments, great dialogue, and good camera moves, but he also notes the connective tissue: conjunctions such as "but," "and," or "if." These are particularly helpful when editing reality shows, when building scenes where you need to play with the dialogue, move things around, and reconstruct sentences. The overdose of "you know's" and "so's" that you trim out of scripted dialogue can also save you when you need to blend sentences or create new lines. These rebuilt lines are sometimes called "frankenbites." Great editors are invisible cheaters. They rewrite dialogue, revise lines, or play scenes differently from how they were conceived.

For users of Avid Media Composer, ScriptSync is the go-to software when searching for an actor saying a specific word or phrase needed to fix a line. With ScriptSync, it's also easy to audition all the versions of a line in rapid succession, so you can choose a favorite. With improvised dialogue, where every take is different and Script-Sync is not an option, when a producer wants to compare all the versions of a line, we build "stacks" of lines, lining up all the versions of a performance back-to-back for easy comparison.

Automated Dialogue Replacement (ADR, a.k.a. Looping)

If I want to cut half a sentence, but the actor does not come to a natural stop on the ending word, I'll look at all the takes for where that word or syllable did have the right ending cadence and replace it. If the proper cadence does not exist, I will mark it for replacement via ADR. Then the actor can rerecord it and give it the proper feel.

The sound designer and dialogue editor go through our final cut and decide which lines need to be replaced due to overlaps or sound-quality imperfections. If they can't find a better version in the production sound, they record replacement options for nearly everything that is not 100 percent perfect. Most of the time, showrunners prefer the original, imperfect production sound over ADR because it feels more natural than ADR recorded in an isolated booth, where actors don't feel the energy of the original environment. But the sound designer doesn't want to get caught at a mix without a replacement if it is needed, so the backups are gathered.

Sound Effects

Adding sound effects and music is the final step. Sound designer and supervising sound editor Mark A. Mangini (*Anchorman: The Legend of Ron Burgundy* [2004], *Dune* [2021]) has said, "Sound design is all about thinking metaphorically. You ask the question, what *could* this sound like, not what *does* it sound like?" Mangini's philosophy is that a sound effect shouldn't sound like what you're seeing, it should sound like what it means.[1]

I have several libraries' worth of sound effects and musical scores from hundreds of movies. It is time consuming finding the right sound effect (or creating a layered combination of sounds) for a door closing or a body fall or a surprised gasp, but it can make the difference between funny or not funny. Slapstick and pratfalls are augmented with sound effect "sweeteners" to the limit of what verges on overkill. I add backgrounds, ambience fills, birds chirping, dogs barking, car tires skidding, dialogue walla (indistinct talking), clothes dropping, punches, anything needed for a scene to feel fully alive.

In a *Veep* scene backstage at a debate (season seven, episode three, "Pledge"), where Selina throws her book down onto the floor to punctuate a tantrum, the heftier the book sounded when it hit the floor, the funnier it got. So, I added a body-punch thump to sweeten it. As you watch and hear the book hit the floor, your brain considers the ramifications and does the math: If she had thrown that book and hit somebody, it would have hurt! Bonus laugh.

Sacha Baron Cohen did a joke in the first *Borat* movie where Borat is in a Jewish bed-and-breakfast, and when he realizes that the food he's been given is kosher, he spits it out. Sacha felt certain the joke was funny, but at test screenings it didn't get a laugh. When he went frame by frame through that scene, he discovered that an editor had added a spitting sound effect three frames prior to the image of Borat actually beginning to spit out the food. Once the sound effect and visual were adjusted to coincide and made even louder, at the next screening the moment got a huge laugh. Sacha concluded that because the timing was off, "the brain is so sensitive that if anything confuses it, it will prevent the person from laughing." Krista Vernoff agreed with this theory. "The hardest thing in editing is to protect the comedy. Sometimes a joke can be killed by the sound of a door opening or a phone ringing. And if the timing is off, forget it."

Music Spotting

My final step in editing is to add music. Mike Binder sees filmmaking as four seasons: writing, filming, editing, and scoring. Music can make a scene funnier, or it can cancel out humor. The first rule is that a scene should work without music. Then music is added to augment a feeling, to amplify the emotion. Wall-to-wall music means a project sucks. If you need music to make a scene work, you have failed.

When I asked Ivan Ladizinsky what he liked most about editing, he said, "I love being able to take images, sound, and music and create an emotional impact almost immediately. You can take a sunrise and put Aaron Copeland's 'Fanfare for the Common Man' under it and everyone goes 'Whoa!'"

I start with music from the composer's library. If nothing works, I go to my own library of songs and movie soundtracks. Temp music is what I use to communicate with the composer during a "spotting session" (a meeting to discuss all the places where we need music). I want a composer to emulate the feeling, the mood, the scope of the temp music, not copy it. They might use similar instrumentation to my temp cues, or they may try something completely different.

I enjoy it when a composer will try music in a spot where it didn't occur to me. But 90 percent of the score will be in places I have spotted. I often tell a composer, "Don't try too hard to compose the most amazing, complex piece of music ever. Keep it subtle." Sometimes you want a full orchestra. But usually I spend time removing instruments, thinning out the cues. Alec Berg's number one instruction to a composer is, "Don't try to be funny, play it real. Often people's instincts to be funny go to ten. When people go to one instead of ten, it's much funnier."

Music in a minor key feels sad. The stories in my documentaries are based on a positive energy that builds, and the music has to do likewise. For comedy I never want anything in a minor key, unless a scene truly is sad. If you listen to the music in my documentary *The Nature of Existence* (2010), some of the temp-score inspirations were from Thomas Newman's scores for *Scent of a Woman* (1992) and *American Beauty* (1999). The new music that replaced the temp cues had no apparent connection to these movie scores, but our goal was to evoke similar feelings.

If there's one music instruction Larry David gives the most on *Curb Your Enthusiasm*, it is, "That cue is too down." He doesn't like to go into drama, so we keep the cues bouncy. Larry said the music helps the audience know they're supposed to laugh. "When you put the right kind of music underneath, it changes the tone and people are all of a sudden enjoying it, whereas if there wasn't music, they wouldn't know how to take it." Steven Rasch noted, "If Larry's tapping his foot, then I know it's a cue he likes. If we put in slower-tempo cues, his yelling and arguing quickly gets depressing or sad. We bring in the tuba to remind people that we're having fun. 'Don't worry, it's okay.' It counters the extreme emotion that's going on in the horrible way people are speaking to each other."

Larry David has made an entire style of Italian music recognizable as signifying comedy on *Curb Your Enthusiasm*. One day Larry heard a song by pianist Luciano Michelini in a bank commercial and thought, "That's the sound I want!" Larry said, "It just sort of introduces the idea that you're in for something pretty idiotic."[2] They licensed the song from the Killer Tracks library (now Universal Production Music), which had a lot of other similar-sounding cues, grouped mostly with Italian composers from the 1970s and 1980s, who were repurposing their tracks. Steven Rasch called Killer Tracks and asked for everything they had in that style. They sent over a box of ten CDs and that's now the musical basis of *Curb Your Enthusiasm*. There originally was a composer on the pilot, but they fired him because he couldn't replicate a good tuba on his synthesizer. Steven tries to find a few new cues each year. He is mostly successful at finding new stuff when he searches for "tuba" or "Italian" or "gypsy music." More recently he's been getting hits by searching "Serbian folk music."

When a specific cue we need isn't in a library, we go to a composer to create exactly what we need. In one episode, Larry catapults a woman from her wheelchair into bed before they make love (season seven, episode five, "Denise Handicapped"). We needed just the right sensual music for the love scene between Larry and a paralyzed woman. I couldn't find anything with the appropriate nuance in the library, so I called Billy Sullivan, composer for most of my films. I asked Billy if he happened to have anything with the feel of Barry White.

Billy said, "No. But you'll have it by Wednesday." When he saw the scene he said, "What you want is Burt Bacharach." He worked up a spec cue titled "Love All Around" and sent it over. The sensual flügelhorn he used hit just the right tone and made the scene work—and most importantly made Larry David laugh, so it stayed in.

Sometimes songs come first and are written into the scripts. Alec Berg said he will have a song in his head for years, as he keeps trying to find a place for it. "There was this old Ennio Morricone song that Jeff and David and I loved called 'A Gringo Like Me,' from *Gunfight at Red Sands* (1963). It's so earnest and campy that it's now hilarious. Bill Hader will constantly be coming in and saying, 'Hey, I found a song for this,' or 'Here's the song that I think plays for that scene.'

Sometimes the music inspires the story rather than just supporting the comedy. The entire plot of the movie *Crossroads* (1986) is a lead-up to the incredible musical ending, where Eugene Martone (Ralph Macchio) duels with the Devil's (Robert Judd) best guitarist (Steve Vai).

Music can also ruin a scene. Krista Vernoff is heavily involved during spotting sessions, giving notes on the songs and the score. "You can destroy an otherwise beautifully crafted scene—whether comedic or dramatic or both—with the wrong score." Judd Apatow loves to have the music supervisor and the editors throw a lot of music at him until something resonates. He sees music as an equal partner in the success of his projects. "That's the only thing I regret when I look back, is song choices. Sometimes late at night I'll wake up and go, 'I think I picked the wrong song!'" The entire tone of a film is set by music. In *The King of Staten Island*, they added emotional rap music, the kind where people are talking about their struggles, rapping about pain, and trying to do better, and that music supported the drama.

The choice *not* to have music can also have a big effect. The last episode of *Girls* (2012–2017) had only a couple of music cues in it. Judd said to Lena Dunham, the series creator, "Maybe we should make a choice that there's no score in the last episode of *Girls*." There's no music track telling the audience what to feel. It ends on a sound effect of Lena's character, Hannah, breastfeeding a baby.

Akira Kurosawa's *Seven Samurai* (1954) has thirty-nine music cues. There is dramatic music in the heavier scenes, something lighter during comedic moments, and sometimes only a simple drumbeat in tense moments leading up to violence. But the climactic battles at the end of the film have no music at all, and it works. The stage has been set so masterfully by everything preceding the final act that there is no need to push the emotion and the energy higher with a music bed.

Less is more is an old cliché, but it will become your mantra.

CHAPTER NINE

Building a Scene

The Building of a Scene Begins at the End

Now that you have added the techniques from the prior chapters to your repertoire, this chapter is about the nuts and bolts of putting a scene together.

Make a List

My first step is to list all the takes on my half-size legal pad so I can check them off one by one after I review each. That way I don't get lost or forget which takes I've viewed. It's easy to lose your place when there are twenty or thirty takes in a large scene.

Clear the Markers

Because my assistant may have left markers when syncing sound or grouping clips, I select all the takes and erase existing in-and-out markers. While working, it is easy to forget: Is that a new or old marker? Now when I add an in-point, I know it's new.

Circled Takes

Circled takes are at best a hope, not a guideline. Generally, I don't care which takes have been circled, which performances they thought

A typical page from Roger Nygard's list of viewed takes.

were best on the day of the shoot. On set, they don't know what will work in the editing room within the context of all the takes. They also have no idea how I do what I do. They just know that when they look at my cuts, either they're workable or not. They hire an editor

208

they can rely on to get them the best head start possible; not some-body they have to micromanage.

Actors tend to steer closer to the script in later takes, as they better remember lines, and as the script supervisor steps in to whisper in their ears. Some actors give their most genuine takes in early rounds, but mostly, as the takes progress, performances tend to get better—and funnier. By the final take, the director and the actors have usually arrived at something with which they are happy, where they felt like they got it and moved on. Therefore, I start at the end.

Start at the End

I begin by selecting the best complete take, usually the last one. I shape this take into a whole scene (or as much of the scene as possi-ble). Because most "single-camera" filming is done with two or three or four cameras, there are multiple angles available, leading to a fire hose of coverage on every take.

In the old days, single-camera actually meant one camera, as dis-tinguished from multi-camera shows, which are filmed in a studio with an audience providing reactions for a laugh track. In the old days, with that one camera, they would shoot a wide shot (or master shot) and then move in for closer coverage, one angle at a time. And then if needed, they might do a "turnaround" and shoot from angles on the other side of the 180-degree line (from behind the action). As cameras got smaller and lighter and prices dropped, productions added cameras. Now television directors often focus on the acting, leaving the details of coverage to the camera folks.

When possible, I like to edit scenes in sequential, story order. I don't skip over difficult scenes; I take them as they come. Beginning with that best take, I remove mistakes, restarts, or anything duplicative. I focus on the words first and then change angles second, until I have the best version I can make from that one take. Sometimes I have had as many as eight or ten camera angles to choose from in each take, such as the presidential debate scene in *Veep* (season seven, episode three, "Pledge"). This first pass provides a framework to begin adding improvements.

If I had started with the first take, I'd be using early performances, most of which are going to be replaced by better, later work. If the best jokes arrive in the last take, it is much faster to start with those keepers in place. When I put the best stuff in first and then work toward the front, I already know I've found the best version of a line when I see earlier, inferior attempts. That's a timesaver. If I were to start at the beginning, I would end up replacing almost everything. My process of beginning with the last, best take and working backwards means I replace much less. And I don't need to look at the script, or the transcript, until later. I don't need to watch all the dailies before beginning.

Starting at the Beginning

Now that I've explained how most of the good stuff is in the later takes, I'm going to explore an opposite approach, which demonstrates how there are no ultimate rules. The earlier takes have a different essence, and they are occasionally better. When we were editing a scene from season ten of *Curb Your Enthusiasm* and we went back to the first take, Jeff Schaffer said, "Oh, that's before I gave him a note that ruined the scene. Often the first take is invaluable—but never for the reason you expect. On the first take people are doing things in different ways that we often think are wrong. But later when we're trying to take out time or look for something different, we realize, 'Oh, that's what we actually wanted.'"

Steven Rasch is an editor who likes to look at the dailies in order of shooting, first to last. He marks takes as he goes, making notes:

"If something is funny or touching, or clearly delivered, or a shot is unusual or good, I'll write down the timecode." He uses a star system of one through four: one is just okay, two is usable, three is good, four is must use it. Zero stars means ignore it. After viewing all the dailies, he builds a cut based on his notes. When he was learning to edit, he used to cut long assemblies, with three versions of each line, because he didn't know which was best. But unless it's a difficult action scene, he doesn't do that anymore. He has the confidence to cut based on how he initially reacts. "Now I know just what I want. I don't have to look at everything five times. I go with my gut from the first viewing and cut it that same day, right away, while the subtleties are in my brain."

Is one approach better? Start at the beginning or start at the end? Each way is best for each of us. Both roads get to the destination.

Duplicate the Timeline

After I've built an entire scene from one take, I'll duplicate it. I always save my current version when I start work on a new version, especially when I'm going to try something radical. I keep the early versions of each sequence in case I want to go back to an original instinct or quickly find a piece of footage I removed.

When working with producers, get used to duplicating timelines often. They may want to jump back one, or three, or ten versions, and you have to be able to do that quickly.

The Second Pass

For the second round, I watch the next-to-last take to try to improve the performances in my timeline. If the final take was the tightest coverage, I may move to the last, best version of the wider coverage, before looking at the rest of the tighter takes.

The Third Pass

After I have utilized a full take from each of the main setups, duplicating my timeline each time, I do a quick polish pass of this version to see what's working and to get a feel for what's missing.

The typical cutting pattern for a scene is to start on a wide shot to establish the location and then move in closer. Sometimes I will change things by opening on one or several tight shots. But even so, I will make sure to cut wide within the first few shots to establish the scene's geography. If you wait too long to show where you are, the audience will begin to wonder.

Watch All Takes

Jon Corn found that working on an improvised show taught him to look at everything, because any piece of footage can go anywhere. "I don't feel bound by the script, or where something happened in a take," said Jon. "I learned to look at every bit of the dailies. From when the camera starts rolling until it stops."

You will find gems in every take, circled or not. You are going to miss things, no matter what you do, so make sure your search is as comprehensive as possible. It's embarrassing to sit there like an idiot and wonder, "How did that happen?!" when you find out you didn't include an important take, or you missed an insert, or you skipped over an entire line of dialogue. Sometimes an errant take does not make it into a scene bin due to an error of paperwork. I tell my assistant to always cross-reference all takes with the script supervisor's notes, and the camera department notes, and the sound mixer's notes. Triangulating all three should turn up any straggler takes that might have fallen through the cracks (and made you look bad).

Evaluate Alternate Lines

As I work through the takes, I may line up two or more choices of the same line or punch line when I encounter alternates, to decide later which one I prefer. At this stage, I'm grabbing options and possibilities. By the time I'm done going through all the takes, it becomes clear which is the best. When an alternate joke is tried in later takes, that means the scripted line it replaced is probably no longer operative. The showrunner improved it during shooting.

The comedy script is a living document; it is continually changing. After the readthrough, the writers will get a lot of information and ideas from the actors. The writers are watching every take on set and constantly suggesting new lines. On *Veep*, when there was a scene scheduled the next day with the characters Jonah or Amy or Dan, David Mandel knew there would be a lot of insults flying, so his assignment to the writers was to come in the next day with ten new insults for each character. Then he would have scores of insults to narrow down to his most ridiculous favorites.

The Baggage Pass

After I finish a version of the scene that incorporates the best performance nuggets from every take, I go through and use all the finishing tools in my editor's bag of tricks: improve performances by removing word baggage, correct grammar, adjust diction, and trim all inessential detritus. I will now closely reread the scene in the script, because there may be specific things written in the description that I missed. I make sure that everything written is included.

The Visual Pass

Up to this point, I have been focused mostly on choosing the right performances. After I have seen all the takes, next I make sure the scene works visually. I ask myself, is it too cutty? Should I slow it down in spots? Is it in close-ups too much? Did we cross the 180-degree line? Are there any outgoing blinks? Where will a four-frame delay in the visual make the edit feel more natural? What else does it need to make the visuals flow elegantly?

The Reaction Pass

I do a specific reaction pass, looking for opportunities to add shots of all persons in the room who are witnessing the madness. There are entire YouTube channels dedicated solely to people reacting to things. "Elders React to Llamas with Hats" has more than eight million views. Sacha Baron Cohen likes to remind editors of a priority: The camera needs to be on the person *reacting* to Sacha's character. "The laughs come on the target; on their naturally timed reaction to the crazy thing they've just heard."

There was a scene in *Silicon Valley* (season three, episode ten, "The Uptick") where Alec Berg discovered that something that seemed funny on the page played differently on set. Richard Hendricks (Thomas Middleditch) discovered that Jared Dunn (Zach Woods) was buying fraudulent uses via a click-farm to give the guys a fake morale boost, because they thought their company was dead in the water. Richard finds out about this lie and then says to Jared, "It's okay, we'll quietly go out of business and the guys will feel better."

Then Erlich Bachman (T. J. Miller) gives a big speech saying he took this information and traded one venture capitalist off another and got a bidding frenzy going to bring more money into the company. The joke is that Erlich is over the moon with himself for doing something good, but Jared and Richard know what he did is the worst thing that's ever happened. The speech was supposed to be the main point of the scene. But because of the way the schedule laid out, they had to shoot the reactions first. As Alec watched the reactions, he realized the scene was actually about Richard, who learns he is in big trouble because of the lie. Alec said, "If I'd shot the speech first, I would have spent a lot of time worrying about making the speech funny, and then cut in some reactions as an afterthought. Having shot the reactions first, I discovered I didn't need to spend an enormous amount of time on this speech because I knew we would be on the reactions."

Eliminate Repetition

If David Mandel suspects he is doing a riff on a joke he used before ("Did we do something like that in season five?"), if the joke is not substantially different, those jokes are targeted for removal. This comes from the Larry David ethos. Larry tries never to repeat a joke from anything he has done.

Remove redundancy in exposition. Don't tell the audience what they have already seen. There is a tendency for redundancy to occur when characters tell other characters what happened in a prior scene. Because the audience has seen this, they tune out.

One exception would be if we are deliberately building a running gag—a rhythmic repetition of an idea that gets funnier each time we come back to it, or it gets bigger and more extreme. Another exception is when Larry David makes sure in every instance he is sufficiently "celebrating the premise." He ensures we have fully explored all the comedic possibilities opened up by a strong premise. Sometimes characters on *Curb Your Enthusiasm* will talk about what just happened in a prior scene in order to unlock more humor than they got out of the primary scene where it first occurred.

I also remove word duplication. The goal is to never reuse the same word or phrase within a scene. Word repetition makes a sentence less funny. Each scene should be a collection of freshness. David Mandel feels this concept works on a subliminal level. "I don't think the audience at home is going: 'How dare you use the same word twice?!' But it hurts you, whether you know it or not. And if we can put a different word in the character's mouth just so we're not using the same construction, it's better. When the words are working, it's like a piece of music. When you hit the same word again, or use the same joke again, it's like hitting the wrong key. It breaks the hidden flow."

Having made all the above adjustments and trims, the scene gets a tiny bit funnier every time it's shaved down by a hair, and the bonus grows as you multiply that across the episode.

Do a Full Sound Mix

When I am happy with the scene, I add sound effects and do a full (temporary) sound mix. I balance everything in the scene to peak at the same level so it matches the rest of the episode. I pick a level that's closest to the average peak of what the location mixer is delivering (usually −8 dB), so I have less work to do.

Digital Effects

If the color of a shot looks egregiously different from the rest of the scene and pulls me out of the story, I'll do a temporary color correction to bring everything in line. I may reframe shots to remove audio booms, cameraman's arms, and floor marks and then note it for the digital effects specialist to fix properly.

Occasionally an actor has to be removed entirely from a scene, even though he's standing right next to the lead. When scenes get moved around, and it no longer makes sense for that person to be present, or the continuity is entirely wrong, that character has to be erased. There is a scene in *Veep* (season seven, episode one, "Iowa") when Amy Brookheimer (Anna Chlumsky) is in bed in her hotel room and Dan Egan (Reid Scott) knocks. She decides to change shirts before answering the door. David Mandel wanted to speed up the scene, so we digitally changed the color of her shirt so we could remove the twenty seconds of her running around changing her shirt. That savings opened up twenty seconds to keep other things in the show.

If there are phones or computers or television screens, that means whatever will be seen on those screens has to be created and tracked for placement, including any graphics and artwork. Tracking is time consuming, especially if a camera is not locked off, so after I choose the elements, the compositing and tracking job is something I will put on my assistant's plate.

Sometimes we have to deal with a "previs," which is short for previsualization, a temporary version of a visual effect. An animated scene, or a special-effects-laden scene, or a complex action scene may have many pieces that are not yet available. In that case if you scan the storyboards or import the digital sketches, as well as a temporary dialogue track, then you can build an approximation of the scene, either before filming or while editing, until you get the missing pieces.

Do Whatever It Takes

I'm not shy about getting my hands on whatever is needed to make a scene work, whether it's a unique sound, a temporary voice, some stock footage, or an exterior establishing shot. When I was in New York, I happened to film the exterior of Rockefeller Center with my GoPro camera for one of my documentaries. On *Veep*, when we couldn't find any shots of Rockefeller Center that we liked at stock footage houses, I remembered I had my own shot and I dropped it into the cut. On the pilot for *Dave* (2020–TBD), we needed an exterior of a recording studio, so on my way into the office I stopped and filmed the building. The *Dave* exterior was reshot for the final version once the series got picked up, but my *Veep* shot stayed in. I never expect any of it to stay in, but my goal is to deliver the most complete cut possible.

Once we turn the episode over to the sound designer, the sound team will probably replace or improve most of my temporary sound effects, although many of the sounds I've added have made it through the final mix. My temporary voice-overs sometimes make it into episodes. I have been announcers, airline pilots, and a multitude of miscellaneous off-camera voices. I think the showrunner sometimes gets used to my simple, deadpan performance. When a voice talent comes in to replace my track and tries too hard, they occasionally revert to my straightforward temp at the mix.

The Finished Scene

Once my cut of a scene is finished and fully mixed, I put it aside. The next day I take a second look, with fresh eyes, and do another polish pass. That's also a good time to do another air pass, to look for pauses or leftover word-baggage I missed the first time around, or to put pauses back in where it feels too rushed.

Then I put the finished scene into a "scene cuts" bin in my "current cut" folder. All along I have been putting the old versions into an "old cuts" bin.

The Music Pass

Once I finish all the scenes, I assemble the show. Most of the time I will wait to do a music pass until I am putting the show together. I want to make sure everything works first without music. If we have a compressed schedule and are strapped for time, I'll ask my assistant to do a sound effects, ambience backgrounds, and temp-music pass. Then I will add to it or polish it. But usually, I do all the sound work myself.

The Pre–Test Screening

It was common on *Curb Your Enthusiasm* and *The League* and *Veep* to show our cuts to the post-crew and other editors to get notes or ideas for improvement. Insecure editors are sometimes afraid to do this. Grady Cooper loved to share his work. He said, "It makes the end product so much better. Editing can be an amazing collaborative effort."

Grady would also take cuts home and watch them. "It gives you a totally different feeling from what you experience in the editing room. You can see the flaws that were previously hidden." Sometimes he will turn the volume off and watch the finished cut to evaluate it on a purely visual basis. "I notice things like: 'There's got to be a better reaction here,' or, 'Oops, I crossed the line.'"

After testing the episode on coworkers, I make a few more improvements and then call it done. I now label it the Editor's Cut.

CHAPTER TEN

The Editor's Cut

*In Movies the Director Is the Boss, but in Television
It's All about the Showrunner*

Working on movies and television shows are different experiences. Editors need to be aware of all the different crew departments they will be dealing with and what each job is like. In feature films, the director's creative vision prevails. I love directing my own feature films and documentaries, but the higher the budget, the more the stress level rises. If you find yourself asking, "Why am I doing this?" you better have an answer ready. For me it's a compulsion, a need to express myself creatively. There was never a question of not doing it. When I stepped into the television directing arena, the differences required getting used to, because in television the director is no longer in charge.

The Television Director

A television director is often described as being like a traffic cop, helping everybody successfully get to where they're supposed to go. I also like the metaphor of an enzyme, where nothing happens without the enzyme's work. The television director supports everybody in their tasks.

The television director's first job is to encourage the actors, to make them feel supported. You can't really tell television actors a lot that they don't already know, because they've probably been playing their role for many seasons and know far more than the new director about the nuances of their characters. While dealing with the actors, you have to keep the production moving and get the necessary coverage in the time allowed. That's called "making your day." If you don't make your day, and if you don't make the actors feel good, you won't be coming back. These two things are often at odds. Actors want more time. Producers want you to have less time (so they will spend less money). How do you give actors more time for more takes while simultaneously spending less time on scenes so you make your day? You're fucked. The best answer is to placate the actors if you want to come back. The bean counters have less say than stars over who returns. So, in terms of your directing career, soothing a star's feelings is more valuable than preventing wasted production dollars.

The Showrunner

The showrunner (the executive producer) is the creative boss in television. Their creative energy steers the ship. A director has to absorb a showrunner's style. Usually a showrunner is present during filming. When I was directing *Zeke and Luther* (2009–2012), creators Matt Dearborn and Tom Burkhard took turns on the set, while the other one supervised the writers' room.

The secret of the writers' room is speed. Television scripts must be delivered on a rigid schedule. Writing good stories takes time, "but because you have a room full of writers," according to Mike Binder, "you can help each other so you can move it along faster: 'Okay, everybody take your shot at it.' With eight or nine good writers who all know the show, you can do in a couple of weeks what could take one screenwriter years. The shows go wrong when they don't have a strong showrunner, or if they have a network or a star who's running the room from outside. The lens has to be focused all the time on the right thing. And you can't do that with a bunch of people grabbing for the camera and saying, 'No focus on this, focus on that.' You've got to have someone who understands where this thing is going."

Good art is the result of a singular, clear voice. With a writers' room, everything is filtered through the showrunner's perspective. Jeff Schaffer has become a major creative force behind *Curb Your Enthusiasm*, but Larry David is the star and a showrunner. Alec Berg co-created and runs *Barry* with the star Bill Hader, and in this case, two people share the voice.

Bernie Mac

When I directed *The Bernie Mac Show* (2001–2006), I found it to be an exception to other shows I had directed. Bernie Mac, Warren Hutcherson, and Steve Tompkins (the executive producers) let me shoot my episodes however I thought best, which was atypical and amazing.

But that's partly because Bernie was the creative force. If Bernie approved of you, you had free reign. Rarely did Bernie need more than two takes, sometimes only one. Occasionally we'd do take three if camera or sound had an issue. In every take you got Bernie's style; there was no changing it or making it different. It came out of him wonderfully, in just the way it worked best.

When I first went to the set, they said, "It's time for you to meet Bernie." As much as I hung back so as not to interfere, Bernie spotted me immediately. He rarely left the shooting stage. It was his domain, and if there was a new element, he sensed it. After finishing a scene, he pointed at me and yelled, "Hey you!" Everybody stopped what they were doing, all eyes suddenly on me. I looked behind, like an idiot, to see who Bernie was pointing at. There was no one. He walked closer as he looked me over and asked, "Who are you?"

Feeling like the sacrificial deer in the headlights, I replied, "I'm Roger Nygard. I'll be directing an episode next week."

"Is that so? What are your credits?"

"Oh, uh . . . I directed *The Mind of the Married Man* and the documentary *Trekkies*—"

"Get me the box offices grosses on *Trekkies*," he called out to his assistant. His eyes narrowed. "Well, we'll see how well you do."

Then he put out his fist. At first, I was confused. I had never encountered a fist bump. 2005 was the year of my first fist bump. I figured it out quickly—evolve or die—I returned his bump.

Then he walked off to his dressing room. I was a bit shell-shocked, but I hadn't withered from the public scrutiny. He enjoyed putting people through the paces.

The crew tried to make me feel better. "He does that to everybody."

I thought, "You could have warned me!"

My shoot went well. After the final take when I yelled, "cut," and the first assistant director, Joe Moore, called, "that's a wrap," Bernie did it again.

He announced in his booming voice, "Okay everybody, let me tell you something!" Everybody was looking at me again. "When I met you, I didn't think you were going to make it." A long pause and more of his intense stare. Then Bernie's big smile bloomed. "But you did it. You did a good job. You earned your props."

You had to earn Bernie's respect, but he was willing to give it. Another fist bump, followed by: "Let's go party!" Bernie always threw a Friday-evening "Bump and Grind," a weekly wrap party for the crew.

I've been a fist-bumping convert ever since, and every time I think of Bernie. Fist bumping is certainly more sanitary than shaking hands. I've been in men's bathrooms and seen the lack of precision men put into their hand washing, when they even bother.

Bernie Mac and Roger Nygard on the set of *The Bernie Mac Show* in 2005.

Bernie suffered from sarcoidosis most of his life, a disease with genetic origins that causes inflammation of the body's tissues, especially the lungs. Treatments can suppress the immune system, so Bernie was cautious about avoiding cold or flu viruses. It was heartbreaking when he died in 2008 from complications caused by pneumonia.

Editing and Directing

I enjoy both editing and directing, but I enjoy alternating. Each discipline informs the other. Of the two, directing television is more stressful, mainly because of the lack of control. Even though you can't control everything, it's still your fault if something goes wrong. It feels like the stress of directing television takes years off my life. But I found that editing puts those years back on. In the edit bay, I enjoy daily creative input.

Directing is a high-paying gig, and it *is* satisfying, especially if it's your show or your movie, or if the environment is supportive. But unless you make it into the top tier of directors, who can get hired repeatedly, work is sporadic. Competition for the limited openings is huge. Whereas, an editing job means six to nine months of continuous, enjoyable work. I still love alternating between directing and editing television, features, and documentaries, but whatever the project, editing has captured my heart.

The Cinematic Look

One key distinction that differentiates television from feature films is the look. Higher-budget movies look "cinematic" because more time is spent lighting each angle, so that every shot is beautiful. With only one angle to worry about, the camera crew can light the actor in the absolute best and most distinctive manner.

Because television budgets are lower, and in order to move quickly, it helps to have two, three, or four camera angles shooting simultaneously. Shooting multiple angles requires a uniform, overall lighting scheme, which allows cameras to photograph in almost any direction. That type of lighting flattens the overall appearance, making it look like television instead of cinema. If you're covering multiple angles, there is no way to light with the same nuance as you could for a single camera angle.

Dollying versus Panning

In features, another aspect that adds to the cinematic feel is the use of fluid-looking shots where a dolly (or crane, or drone) is used to reframe. It may require dozens of takes to perfect the timing for a move. Panning, tilting, and zooming is eschewed in favor of moving and reframing the camera.

In his memoir *Barry Sonnenfeld, Call Your Mother: Memoirs of a Neurotic Filmmaker* (2020), director-cinematographer Barry Sonnenfeld wrote, "The one thing I begged a director not to do was pan. I loved to track, but hated to pan. Panning is a lazy way to block scenes and frame shots." After a premiere screening of Martin Scorsese's *Gangs of New York* (2002), filmmaker Ethan Coen asked Sonnenfeld, "Why was that so bad?" Sonnenfeld replied, "Too much panning."[1]

There is a visual trade-off that is made to create the more spontaneous filming process of a show such as *Curb Your Enthusiasm*. The cameras are there to capture what's happening, to receive what the actors are doing, not to control the filmic look. "Anytime we tried to get even a little cinematic on *Curb Your Enthusiasm*," said Alec Berg, "we'd get into the edit and go, 'What the hell is that doing in there? That doesn't feel like the show.' I remember when we shot with a Steadicam for the first time. As soon as we looked at that fluid move, we went, 'Nope. That's not the show.' It was weird. It knocked us out of our chairs."

Swingles

Handheld cameras have become a popular style. One reason is because cameras can move faster because crews don't have to set up dolly tracks and tripods and make every shot perfect. *Veep* was known for its panning shots, which they called "swingles"—short for swinging singles. Jimmy Lindsey was the director of photography on the *Veep* pilot, and he believes he brought the term swingles into the *Veep* camp. He said, "I probably picked it up early in my career, maybe as a camera assistant on *Rushmore* (1998)." *Curb Your Enthusiasm* utilized a lot of swingles from the very beginning (often panning out of necessity). Armando Iannucci also liked the panning style when he created the look for *Veep*. The original rule from Armando's era was: You must not pan before a line begins. In other words, don't anticipate a line. The actor starts the line and then you can begin the pan. Otherwise, it wouldn't feel appropriate, as if it was a documentary camera following the action. But that rule was demoted when it became more important to David Mandel to make sure we used the funniest version of a line, even if the camera operator anticipated a move. Visual look was sacrificed for increased comedy.

On an improvised show, the camera has to be on the actors when they say the unique hilarious line or it's lost forever. The first reaction to a line is often the most natural. There's always a camera on Larry David, so we can cut to his reaction because it might happen that way only once. When there were only two cameras used on *Curb Your Enthusiasm*, and when a panning shot missed the funny moment, we would be cursing in the editing room. The solution was to add more cameras. That's expensive, but how do you put a price on hilarious lines?

When filming a scene on *Curb Your Enthusiasm*, they start by keeping it wide during the early takes. At first the actors don't know exactly where they're going within the scene. As the takes develop, the camera crew senses how Larry is going to react. Then they move in for closer coverage.

Save the Wide Shot

Something they did during *Veep* season six was to shoot closer coverage first and then pull back and get the extreme wide shot during the last setup. It reverses the traditional approach, where they usually shoot the master first and then move in for coverage. In season five we were not able to use wide shots in the cuts as much as we wanted, because the wides were filmed first, before they had arrived at the best performance and the funniest jokes. The master shots filmed early didn't have the overall effectiveness that came in later takes.

Veep executive producer Morgan Sackett said they started the ethos of doing the wide shots last on *Parks and Recreation* (2009–2015). "Often we would shoot wides. But then doing improv would change the blocking in the tighter shots and so we would have to reshoot the wides. I noticed the same thing was happening on *Veep* because the dialogue was changing due to rewrites and the use of alt lines and so I suggested it as a strategy." David Mandel and Julia Louis-Dreyfus jumped on board for that idea. Julia said, "On *Veep* the wide shot was our friend. That's a big takeaway. Moving forward in my life, I'm going to rely on the wide, given how much a scene changes shape during shooting, from the beginning of your first shot until the end. You don't walk away from a scene until it works. So, you have to get the wide at the end as a result."

Rehearsals

The television production pace moves too fast to allow for in-depth rehearsals. Feature films have more time, and rehearsals often provide unexpected gold. While making *Black or White* (2014), Kevin Costner said to Mike Binder, "Sometimes when I shoot a scene, I get an idea driving home and I go, 'I wish I did that in the scene.' But we're done; we moved to another location. When you rehearse, you give the actors a chance to experience it, and then come back to it later. It sinks into their consciousness. They have time to live with it, and if they think of ideas, they can bring them to the shoot. But sometimes we move too fast."

Writing Television versus Feature Films

On a television series, Judd Apatow doesn't worry about resolving a character's largest issues. But when he's writing a movie, it has to be fully self-contained to complete a story. His protagonist must show some sort of emotional change. All questions raised by the story must be resolved. In *Knocked Up* (2007), Ben Stone (Seth Rogen) is a pothead who finds out Alison Scott (Katherine Heigl) is pregnant. He takes a journey to find enough responsibility within himself to cope with a baby when it arrives. With a television series, you have a longer timeline. If two strangers decide they're going to try to raise a baby together, they could break up in episode two, without resolving the questions, keeping story threads open. You could spend an entire season trying to figure things out. They're completely different mediums.

Overwriting

During each season on *Curb Your Enthusiasm* and *Veep*, stories got longer and longer, which created ever-bigger challenges to fit them into their time slots. At the end of season seven on *Veep*, I asked David Mandel, "Have you learned your lesson, to write less for the next show?"

David said, "No. I'll just do it again and hire you, so there's your problem."

One reason these shows are overwritten is because it's easier to worry about fixing it in the editing room than be disciplined in the writing stage. Comedians are not necessarily known for their discipline. Comedic writers are sort of like five-year-olds who never quite have to grow up. But even a five-year-old with constraints will stay within the constraints. If you slowly remove the constraints, that

230

five-year-old is going to get into everything. Due to streaming, running-time constraints have loosened. Like when someone's expenditures rise to meet their income, the writing rises to meet the volume available. And so, episodes of *Curb Your Enthusiasm* started regularly coming in at more than thirty minutes. But you can't get the type of comedic moments you see on *Veep* and *Curb Your Enthusiasm* any other way. You have to let the writers and performers play in the sandbox and see what happens. The script is a seed that blooms during shooting and is heavily pruned in the editing room.

However, there is a financial incentive to keep shows shorter, because once an episode exceeds thirty-one minutes or thirty-six minutes, in different cases, it may trigger additional guild payments because it's no longer considered a half-hour program. It also takes more time to shoot more scenes with more locations, more props, more actors, and more post-production. More time costs more money.

The Editor's Cut

First cuts of a half-hour show may be as long as fifty or sixty minutes. On my first round, I try to deliver a "kitchen sink cut," with every idea and joke included. I don't want to remove jokes, dialogue, or story points yet. My goal is to show them the best version of everything they shot. Larry David prefers the longer cut: "I'd rather see more stuff because it's easier to say, 'take that out,' rather than missing something and wanting to add bits." But Jeff Schaffer acknowledged that having everything gives you less. "Even with the best editors, the first cuts are depressing. The reason is simple. You're dumping everything in. We're not letting you cut it to the correct pace."

My cut of the first scene in the *Veep* episode "Iowa" (season seven, episode one) was four minutes and twenty seconds long. By the time David Mandel got through revising this scene, it came down to half that length at two minutes and three seconds. It can be scary for an editor to show something that could be better. But even when you feel like you can improve a scene by trimming, you have to include the producers in the cut-down process.

The goal is to get a half-hour episode down to 28:30 for pay cable (it can be under that, but it can't go over, though occasionally a dispensation is granted by a network for extra length) or 21:30 for a broadcast network (which is pretty firm, to preserve room for commercials). If you begin with a forty-five-minute rough cut, that means you have to throw away a third to half of what was shot. David Mandel said that once he gets an episode down around thirty-five minutes, "that's where you start to get a sense of, 'what is this show?' That's when you may feel like an entire storyline isn't working because it's kicking in way too late. Then you move it and it's a different show."

A scripted half-hour show, in which we are building a scene favoring circled takes, may need only a week to prepare a first cut. A fully improvised show such as *Curb Your Enthusiasm* or *The League* takes about three weeks for a first cut, because there is less script

Author's collection.

Kent, Selina, Gary, and Ben on their way to a campaign event, in *Veep*.

guidance and more to construct. You have to figure out how to build consistent scenes from continually changing performances. A scripted show such as *Veep*, with a lot of overshooting and alternative lines, falls somewhere in between and takes around two weeks for an editor's cut. Comedies tend to overshoot, because they are not always certain which bits may or may not work. Mike Binder dreads viewing the editor's cut. "When I saw the first cuts of my first two movies, I went home and got sick. Over the years, you realize that it's just a starting point."

The Director's Cut

Before the producers see the episode, I deliver a fully finished editor's cut to the director. No editor catches everything the director intended. Only the directors know what they had in mind for any given shot. The editor brings a fresh eye and maybe conceives of a different use. But the director brings adjustments, improvements, and course corrections before an episode is turned over to the producers.

The television director has two days to craft a half-hour cut. Four days for an hour-long episode, and fifteen days for a feature-length program. On some shows, the directors come in for their two days, and sometimes they don't bother. Some only send notes. It depends on the director and the show. But they all know who's show it is—*not theirs*.

On *Veep*, Brad Hall had the record for the most director's cut days, working ten days with Steven Rasch on "C★★tgate" (season five, episode six). Brad was able to spend that amount of time because David Mandel wasn't ready yet to start work on his producer's cut. When I asked Brad why he put so much effort into the editing, he said, "I like the feeling of watching things over and over, then not knowing you've been in there ten hours. I defy anybody, once they're actually cutting, to have any idea how long they have been in the room. You lose all sense of time. I'm amazed at how much better things get. There is a point where you start hurting scenes. But if you've got a great editor, they'll say, 'What are we doing here? We're ruining this thing.' And then you go back a couple versions. It's all right. It's all there. It's nondestructive."

The Producer's Cut

Once the director finishes, then it's up to the showrunner to complete a final version. Typically, they will view the director's cut and work from there. There have been instances where the showrunner had no faith in the director's changes and tossed the director's cut sight unseen and started with the editor's cut. When that happened, I would create a hybrid, where I added the changes I thought were indeed improvements that came out of the director's cut process.

On *Curb Your Enthusiasm*, we spent as much time as Larry David needed to finish editing an episode. Typically, it's about three weeks. Jeff Schaffer has been Larry David's right hand on the later seasons, directing most of the episodes, and Jeff will get many of his changes into an episode before Larry watches it.

During his first week in editing, Larry David views all the raw footage. Jeff Schaffer joins when available. Few producers have the time (or inclination) to watch all the footage. Larry is different. He wants to see every take. Even the best editor doesn't find every gold nugget. As we watch, Larry shares his thoughts about the footage, mainly ideas for trying more jokes or alternate lines. Larry and Jeff debate preferences. I'll jot down notes in the transcript and then squeeze all the new stuff they select into the expanding cut, until we have a forty-five- to fifty-five-minute cut. And then we devote another two weeks to cutting it down, fine-tuning as we go.

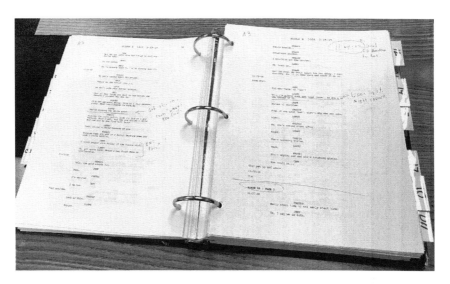

Each improvised take is transcribed on *Curb Your Enthusiasm.*

Jeff Schaffer was really good at multitasking on *The League*. He would pop in and give batches of notes and then leave to write, or shoot, or work with other editors, and keep things moving. As a writing and directing showrunner, he didn't have time to sit in one place for long.

On *Veep*, David Mandel concentrated on writing and directing during the shooting of the show. When it was time for him to sit in the editing room, he focused on one episode for about ten days, in sequential order, until he finished each cut. David thinks of editing in terms of micro and macro approaches. In the micro realm, he trims things within a scene. In the macro, he considers moving scenes around and removing scenes. There are some scenes in *Veep* that were completely revised, sections shifted around, lines revoiced, until that scene was radically different from what was shot.

Why is it so difficult to find the right concoction? Sometimes a scene reads one way, but when performed, it has a different feel. Or on set they may add four great jokes, expanding the length. Even if the scene works great unto itself, if you need to be moving faster toward the end, concern for pacing takes over. According to David Mandel, "It could be a nice little scene, the performances are great, every joke is funny, but if we don't cut it in half, we're destroying the back end of our show. It's not until you watch the show top to bottom that you can feel what each scene should be. That's why you can make, remake, or break something in editing."

On *Grey's Anatomy*, since the shows are cut close to what's scripted, there's not a lot of handwringing about restructuring episodes. If I had cut one line out of an episode, Krista Vernoff noticed. With comedy, when actors' performances varied, she often preferred to find the scripted version. "Because we worked hard on the rhythm of the line and on the combination of sounds within the line, it's usually funnier as scripted. But I don't stick to rules and I don't keep it my way just on principal. If the actor tried it different ways and one of their ways is funnier than mine, I'm using it. With drama it depends on the actor. Some actors can say whatever words they want to say and still land a moment. Some can't."

When Jon Corn worked on the first season of *Parks and Recreation* (2009–2020), he ventured off script on his first episode. Because Greg Daniels and Michael Schur had come from *The Office* (2005–2013), which had a loose-looking semi-documentary feel, Jon thought, "I'm going to do my best version of the episode. I'm going to try experiments, move things around, look for the best solutions."

When he turned in his editor's cut, he got a frantic call from Greg Daniels's assistant. "Where's the scripted cut?! Greg needs to see the scripted cut!"

Jon had to go in and hurriedly reassemble a cut that hewed closer to the script. "I was surprised to find that show was so tightly controlled," Jon said. "The ability to make something appear so loose is a skill. *Curb Your Enthusiasm* was so different. Larry says: 'Have at it, man. Put everything you want in it.' My first cut is a guide track. Larry

David is precious about very little. Seventy five percent of the jokes are left on the floor. Not because they didn't work, you just have to choose favorite tangents."

There are airdates and commensurate deadlines. Post-production supervisors make schedules and then tear their hair out if we don't stick to them. With *Curb Your Enthusiasm*, the deadline is looser because it takes longer to do it Larry's way. A network series such as *Grey's Anatomy*, where they produce twenty-four episodes per season, has firm airdates. That forces everyone to adapt to the schedule and move quickly.

The Network Cut

After David Mandel finished his producer's cut of an episode of *Veep*, it would simultaneously go to the network, executive producer Frank Rich, and Julia Louis-Dreyfus for their notes. It can sometimes be alarming when actors are allowed to give notes, but Julia is an exception; her notes on *Veep* were helpful. David would come in with several handwritten pages after he talked to everybody. That round of notes took about a day to address. You can't fix every note. But you at least give each one a hearing. Sometimes we decided that what was there played better in context compared to the requested change. And then David would explain that we tried, but sometimes we couldn't do it. David Mandel had final cut, so he was the tiebreaker when notes were conflicting. If you bring the awards, they'll let you make the call. But you better bring awards. Or lots of eyeballs. Or both.

CHAPTER ELEVEN

Success in the Film Business

If You Enjoy Your Work, and You Work Hard,
You're Not a Workaholic, You're a Funaholic

The prior chapters focused on how to become a better editor, how to be more creative, and how the editing room works. This chapter contains specific advice on how to actually land that dream job. Jobs in production come three ways: through a good agent, word-of-mouth connections, and your own initiative. The last is the most important. Even when I'm not working, I'm working—writing, pitching, shooting, editing my own projects, and networking. Let's say you earned excellent grades in college and you feel ready to join the film industry. What do you do next? Let's review the essential ingredients in this plan.

The Plan for Success

1. **Have good timing.** You don't know when it's good or bad timing, so try every avenue, repeatedly, until you happen to turn up the day they are looking for somebody. There is always room for quality. You are needed somewhere right now. You just don't know where. Research and find companies that make the product you love and contact them.

2. **Be persistent**. Until you get a job in your field, don't stop. If they say no, move on to the next. Luck is another word for persistence. If you stay in the game long enough, you will get that break. As long as you keep making whatever you do a little better, you will get noticed.

3. **Be well-rounded**. Be a filmmaker, not just an editor. Start making films. Be creative daily. That's how you stay in shape.

4. **Understand storytelling**. Editing is rewriting. Study great films. Read great novels. Practice writing (it doesn't matter if your writing is not great at first).

5. **Learn the software**. Learn new software and different workflows. Be an expert. My assistants must be technical aces.

6. **Move to the work**. Atlanta, Chicago, Houston, Kansas City, Minneapolis—they all have media-production work, but New York has a hundred times more. And Los Angeles has triple what New York has. Are you fishing in a small pond?

7. **Network**. Force yourself out of your introverted mindset. Meet your peers. Take classes, send e-mails, attend events, throw events. Nobody succeeds on their own. To get there, you need help from the contacts and friends you will make.

8. **Get an agent**. This is one of the last things you will do. Agents are like bankers, they're not available until you don't need them. Once you start getting successful, you'll get an agent. They will help you move to the next level.

9. **Join MPEG and ACE**. The Motion Picture Editors Guild (MPEG) is a part of the International Alliance of Theatrical Stage Employees (IATSE). You have to be a guild member to work on union shows. MPEG includes animation editors, apprentice editors, assistant editors, colorists, engineers, foley artists, librarians, music editors, picture editors, recordists, rerecording/scoring mixers, sound editors, story analysts, technical directors, trailer editors, and more. They negotiate contracts covering wages, health

insurance, retirement and pension, safety, and artistic integrity. To join you have to prove you have a certain amount of work experience. For example, to join as an assistant editor, you have to demonstrate one hundred days of non-union work experience within the last three years. Save your pay stubs. You can find membership requirements on the MPEG website. The American Cinema Editors (ACE) is a society formed to advance the art and science of the film-editing profession. To apply, you need to have been employed for a minimum of seventy-two months as an editor and be sponsored by two members. You can find membership requirements on the ACE website.

10. **Write an amazing introduction**. You need to introduce yourself to the production world. Keep your cover letter short, grammatically perfect, and pleasant. Then begin selling your talents.

The Magic E-Mail

This is an e-mail that works. I fall for it every time. Willingly. This example is similar to some I have received:

> Dear Roger,
>
> You have edited some of my favorite shows, such as *Curb* and *Veep*, and I really respect the work that you do. I am a trailer editor looking to transition to scripted as an assistant editor or apprentice editor, and your advice would be invaluable. I was wondering if I could ask you a couple of questions? Would you be open to a phone call or video chat sometime?

Yes, of course I would be open! Why? Because this person followed the magic formula: start with praise, then a very short self-description, then a call to action—ask for a phone conversation. Don't ask to meet for coffee. That's too much time investment. Ask for advice. Just a few short questions. As a fellow human being, I like to be helpful to other nice humans. It's hard to turn down somebody who is praising your work and asking for wisdom. Do the research; look up my work and mention specifics. Don't ask me to read your script, watch your film, or anything else that will take more time or work.

Make a list of companies that are vibrant, with recent releases, that have new product in development, and send your letter to a specific person(s) there; send it by snail mail if you really want to stand out. Don't attach a résumé to an introductory e-mail, but put your website at the bottom, which has essentially the same information as a résumé. Go ahead and include a résumé with your cover letter when it's snail mail.

Once you get somebody on the phone, don't overstay your welcome. Prepare your questions in advance and learn what you can. And now that you have made an acquaintance in the business, it's on you to nurture that connection. Send a thank-you afterward with a specific comment about what you learned. Follow up again in three to six months, and then again in nine to twelve months. Just a short line to mention what you have learned or accomplished since we last spoke. Did you watch a movie I recommended? Did you read a book? What did you think? People love to hear they may have affected you in a positive way. And by doing so, you are staying on their radar. I maintain hundreds of connections via e-mails and text check-ins. I utilize such social conventions as holiday cards. A holiday gives you an excuse to send a funny photo or note to everybody you know in the business. They will enjoy the chuckle, and your goal is for them to remember you next time there's a job opening.

The Successful Job Interview

When you go in for an interview (or an audition), they want you to win, because then they can stop working on this task and go home.

Don't look at them as an adversary; they are on your side. Once you schedule a meeting, go in prepared. Learn everything about that company (names of the principals, history, credits), have a specific goal (to get an offer), and be 100 percent interested in taking the job and giving it your all. Don't meet if you don't want the job. Your feeling toward the job will suffuse your demeanor in the interview. They notice; they meet with people all day, and differences are clear.

Here's the advice that bears repeating: praise and flattery work—whether on a date, a business meeting, or maintaining friendships. We are social creatures and need support from peers. We shy away from negative people. Human beings like people who support and compliment them. It makes them feel good about themselves and about the person who is making the comment. Steven Rasch said of Larry David, "He likes real appreciation. And if you see him on the street, just say, 'Hey, Larry, I love your show.' And he will give you the time of day. He will respond well. But if you try to be funny or mock him or call him out for no reason, he will avoid that. But he loves compliments." Studies have found that praise activates the same reward-related areas of the brain (the ventral striatum) that light up when we receive monetary rewards. Offering a compliment achieves the same result as handing somebody cash.[1,2] And praise is somewhat more ethical than bribery.

Remember that an interview is a conversation, not an interrogation. As soon as possible, open with your "spontaneous" flattery. Verbalize how much you genuinely love their project and then give specific, concrete examples of what has impressed you about their work. If you can find a point of personal overlap with yourself and the interviewer, that's a bonus. Scan the room as you enter to look for family photos, sports memorabilia, award statues, anything upon which you can connect. If you see a signed Clayton Kershaw jersey on the wall, you might say: "I love the Dodgers! Did you see game seven of the series?" Do you notice a photo of people in front of the Cloud Gate sculpture? Try: "Is that the Bean? My family lived in Chicago when I was a kid. How do you like Chicago in the fall?" If you see photos of children, you can never go wrong with any version of: "You have such beautiful children! What ages are they?" If you genuinely notice anything personal that you have in common, make this person feel good about their life choices; it warms up the room.

The first few minutes of any meeting are the "get to know you" happy talk. Don't worry about wowing them with your achievements or technical prowess. They already know enough about your history to have you in the room. This is your opportunity to be *likable*. People hire those they feel good around. Simply be personable and charming. Did you notice that I ended each example above with a question? Keep the focus on the interviewer, not on yourself or your anecdotes. The more they talk about themselves, and the less that you talk, the more likely you are to get the job.

Keep in mind that the meeting starts in the waiting room. Be nice to the receptionist, the assistants, the entire staff. If you are a jerk to the employees, they will make note of it. If there are multiple people in the meeting, don't ignore anybody. That quiet person in the corner may have the final say. Never apologize in advance; don't admit deficiencies unprompted. ("I forgot my résumé." "I can't parallel park." "I'm afraid of frogs.") Don't point out mistakes you made in the meeting. Chances are, only you noticed, so why bring it to their attention?

To prepare for my interview with Lisa Taylor, producer of *Grey's Anatomy*, I asked a friend who had watched all seasons of *Grey's Anatomy* which episodes were most memorable. There was no way I could watch three hundred hours in three days. I received a list of five key episodes: the pilot, which sets up an ensemble cast and the tone of the show, one episode that took place in real time over the course of an hour, an episode that has time jumps, a musical episode, and a documentary-style episode. I was surprised at the creative chances they took, sometimes breaking their usual format. I also watched as many episodes of the most recent season as possible. I found the series to be truly impressive, well-written, emotional, and exciting. Because I had watched twenty episodes before I went in, I was able to be honest, specific, and genuine in my flattery.

The Wrong Way to Interview

The next season on *Grey's Anatomy*, when I got booked on *Veep* and was unable to return, Lisa Taylor asked if I could recommend somebody. I suggested Grady Cooper, who I knew was excellent. At Grady's interview, when Lisa asked why he wanted the job, he said, "I really need the work." The interview was over when he said that. Grady sabotaged himself by saying he didn't specifically want to work on that show. He admitted to me afterward that he had made a mistake: "You have to be a little bit of an actor in the job audition phase."

Several years prior, Grady's wife, Jane Cooper, had been diagnosed with glioblastoma, the worst kind of brain tumor. Grady took a year off in 2014 to help take care of her. It was a scary time, existing on savings, not knowing when he would be able to work again. After Jane died in 2015, Grady decided he wanted to be home more to take care of his two daughters. When he returned to editing, he told producers: "I'll come in early, I'll skip lunch breaks, but I need to leave by five p.m. so I can be with my kids." As long as he mentioned it up front, most were okay with that. The shows that took him on weren't always his favorite jobs. But his primary criterion was being able to leave early. Grady felt like he was in a creative decline and the money was running out. It's hard to act enthusiastic when the walls are closing in. And in an interview, desperation is not attractive.

On one occasion, when my agent booked a meeting for a potential directing job, the producers arranged for me to watch their pilot for a new FOX series called *Unhitched* (2008). It was all very secretive, so I had to watch in a conference room just before the meeting. Because it was executive-produced by the Farrelly brothers, who wrote and directed the hugely successful comedy *There's Something About Mary* (1998), and because the series starred Rashida Jones, whom I had worked with on *The Office*, I had high hopes. The assistant showed me to the conference room, inserted a disc, and left. As I watched I became increasingly anxious because I thought the pilot was terrible. For example, the first scene began with a guy returning to a potential girlfriend's apartment after a date. Both are flirtatious and upbeat. The woman excuses herself to freshen up. After she exits, her pet orangutan enters and rapes the boyfriend. I was shell-shocked that somebody thought this was funny. When I was led to the meeting with the producers, I tried to rise to the occasion, but I was so disturbed I couldn't bring myself to praise the pilot. I didn't make any big mistakes or say anything wrong, but in meetings you are required to rave. Any praise that is less than all-out gushing is insulting. As Jeff Shaffer puts it, "If you say, 'It's great,' that's the equivalent of saying, 'it exists.'" I didn't get the job. Maybe the series got better after the pilot. They filmed six episodes and then FOX canceled it.

Keep Your Mouth Shut

My final advice for the job seeker is this: When you get to the meeting, shut up! You may think the interview is about you talking about your qualifications. It's not. Don't offer anything until asked. Do not interrupt the interviewer. Sit quietly and actively listen. Make eye contact. Smile. Nod. Avoid nervous movements: no toe tapping, leg shaking, or shifty eyes. Don't touch anything. When it's your turn, don't leave any awkward pauses. Answer immediately, clearly, and with confidence. Look people in the eye. But keep it short. No shaggy dog stories. If you don't know what that is, look it up. Turn the conversation back around as much as you can and ask questions about the interviewer, questions you prepared in advance.

I forwarded a draft of this chapter to a friend just before he jumped into an interview. Two weeks later he said: "Those tips didn't hurt. I landed the job."

Be the Greatest Peon in History

Once you get that job, be the first to arrive and the last to leave. Nobody should ever have to tell you something twice. Whatever they put on your plate, it gets done quickly and correctly. Double- and triple-check your work. Don't be known as the person who made The Big Mistake. Be easy to get along with. Keep your opinions to yourself. Don't tell anybody what you think of politics, religion, or abortion. Listen. Never argue. Word of mouth is going to be your best currency. People refer reliable people who are easy to work with and get things done. Enthusiasm will get you promoted; a negative attitude will get you shown the door.

You are going to be compared to every person who has been in that job before, and your mission is to stand out. David Mandel put it this way: "I have to be in that room so long that I don't have a lot of patience for slowness. I need these edits to get done. When somebody is doing something simplistic and it's taking longer and I know in the other room I've got a person who can be doing it like this"—he snaps his fingers—"it's hard. It's painful."

All it takes is one day where you take a job for granted, and your stock can plummet, faster than it rose. I didn't go to college to become a messenger, but when I accepted my first job as a runner at Rollins, Joffe, Morra and Brezner, I tried to be the best runner they

Roger Nygard's first job as a messenger, on the Paramount lot, in 1985.

ever had. Eventually they noticed my enthusiasm and reliability. If you can't be a great assistant, you won't be a great leader. Whichever opportunity you say yes to, give it your all. My job is perpetually difficult, but it's also fun. It's easy to work hard when you like to wake up and do it again. I love what I do. I'm blessed to be able to say that about my career.

Jonathan Vogler, the producer of the docu-series *The Comedy Store* (2020), once said, "I like to hire people who fought to be here, who did whatever it took to get to Los Angeles. If you hire somebody who went into the business because it was convenient, you're going to get a worse attitude about doing a great job." If the boss hires the offspring, if the job doesn't resonate, if an employee has no concern about being fired, that removes some of the incentive to do a stellar job. When you choose a career, go at it with everything you've got.

The Résumé

When he moved to Los Angeles, Jonathan Vogler was unsuccessful in getting a response to his résumé. Confused and demoralized, he wanted to find out why, so he placed his own test ad. He was inundated with job applicants. When he analyzed their résumés, he discovered they didn't have more bona fides than he did, but their résumés *looked* better.

The first lesson he learned was to fill up the page with experience; add all your industry credits, no matter how small. He had left off jobs that were of short duration or that he was embarrassed by because they were in Georgia. People look at quantity and move on.

The second lesson: Only include work that is related to the industry; remove irrelevant jobs. He had assumed that working for two years in a warehouse would show a good work ethic, but nobody interprets it that way. People group like with like. Typecasting is the rule of the land. When I wrote and directed *Warped*, my first short film that had a decent budget, a mutant baby briefly made an appearance at the end. When I sent the film out as my demo, my first job offer was to direct an episode of a low-budget television series called *Monsters*. Why did

Kevin Nealon, mutant baby, Julie Brown, David Spade, and Roger Nygard, on the set of *Monsters* in 1990.

they think I was qualified? Because their episode also had a mutant baby in it. I thought it was crazy for somebody to think I'm a mutant baby expert because there was one briefly in my first short. But I was thrilled to be typecast because it got me a job, so I dove in eagerly.

Jonathan Vogler's third lesson: Dump the standard template and design your own, clean, stylish résumé. Put effort into creating a clean look. Some of his favorites looked elegant, nicely designed, and pleasing to the eye. He changed his stuffy Times New Roman font to a more modern sans serif. He balanced out the page, spread things to all four corners, and didn't try to space the text so tightly. Once he made the résumé tweaks, he began getting responses and quickly landed his first job as a production assistant on a Nike commercial.

Unicorns Exist

A way to get in the room for that interview is to become the best at what you do. You have to practice more than your peers. Keep making films. Keep writing. Keep editing. In his book *Outliers: The Story of Success* (2008), Malcolm Gladwell describes the 10,000-hour rule, asserting that the way to expertise is by practicing your specialty. If you are the best, producers will keep you around. And to do that they will have to offer you more money and better perks. If you have the stamina to stick with it, eventually you will be calling the shots.

After Grady Cooper blew his *Grey's Anatomy* job interview, things did work out. After his wife passed away, he slowly began dating again. At the same time, he was focusing on getting one kid through high school and the other off to college. He said, "I had been married twenty years, and it felt like a bizarre return to a different reality." Grady started journaling his thoughts and feelings about what his experience was like, mostly as a cathartic process. "I called it being an 'only parent,' not a single parent."

In 2015, Grady ran into showrunners Bill Martin and Mike Schiff (*Grounded for Life*, 2001–2005) while getting a sandwich in Studio City. Grady knew Bill from college. "He was in a smart, cool, nerdy fraternity. They hosted these really great drug parties and I would get invited. Everybody there was cut from the same cloth, all smart, goofy people." Funny enough, I had also worked with Bill Martin and Mike Schiff when I directed an episode of a short-lived series they had created called *The Singles Table* (2006), starring John Cho, Alicia Silverstone, and Rhea Seehorn. Grady couldn't have bumped into a better pair of easygoing, good-natured, funny guys.

When Grady shared some of his poignant stories, Bill said, "Wow your life is so different now."

After they parted, Bill and Mike talked about Grady's life and agreed it could be a great idea for a series, but they felt it would be tacky asking Grady, given his personal circumstance. Grady also chewed it over and arrived at the same conclusion. A few days later he called them and asked, "Do you think it could be a show?"

Mike replied, "We are so glad you asked. We were hoping you would pitch this to us." They said they were tired of fictionalized stories and wanted to dig into something based on real life. Together they worked up a pitch called *The Unicorn* and took it to Aaron Kaplan, CEO of Kapital Entertainment. Kaplan responded strongly, partly because his brother had recently passed away; he was sensitive to what it felt like to be an adult and grieve. The "widower dad" had been a common archetype in pitches over the years, and so it was not an easy sell, but the final piece of the puzzle fell into place when they pitched at CBS Studios. Grady had worked with executive Kate Adler on *Survivor*, and she said, "Oh, I love Grady, I love Bill and Mike, we should do this show!" Next, this team brought the show to Julie Pernworth at CBS network, and she went out on a limb and bought it. Grady the editor, who was also a filmmaker who kept writing, said he now had his own show that he had co-created with friends. "I blame

Kate entirely for getting me into this amazing mess." Kate demurred, saying, "I don't deserve any credit for the show. It's really good and that is 100 percent because of Grady, Mike, and Bill."

Grady Cooper said he would never have even had the idea to pitch a show like *The Unicorn* if he hadn't worked on *Curb Your Enthusiasm*, because in that show, Larry David is an extension of himself.

Photo by Mike Schiff.

Walton Goggins and Grady Cooper, on the set of *The Unicorn* in 2019.

"I constantly heard Larry talking about storylines based on his own life experiences. Once I got to know him, I fell in love with his perspective on life. He has his own rules and behaviors—but they are based on a relatable reality. That's what makes him special." Thanks to Grady's change in fate, he was able to pay for his girls' college and take a breath. "In a sweetly sad way, it was my wife's contribution. And I'm forever grateful. I'm lucky to be a part of a creative community that cares for each other. And whenever I can repay the favor, I'm there. So, for anyone wanting to contribute to the film business, the bottom line is to not give up. Seek mentors wherever they are."

Start Now

I often hear a version of this question: "How do I become a film-maker/director/writer/editor?" My answer is, "Start today." There is a Chinese proverb: *The best time to plant a tree was twenty years ago. The second-best time is now.* Even if you do not have enough money to make a feature film, make what you can afford, even if it is only a one-minute short. Practice your craft. Be creative. Alec Berg shared his sentiment: "If you want to be a writer there's nothing stopping you from being a writer except yourself. Which is really one of the bummers about being a writer: You have no excuses. The compulsion to do it has to be the biggest thing."

Whatever it takes, you need to be shooting and editing. I learned to operate a video camera and record sound so that I could get the footage I needed to edit. With some of my projects, such as *Trekkies* (1997) and *Six Days in Roswell* (1999) and *Suckers* (2001), I had a full production team. But for others, such as *The Nature of Existence* (2010) and *The Truth About Marriage* (2020), I mostly did everything myself. If you are making films, you are a filmmaker. No matter what department you gravitate toward, start writing, shooting, and editing. Start now. As soon as you put down this book.

Notes

Introduction

1. Sven Svebak, Solfrid Romundstad, and Jostein Holmen, "A 7-year Prospective Study of Sense of Humor and Mortality in an Adult County Population: The Hunt-2 Study," *The International Journal of Psychiatry in Medicine* 40, no. 2 (July 7, 2010): 125–46, https://doi.org/10.2190/PM.40.2.a.

2. "Greek Police Arrest Monk Wanted for Fraud," *Irish Examiner*, October 5, 2005, https://www.irishexaminer.com/world/arid-30224016.html.

Chapter One

1. Marina Davila-Ross et al., "Chimpanzees (Pan troglodytes) Produce the Same Types of 'Laugh Faces' When They Emit Laughter and When They Are Silent," *PLoS One* (June 10, 2015), https://doi.org/10.1371/journal.pone.0127337.

2. Jaak Panksepp, "Neuroevolutionary Sources of Laughter and Social Joy: Modeling Primal Human Laughter in Laboratory Rats," *Behavioural Brain Research* 182, no. 2 (September 4, 2007): 231–44, https://doi.org/10.1016/j.bbr.2007.02.015.

3. E. B. White and Katharine S. White, *A Subtreasury of American Humor* (New York: Coward-McCann, 1941), preface, xvii.

4. John Gallishaw, *The Only Two Ways to Write a Story: A Book for Writers Which Cites Cases in the Craftmanship of the Modern Short Story* (New York: G. P. Putnam's Sons, 1928), 4–24.

5. A. E. van Vogt, "A. E. van Vogt: A Writer with a Winning Formula," interview by Jeffrey M. Elliot, *Science Fiction Voices 2: Interviews with Science Fiction Writers* (San Bernardino, CA: Borgo Press), 32.

6. Sigmund Freud, "Humor," *International Journal of Psychoanalysis*, vol. 9 (1928): 1–6.

7. Steve Allen, *Steve Allen's Almanac* (New York: Hearst Corp., Cosmopolitan, vol. 142, February 1957), 12.

8. Ricky Gervais, "#237—Another Call from Ricky," *Making Sense*, interview by Sam Harris, podcast recorded February 16, 2021, audio, 14:00, https://samhar ris.org/podcasts/237-another-call-from-ricky/.

9. Michael Bala, "The Clown: An Archetypal Self-Journey," *Jung Journal: Culture and Psyche* 4, no. 1 (Winter 2010, published online February 1, 2013): 50–71, https://doi.org/10.1525/jung.2010.4.1.50.

10. John Cleese, "John Cleese and the Key to Comedy," interview by Devon Ivie, *Interview Magazine*, November 11, 2014, https://www.interviewmagazine .com/culture/john-cleese-so-anyway.

Chapter Two

1. Harrison Blackman, "In 'Barry,' Tragedy Masquerades as Comedy: Genre-Bending Show Shines When It Commits to Its Premise," review of *Barry*, *Medium*, May 16, 2018, https://medium.com/@harrisonblackman/in-barry-trag edy-masquerades-as-comedy-be07ce1e6a17.

Chapter Three

1. Shai Danziger et al., "Extraneous Factors in Judicial Decisions," *Proceedings of the National Academy of Sciences* 108, no. 17 (April 26, 2011): 6889–92, https://doi .org/10.1073/pnas.1018033108.

2. Kenneth Tynan, "Playboy Interview: Orson Welles," *Playboy*, March 1967, published online May 19, 2017, https://scrapsfromtheloft.com/2017/05/19/ orson-welles-playboy-interview/.

3. Oliver Wendell Holmes Jr., *The Occasional Speeches of Justice Oliver Wendell Holmes*, edited by Mark De Wolfe Howe (Cambridge, MA: Harvard University Press, 1962), 28–31.

4. Eddie Van Halen, "Is Rock 'n' Roll All about Reinvention?" interview by Denise Quan, The Smithsonian's National Museum of American History and Zócalo Public Square, March 9, 2017, video, 11:20; 39:25, https://www .zocalopublicsquare.org/2015/02/14/necessity-is-the-source-of-eddie-van-hal ens-inventions/events/the-takeaway/.

5. Ben Sachs, "An Interview with Composer John Corigliano (Part One)," *Chicago Reader*, April 18, 2013, https://www.chicagoreader.com/Bleader/archives/2013/04/18/an-interview-with-composer-john-corigliano-part-one.

Chapter Four

1. Scott Conrad, "#2—Scott Conrad, A Conversation with Scott Conrad, One of the Oscar Winning Editors of Rocky," *The Road to Cinema*, podcast recorded August 12, 2014, audio, 15:25, https://jogroad.podbean.com/e/the-road-to-cinema-podcast-2-scott-conrad-editor/.

2. Alfred Hitchcock and Sidney Gottlieb, *Hitchcock on Hitchcock: Selected Writings and Interviews* (Los Angeles: University of California Press, 1995), 144.

3. Jackie Chan, "Faster Than a Speeding Bullet, But Also Humanly Fallible," interview by Neil Strauss, *New York Times*, January 30, 1995, section C, 13, https://www.nytimes.com/1995/01/30/movies/faster-than-a-speeding-bullet-but-also-humanly-fallible.html.

4. Arnold Samuelson, *With Hemingway: A Year in Key West and Cuba* (New York: Random House, Henry Holt and Co., 1988), 11.

5. Ernest Hemingway, *A Moveable Feast* (New York: Charles Scribner's Sons; London: Jonathan Cape, 1964, 2021), 77, Kindle.

6. George Plimpton, "Ernest Hemingway, The Art of Fiction, No. 21," *The Paris Review*, issue 18, Spring 1958, https://www.theparisreview.org/interviews/4825/ernest-hemingway-the-art-of-fiction-no-21-ernest-hemingway.

7. Cameron Crowe, *Conversations with Wilder* (New York: Knopf, 1999), 168.

8. Crowe, *Conversations with Wilder*, 168.

9. Patrick Heal, "Guare's Gamble of Epic Proportions," *New York Times*, November 14, 2010, section AR, 6, https://www.nytimes.com/2010/11/14/theater/14guare.html.

10. William Foster-Harris, *The Basic Patterns of Plot* (Norman: University of Oklahoma Press, 1959), 40.

11. Foster-Harris, *Basic Patterns of Plot*, 12, 35–46.

12. Douglas E. Richards, *Seeker* (Paragon Press, June 3, 2018), 340, Kindle.

13. Jason Blum, "The Purge/Get Out Producer—Jason Blum," interview by Todd Garner, *The Producer's Guide, Todd Garner and Hollywood's Elite*, podcast recorded December 20, 2018, audio, 19:30, https://podcastone.com/episode/Jason-Blum.

Chapter Five

1. Hemingway, *A Moveable Feast*, 6.

2. Stephen King, *On Writing: A Memoir of the Craft* (New York: Charles Scribner's Sons, 2000), 154, Kindle.

3. Anita M. Busch, "McConaughey Near 'Amistad,'" *Variety*, January 6, 1997, https://variety.com/1997/scene/vpage/mcconaughey-near-amistad-1117433944/.

4. Anita M. Busch, "DreamWorks Taps Cooper for Prod'n," *Variety*, May 28, 1997, https://variety.com/1997/film/news/dreamworks-taps-cooper-for-prod-n -1116677963/.

5. Adam Sandler, "Battle over *Amistad* Credit Intensifying," *Variety*, December 3, 1997, https://variety.com/1997/film/news/battle-over-amistad-credit-intensi fying-111733906/.

6. "Discipline Report," *California Lawyer*, Daily Journal Corporation, June 2003, 45.

Chapter Six

1. Albert Mehrabian and Morton Wiener, "Decoding of Inconsistent Communications," *Journal of Personality and Social Psychology* 6, no. 1 (1967): 109–14, https:// psycnet.apa.org/doiLanding?doi=10.1037%2Fh0024532.

2. Albert Mehrabian and Susan R. Ferris, "Inference of Attitudes from Nonverbal Communication in Two Channels," *Journal of Consulting Psychology* 31, no. 3 (May 31, 1967): 248–52, https://doi.org/10.1037/h0024648.

3. Sir Arthur Quiller-Couch, *On the Art of Writing, Lectures Delivered in the University of Cambridge 1913–1914* (Cambridge: Cambridge University Press, 1916), chapter XII, 6, https://www.bartleby.com/190/12.html.

Chapter Seven

1. Crowe, *Conversations with Wilder*, 165.

2. Billy Wilder and I. A. L. Diamond, *One, Two, Three: Screenplay* (Beverly Hills: Margaret Herrick Library, Academy Library, 1961), https://gointothestory.blcklst .com/daily-dialogue-june-17-2010-c136505bf9ef.

Chapter Eight

1. Mark Mangini, "Oscar-Winning Sound Supervisor Mark Mangini Gives You the Keys to the Kingdom," interview by Jeffrey Reeser, *The No Film School*, podcast recorded December 16, 2020, audio, 12:15, 20:20, https://nofilmschool .com/master-sound-supervisor-mark-mangini-gives-you-keys-kingdom.

2. Larry David, "Curb Your Enthusiasm—Larry David on Theme Song," The Paley Center for Media, July 29, 2009, video interview, 00:10, 01:20, https://www .youtube.com/watch?v=U4z0y4vTLok.

Chapter Ten

1. Barry Sonnenfeld, *Barry Sonnenfeld, Call Your Mother: Memoirs of a Neurotic Filmmaker* (New York: Hachette Books, 2020), 249.

Chapter Eleven

1. Sho K. Sugawara et al., "Social Rewards Enhance Offline Improvements in Motor Skill," *PLoS ONE* 7, no. 11 (November 7, 2012), https://doi.org/10.1371/ journal.pone.0048174.

2. Keise Izuma et al., "Processing of Social and Monetary Rewards in the Human Striatum," *Neuron* 58, no. 2 (April 24, 2008): 284–94, https://doi .org/10.1016/j.neuron.2008.03.020.

Bibliography

Adams, Douglas. *The Hitchhiker's Guide to the Galaxy*. London: Pan Books, 1979.

Allen, Steve. *Steve Allen's Almanac*. New York: Hearst Corp., Cosmopolitan, Volume 142, 1957.

Allen, Woody. *Getting Even*. New York: Random House, 1971.

American Cinema Editors. https://americancinemaeditors.org/.

Anderson, Poul. *Call Me Joe*. Astounding Science Fiction. 1957.

Anonymous Anglo-Saxon poet. *Beowulf*. 1000.

Aristophanes. *Lysistrata*. 411 BC.

Aristotle. *Poetics*. 330 BC.

Bala, Michael. "The Clown: An Archetypal Self-Journey." *Jung Journal: Culture and Psyche* 4, no. 1 (Winter 2010, published online February 1, 2013): 50–71. https://doi.org/10.1525/jung.2010.4.1.50.

Beckett, Samuel. *Waiting for Godot*. Paris: Les Editions De Minuit, 1952.

Blum, Jason. "The Purge/Get Out Producer—Jason Blum." *The Producer's Guide, Todd Garner and Hollywood's Elite*, podcast recorded December 20, 2018, audio, 19:30. https://podcastone.com/episode/Jason-Blum.

Booker, Christopher. *The Seven Basic Plots: Why We Tell Stories*. London: Bloomsbury Continuum, 2019.

Box Office Mojo, by IMDbPro. https://www.boxofficemojo.com/title/tt0118607/?ref_=bo_se_r_1.

Brontë, Charlotte. *Jane Eyre: An Autobiography*. London: Smith, Elder and Co., 1847.

Cameron, Julia. *The Artist's Way: A Spiritual Path to Higher Creativity*. New York: J. P. Tarcher/Putnam; Hardcover, 10th Anniversary edition, March 18, 2002.

Campbell, Joseph. *The Hero with a Thousand Faces*. Princeton, NJ: Princeton University Press, 1949.

Chan, Jackie. "Faster Than a Speeding Bullet, but Also Humanly Fallible." Interview by Neil Strauss, *New York Times*, January 30, 1995, section C, 13. https://www.nytimes.com/1995/01/30/movies/faster-than-a-speeding-bullet-but-also-humanly-fallible.html.

Cleese, John. "John Cleese and the Key to Comedy." Interview by Devon Ivie. *Interview Magazine*, November 11, 2014. https://www.interviewmagazine .com/culture/john-cleese-so-anyway.

Conrad, Scott. "#2—Scott Conrad, A Conversation with Scott Conrad, One of the Oscar Winning Editors of Rocky." *The Road to Cinema*, August 12, 2014. Audio, 15:25. https://jogroad.podbean.com/e/the-road-to-cinema-podcast-2 -scott-conrad-editor/.

Copyright Registration. https://www.copyright.gov/registration/.

Crowe, Cameron. *Conversations with Wilder.* New York: Knopf, 1999.

Dahl, Roald. *Charlie and the Chocolate Factory.* New York: Knopf, 1964.

Danziger, Shai, Jonathan Levav, and Liora Avnaim-Pesso. "Extraneous Factors in Judicial Decisions." *Proceedings of the National Academy of Sciences* 108, no. 17 (April 26, 2011): 6889–92. https://doi.org/10.1073/pnas.1018033108.

David, Larry. "Curb Your Enthusiasm—Larry David on Theme Song." The Paley Center for Media, July 29, 2009. Video, 00:10, 01:20. https://www.youtube .com/watch?v=U4z0y4vTLok.

Davila-Ross, Marina, Goncalo Jesus, Jade Osborne, and Kim A Bard. "Chimpanzees (Pan troglodytes) Produce the Same Types of 'Laugh Faces' When They Emit Laughter and When They Are Silent." *PLoS One* (June 10, 2015). https://doi .org/10.1371/journal.pone.0127337.

Defoe, Daniel. *Robinson Crusoe.* London: William Taylor, 1719.

Dickens, Charles. *David Copperfield.* London: Bradbury and Evans, 1850.

Dickens, Charles. *Great Expectations.* London: Chapman and Hall, 1861.

Dubus, Andre. *Dancing after Hours.* New York: Knopf, 1996.

Dubus III, Andre. *House of Sand and Fog.* New York: W. W. Norton and Company, 1999.

Eggers, Dave. *A Heartbreaking Work of Staggering Genius: Based on a True Story.* New York: Simon & Schuster, 2000.

Field, Syd. *Screenplay: The Foundations of Screenwriting.* New York: Dell Publishing Company, 1978.

Fielding, Henry. *The History of Tom Jones, a Foundling.* London: Andrew Millar, 1749.

Fisher, Peter (translated by); edited by Hilda Ellis Davidson. *Saxo Grammaticus: History of the Danes.* Cambridge, UK: Brewer, 1979.

Fitzgerald, F. Scott. *The Great Gatsby.* New York: Charles Scribner's Sons, 1925.

Flaubert, Gustave. *Madame Bovary.* Paris: Michel Levy Freres, 1857.

Foster-Harris, William. *The Basic Patterns of Plot*. Norman: University of Oklahoma Press, 1959.

Freud, Sigmund. "Humor." *International Journal of Psychoanalysis*, vol. 9, 1928.

Gallishaw, John. *The Only Two Ways to Write a Story: A Book for Writers Which Cites Cases in the Craftmanship of the Modern Short Story*. New York: G. P. Putnam's Sons, 1928.

Gervais, Ricky. "#237—Another Call from Ricky." Interview by Sam Harris. *Making Sense*. Podcast recorded February 16, 2021. Audio, 14:00. https://samharris.org/podcasts/237-another-call-from-ricky/.

Gladwell, Malcolm. *Outliers: The Story of Success*. Boston: Little, Brown and Co., 2008.

Goldman, William. *Adventures in the Screen Trade: A Personal View of Hollywood and Screenwriting*. New York: Warner Books, 1983.

Greek Mythology. *Icarus*. 30 BC.

Guare, John. *The House of Blue Leaves*. New York: Viking Press, 1972.

Heal, Patrick. "Guare's Gamble of Epic Proportions." *New York Times*, November 14, 2010, section AR, 6. https://www.nytimes.com/2010/11/14/theater/14guare.html.

Hemingway, Ernest. *A Farewell to Arms*. New York: Charles Scribner's Sons, 1929.

Hemingway, Ernest. *A Moveable Feast*. New York: Charles Scribner's Sons; London: Jonathan Cape, 1964; 2021. Kindle.

Hemingway, Ernest. *In Our Time*. New York: Boni and Liveright, 1925.

Hitchcock, Alfred, and Sidney Gottlieb. *Hitchcock on Hitchcock: Selected Writings and Interviews*. Los Angeles: University of California Press, 1995.

Holmes Jr., Oliver Wendell. *The Occasional Speeches of Justice Oliver Wendell Holmes*. Edited by Mark De Wolfe Howe. Cambridge, MA: Harvard University Press, 1962.

Izuma, Keise, Daisuke N. Saito, and Norihiro Sadato. "Processing of Social and Monetary Rewards in the Human Striatum." *Neuron* 58, no. 2 (April 24, 2008): 284–94. https://doi.org/10.1016/j.neuron.2008.03.020.

Jerome, Jerome K. *Three Men in a Boat*. London: Arrowsmith, 1889.

Kerr, Jean. *Please Don't Eat the Daisies*. New York: Doubleday, 1957.

King, Stephen. *Firestarter*. New York: Viking Press, 1980.

King, Stephen. *On Writing: A Memoir of the Craft*. New York: Charles Scribner's Sons, 2000. Kindle.

Maguire, Gregory. *Wicked: The Life and Times of the Wicked Witch of the West*. New York: Harper Collins, 1995.

Mangini, Mark. "Oscar-Winning Sound Supervisor Mark Mangini Gives You the Keys to the Kingdom." Interview by Jeffrey Reeser. *The No Film School*, podcast recorded December 16, 2020. Audio, 12:15, 20:20. https://nofilmschool.com/master-sound-supervisor-mark-mangini-gives-you-keys-kingdom.

McKee, Robert. *Story: Substance, Structure, Style and the Principles of Screenwriting*. New York: Regan Books, 1997.

Mehrabian, Albert, and Susan R. Ferris. "Inference of Attitudes from Nonverbal Communication in Two Channels." *Journal of Consulting Psychology* 31, no. 3 (May 31, 1967): 248–52. https://doi.org/10.1037/h0024648.

Mehrabian, Albert, and Morton Wiener. "Decoding of Inconsistent Communications." *Journal of Personality and Social Psychology* 6, no. 1 (1967): 109–14. https://psycnet.apa.org/doiLanding?doi=10.1037%2Fh0024532.

Milton, John. *Paradise Lost: A Poem*. London: Samuel Simmons, 1667.

Molière. *Tartuffe*. 1664.

Motion Picture Editors Guild. https://www.editorsguild.com/.

Orwell, George. *Nineteen Eighty-Four: A Novel*. London: Secker and Warburg, 1949.

Panksepp, Jaak. "Neuroevolutionary Sources of Laughter and Social Joy: Modeling Primal Human Laughter in Laboratory Rats." *Behavioural Brain Research* 182, no. 2 (September 4, 2007): 231–44. https://doi.org/10.1016/j.bbr.2007.02.015.

Perrault, Charles. *Cinderella, or The Little Glass Slipper*. New York: North South, 1697.

Plimpton, George. "Ernest Hemingway, The Art of Fiction, No. 21." *The Paris Review*, issue 18, Spring 1958. https://www.theparisreview.org/interviews/4825/ernest-hemingway-the-art-of-fiction-no-21-ernest-hemingway.

Portis, Charles. *The Dog of the South*. New York: Knopf, 1979.

Quiller-Couch, Sir Arthur. *On the Art of Writing, Lectures Delivered in the University of Cambridge 1913–1914*. Cambridge: Cambridge University Press, 1916. https://www.bartleby.com/190/12.html.

Richards, Douglas E. *Seeker*. Paragon Press, 2018. Kindle.

Sachs, Ben. "An Interview with Composer John Corigliano (Part One)." *Chicago Reader*, April 18, 2013. https://www.chicagoreader.com/Bleader/archives/2013/04/18/an-interview-with-composer-john-corigliano-part-one.

Samuelson, Arnold. *With Hemingway: A Year in Key West and Cuba*. New York: Random House, Henry Holt and Co., 1988.

Schulberg, Budd. *What Makes Sammy Run?* New York: Random House Inc., 1941.

Sedaris, David. *Naked*. New York: Little, Brown and Company, 1997.

Shakespeare, William. *A Midsummer Night's Dream*. London: Thomas Fisher, 1600.

Shakespeare, William. *Twelfth Night*. London: Edward Blount, 1602, 1623.

Shakespeare, William. *Romeo and Juliet*. London: Edward Blount, 1595, 1623.

Shakespeare, William. *The Tragedy of Hamlet, Prince of Denmark*. London: Edward Blount, 1603, 1623.

Shaw, George Bernard. *Pygmalion*. London: Constable and Company Ltd., 1913.

Shelley, Mary. *Frankenstein; or, The Modern Prometheus*. London: Lackington, Hughes, Harding, Mavor and Jones, 1818.

Shepherd, Jean. *In God We Trust: All Others Pay Cash*. New York: Double Day, 1966.

Snyder, Blake. *Save the Cat! The Last Book on Screenwriting You'll Ever Need*. Studio City, CA: Michael Wiese Productions, 2005.

Sonnenfeld, Barry. *Barry Sonnenfeld, Call Your Mother: Memoirs of a Neurotic Filmmaker*. New York: Hachette Books, 2020.

Sophocles. *Oedipus Rex*. 430 BC.

Stevenson, Robert Louis. *Treasure Island*. London: Cassell and Company, 1883.

Strauss, Neil. "Faster Than a Speeding Bullet, But Also Humanly Fallible." *New York Times*, January 30, 1995. https://www.nytimes.com/1995/01/30/movies/faster-than-a-speeding-bullet-but-also-humanly-fallible.html.

Sugawara, Sho K., Satoshi Tanaka, Shuntaro Okazaki, Katsumi Watanabe, and Norihiro Sadato. "Social Rewards Enhance Offline Improvements in Motor Skill." *PLoS ONE* 7, no. 11 (November 7, 2012). https://doi.org/10.1371/journal.pone.0048174.

Svebak, Sven, Solfrid Romundstad, and Jostein Holmen. "A 7-Year Prospective Study of Sense of Humor and Mortality in an Adult County Population: The Hunt-2 Study." *The International Journal of Psychiatry in Medicine* 40, no. 2 (July 7, 2010): 125–46. https://doi.org/10.2190/PM.40.2.a.

Thompson, Hunter S. *Fear and Loathing in Las Vegas*. New York: Random House, 1971.

Tolkien, J. R. R. *The Lord of the Rings*. London: George Allen and Unwin Ltd., 1954.

Tolstoy, Leo. *Anna Karenina*. New York: Thomas Y. Crowell and Company Publishers, 1899.

Toole, John Kennedy. *A Confederacy of Dunces*. Baton Rouge: Louisiana State University Press, 1980.

Truby, John. *The Anatomy of Story: 22 Steps to Becoming a Master Storyteller*. Hardcover. London: Faber and Faber, 2007.

Twain, Mark. *A Connecticut Yankee in King Arthur's Court*. New York: Charles L. Webster and Company, 1889.

Van Halen, Eddie. "Is Rock 'n' Roll All about Reinvention?" Interview by Denise Quan. The Smithsonian's National Museum of American History and Zócalo Public Square, March 9, 2017, video, 11:20; 39:25. https://www.zocalopublicsquare.org/2015/02/14/necessity-is-the-source-of-eddie-van-halens-inventions/events/the-takeaway/.

Van Vogt, A. E. *The Voyage of the Space Beagle*. New York: Simon and Schuster, 1950.

Van Vogt, A. E. "A. E. van Vogt: A Writer with a Winning Formula." Interview by Jeffrey M. Elliot. *Science Fiction Voices 2: Interviews with Science Fiction Writers*. San Bernardino, CA: Borgo Press.

Villeneuve, Gabrielle-Suzanne Barbot de. *Beauty and the Beast*. 1740.

Weir, Andy. *The Martian*. New York: Crown Publishing, 2014.

Welles, Orson. "Playboy Interview: Orson Welles." Interview by Kenneth Tynan. *Playboy*, March 1967, published online May 19, 2017. https://scrapsfromtheloft.com/2017/05/19/orson-welles-playboy-interview/.

Wells, H. G. *The Time Machine*. London: William Helinemann, 1895.

White, E. B., and William Strunk Jr. *The Elements of Style*. New York: Harcourt, Brace and Howe, 1959.

White, E. B., and Katharine S. White. *A Subtreasury of American Humor*. New York: Coward-McCann, 1941.

Wilde, Oscar. *The Importance of Being Earnest*. London: Leonard Smithers, 1895.

Wilder, Billy, and I. A. L. Diamond. *One, Two, Three: Screenplay*. Beverly Hills: Margaret Herrick Library, Academy Library, 1961. https://gointothestory.blcklst.com/daily-dialogue-june-17-2010-c136505bf9ef.

Filmography

Movies

Abbott and Costello Meet Frankenstein. 1948. USA. Charles Barton, director. Robert Lees, Frederic I. Rinaldo, John Grant, screenplay. Robert Arthur, producer. Frank Gross, editor. Universal Pictures.

Adventurer, The. 1917. USA. Charlie Chaplin, director. Charlie Chaplin, Vincent Bryan, Maverick Terrell, screenplay. Henry P. Caulfield, Charlie Chaplin, John Jasper, producers. Charlie Chaplin, editor. Lone Star Corporation, Mutual Film Corporation.

Airplane! 1980. USA. Jim Abrahams, David Zucker, Jerry Zucker, directors, screenplay. Jon Davison, producer. Patrick Kennedy, editor. Paramount Pictures.

Alien. 1979. USA. Ridley Scott, director. Dan O'Bannon, screenplay. Gordon Carroll, David Giler, Walter Hill, producers. Terry Rawlings, Peter Weatherley, editors. 20th Century Fox.

Aliens. 1986. USA. James Cameron, director. James Cameron, screenplay. Gale Anne Hurd, producer. Ray Lovejoy, editor. 20th Century Fox.

Alive. 1993. USA. Frank Marshall, director. John Patrick Shanley, screenplay. Kathleen Kennedy, Robert Watts, producers. Michael Kahn, William Goldenberg, editors. Buena Vista Pictures, United International Pictures.

Altered States. 1980. USA. Ken Russell, director. Sidney Aaron (Paddy Chayefsky), screenplay. Howard Gottfried, producer. Eric Jenkins, editor. Warner Bros.

Amadeus. 1984. USA. Miloš Forman, director. Peter Shaffer, screenplay. Saul Zaentz, producer. Michael Chandler, Nena Danevic, editors. Orion Pictures.

American Beauty. 1999. USA. Sam Mendes, director. Alan Ball, screenplay. Bruce Cohen, Dan Jinks, producers. Tariq Anwar, Christopher Greenbury, editors. DreamWorks Pictures.

Amistad. 1997. USA. Steven Spielberg, director. David Franzoni, screenplay. Debbie Allen, Steven Spielberg, Colin Wilson, producers. Michael Kahn, editor. DreamWorks Pictures.

Anchorman: The Legend of Ron Burgundy. 2004. USA. Adam McKay, director. Will Ferrell, Adam McKay, screenplay. Judd Apatow, producer. Brent White, editor. DreamWorks Pictures.

Ant-Man. 2015. USA. Peyton Reed, director. Joe Cornish, Adam McKay, Paul Rudd, Edgar Wright, screenplay. Kevin Feige, producer. Dan Lebental, Colby Parker Jr., editors. Walt Disney Studios Motion Pictures.

Armour of God. 1986. Hong Kong. Jackie Chan, Eric Tsang, directors. Jackie Chan, Ken Lowe, John Sheppard, Hon Szeto, Edward Tang, screenplay. Leonard Ho, producer. Peter Cheung, editor. Golden Harvest.

Arthur. 1981. USA. Steve Gordon, director, screenplay. Robert Greenhut, producer. Susan E. Morse, editor. Orion Pictures.

Avatar. 2009. USA. James Cameron, director, screenplay. James Cameron, Jon Landau, producers. James Cameron, John Refoua, Stephen Rivkin, editors. 20th Century Fox.

Back to Back: American Yakuza 2. 1996. USA/Japan. Roger Nygard, director. Roger Nygard, Scott Nimerfro, screenplay. W. K. Border, producer. Dawn Hoggatt, Roger Nygard, editors. NEO Motion Pictures, Ozla Productions, Overseas FilmGroup.

Bangville Police, The. 1913. USA. Henry Lehrman, director. Mack Sennett, producer. Keystone Film Company, Mutual Film.

Batman v Superman: Dawn of Justice. 2016. USA. Zack Snyder, director. Chris Terio, David S. Goyer, screenplay. Charles Roven, Deborah Snyder, producers. David Brenner, editor. Warner Bros.

Big Jake. 1971. USA. George Sherman, director. Harry Julian Fink, Rita M. Fink, screenplay. Michael A. Wayne, producer. Harry Gerstad, editor. Batjac Productions, National General Films.

Big Sick, The. 2017. USA. Michael Showalter, director. Emily V. Gordon, Kumail Nanjiani, screenplay. Judd Apatow, Barry Mendel, producers. Robert Nassau, editor. Amazon Studios.

Big Sleep, The. 1946. USA. Howard Hawks, director, producer. William Faulkner, Leigh Brackett, Jules Furthman, screenplay. Christian Nyby, editor. Warner Bros.

Birds, The. 1963. USA. Alfred Hitchcock, director, producer. Evan Hunter, screenplay. George Tomasini, editor. Universal Pictures.

Black or White. 2014. USA. Mike Binder, director, screenplay. Kevin Costner, Mike Binder, Todd Lewis, producers. Roger Nygard, editor. Relativity Media, IM Global.

Blazing Saddles. 1974. USA. Mel Brooks, director. Mel Brooks, Norman Steinberg, Andrew Bergman, Richard Pryor, Alan Uger, screenplay. Michael Hertzberg, producer. Danford B. Greene, John C. Howard, editors. Warner Bros.

Blue Ruin. 2013. USA. Jeremy Saulnier, director, screenplay. Richard Peete, Vincent Savino, Anish Savjani, producers. Julia Bloch, editor. Radius-TWC.

Borat: Cultural Learnings of America for Make Benefit Glorious Nation of Kazakhstan. 2006. USA. Larry Charles, director. Sacha Baron Cohen, Peter Baynham, Anthony Hines, Dan Mazer, Todd Phillips, screenplay. Sacha Baron Cohen, Jay Roch, producers. Craig Alpert, Peter Teschner, James Thomas, editors. 20th Century Fox.

Borat Subsequent Moviefilm: Delivery of Prodigious Bribe to American Regime for Make Benefit Once Glorious Nation of Kazakhstan. 2020. USA. Jason Woliner, director. Peter Baynham, Sacha Baron Cohen, Jena Friedman, Anthony Hines, Lee Kern, Dan Mazer, Erica Rivinoja, Dan Swimer, screenplay. Sacha Baron Cohen, Anthony Hines, Monica Levinson, producers. Craig Alpert, Michael Giambra, James Thomas, editors. Amazon Studios.

Bourne Identity, The. 2002. USA. Doug Liman, director. Tony Gilroy, William Blake Herron, screenplay. Doug Liman, Patrick Crowley, Richard N. Gladstein, producers. Saar Klein, editor. Universal Pictures.

Braindead (a.k.a. *Dead Alive*). 1992. New Zealand. Peter Jackson, director. Stephen Sinclair, Fran Walsh, Peter Jackson, screenplay. Jim Booth, producer. Jamie Selkirk, editor. Trimark Pictures.

Brazil. 1985. UK/USA. Terry Gilliam, director. Terry Gilliam, Tom Stoppard, Charles McKeown, screenplay. Arnon Milchan, producer. Julian Doyle, editor. Embassy International Pictures, Universal Pictures.

Bridesmaids. 2011. USA. Paul Feig, director. Kristen Wiig, Annie Mumolo, screenplay. Judd Apatow, Barry Mendel, Clayton Townsend, producers. William Kerr, Michael L. Sale, editors. Apatow Productions, Relativity Media, Universal Pictures.

Bringing up Baby. 1938. USA. Howard Hawks, director. Dudley Nichols, Hagar Wilde, screenplay. Cliff Reid, Howard Hawks, producers. George Hively, editor. RKO Radio Pictures.

Cameraman, The. 1928. USA. Edward Sedgwick, director. Clyde Bruckman, Lew Lipton, Joseph Farnham, screenplay. Buster Keaton, Lawrence Weingarten, producers. Hugh Wynn, editor. Metro-Goldwyn-Mayer.

Chemical Wedding. 2008. UK. Julian Doyle, director. Bruce Dickinson, Julian Doyle, screenplay. Malcolm Kohll, Justin Peyton, Ben Timlet, producers. Bill Jones, editor. Anchor Bay Entertainment.

Chinese Ghost Story, A. 1987. Hong Kong. Siu-Tung Ching, director. Kai-Chi Yuen, screenplay. Tsui Hark, producer. David Wu, editor. Golden Harvest Company, Golden Princess Amusement Co. Ltd.

Christmas in July. 1940. USA. Preston Sturges, director, screenplay. Paul Jones, Buddy G. DeSylva, producers. Ellsworth Hoagland, editor. Paramount Pictures.

Chronicle. 2012. UK/USA. Josh Trank, director. Max Landis, screenplay. John Davis, Adam Schroeder, producers. Elliot Greenberg, editor. 20th Century Fox.

Citizen Kane. 1941. USA. Orson Welles, director, producer. Herman J. Mankiewicz, Orson Welles, screenplay. Robert Wise, editor. RKO Radio Pictures.

City on Fire. 1987. Hong Kong. Ringo Lam, director, producer. Tommy Sham, screenplay. Ming Lam Wong, editor. Cinema City and Films Co.

Computer Wore Tennis Shoes, The. 1969. USA. Robert Butler, director. Joseph L. McEveety, screenplay. Bill Anderson, producer. Cotton Warburton, editor. Walt Disney Productions, Buena Vista Distribution Company.

Coup de Ville. 1990. USA. Joe Roth, director. Mike Binder, screenplay. Larry Brezner, Paul Schiff, producers. Paul Hirsch, editor. Universal Pictures.

Crossroads. 1986. USA. Walter Hill, director. John Fusco, screenplay. Mark Carliner, producer. Freeman A. Davies, editor. Columbia Pictures.

Cyborg 2087. 1966. USA. Franklin Adreon, director. Arthur C. Pierce, screenplay. Earle Lyon, producer. Frank P. Keller, editor. Feature Film Corp. of America.

Dances with Wolves. 1990. USA. Kevin Costner, director. Michael Blake, screenplay. Kevin Costner, Jim Wilson, producers. William Hoy, Chip Masamitsu, Steve Potter, Neil Travis, editors. Orion Pictures.

Daylight. 1996. USA. Rob Cohen, director. Leslie Boehm, screenplay. John Davis, David T. Friendly, Joseph M. Singer, producers. Peter Amundson, editor. Universal Pictures.

Death Wish. 1974. USA. Michael Winner, director. Wendell Mayes, screenplay. Hal Landers, Bobby Roberts, producers. Bernard Gribble, editor. Dino De Laurentiis, Paramount Pictures.

Delicatessen. 1991. France. Marc Caro, Jean-Pierre Jeunet, directors. Gilles Adrian, Marc Caro, Jean-Pierre Jeunet, screenplay. Claudie Ossard, producer. Herve Schneid, editor. Constellation, Miramax Films.

Die Hard. 1988. USA. John McTiernan, director. Jeb Stuart, Steven E. de Souza, screenplay. Lawrence Gordon, Joel Silver, producers. John F. Link, Frank J. Urioste, editors. 20th Century Fox.

Dr. Strangelove or: How I Learned to Stop Worrying and Love the Bomb. 1964. USA. Stanley Kubrick, director, producer. Stanley Kubrick, Terry Southern, Peter George, screenplay (based on the book *Red Alert*). Anthony Harvey, editor. Columbia Pictures.

Drive. 1997. USA. Steve Wang, director. Scott Philips, screenplay. Mitsuru Kurosawa, Michael Leahy, producers. Ivan Ladizinsky, editor. NEO Motion Pictures, Overseas FilmGroup.

Duck Soup. 1933. USA. Leo McCarey, director. Bert Kalmar, Harry Ruby, Arthur Sheekman, Nat Perrin, screenplay. Herman J. Mankiewicz, producer. LeRoy Stone, editor. Paramount Pictures.

Dune. 2021. USA. Denis Villeneuve, director. Jon Spaihts, Denis Villeneuve, Eric Roth, screenplay (based on the novel by Frank Herbert). Cale Boyter, Joseph M. Caracciolo Jr., Amanda Confavreux, Robbie McAree, Mary Parent, Denis Villeneuve, producers. Joe Walker, editor. Warner Bros.

Escape from New York. 1981. USA. John Carpenter, director. John Carpenter, Nick Castle, screenplay. Larry J. Franco, Debra Hill, producers. Todd C. Ramsay, editor. AVCO Embassy Pictures.

Eurotrip. 2004. USA. Jeff Schaffer, director. Alec Berg, David Mandel, Jeff Schaffer, screenplay. Alec Berg, David Mandel, Daniel Goldberg, Jackie Marcus, producers. Roger Bondelli, editor. DreamWorks Pictures.

Evil Dead II. 1987. USA. Sam Raimi, director. Sam Raimi, Scott Spiegel, screenplay. Robert G. Tapert, producer. Kaye Davis, editor. Renaissance Pictures, Rosebud Releasing Corporation, De Laurentiis Entertainment Group.

Exorcist, The. 1973. USA. William Friedkin, director. William Peter Blatty, screenplay, producer. Norman Gay, Evan A. Lottman, editors. Warner Bros.

Fantastic Voyage. 1966. USA. Richard Fleischer, director. Harry Kleiner, screenplay. Saul David, producer. William B. Murphy, editor. 20th Century Fox.

FernGully: The Last Rainforest. 1992. Australia. Bill Kroyer, director. Jim Cox, screenplay. Peter Fairman, Wayne Young, producers. Gillian L. Hutshing, editor. 20th Century Fox.

Forest Gump. 1994. USA. Robert Zemeckis, director. Eric Roth, screenplay. Wendy Finerman, Steve Tisch, Steve Starkey, producers. Arthur Schmidt, editor. Paramount Pictures.

40-Year-Old Virgin, The. 2005. USA. Judd Apatow, director. Judd Apatow, Steve Carell, screenplay. Judd Apatow, Shauna Robertson, Clayton Townsend, producers. Brent White, editor. Apatow Productions, Universal Pictures.

French Connection, The. 1971. USA. William Friedkin, director. Ernest Tidyman, screenplay. Philip D'Antoni, producer. Gerald B. Greenberg, editor. 20th Century Fox.

Fresh. 1994. USA. Boaz Yakin, director, screenplay. Lawrence Bender, Randy Ostrow, producers. Dorian Harris, editor. Miramax Films.

Freshman, The. 1925. USA. Fred C. Newmeyer, Sam Taylor, directors. John Grey, Sam Taylor, Tim Whelan, Ted Wilde, screenplay. Harold Lloyd, producer. Allen McNeil, editor. The Harold Lloyd Corporation, Pathe Exchange.

From Dusk Till Dawn. 1996. USA. Robert Rodriguez, director. Quentin Tarantino, screenplay. Gianni Nunnari, Meir Teper, producers. Robert Rodriguez, editor. Dimension Films.

Funny Girl. 1968. USA. William Wyler, director. Isobel Lennart, screenplay. Ray Stark, producer. William Sands, Maury Winetrobe, editors. Columbia Pictures.

Funny People. 2009. USA. Judd Apatow, director, screenplay. Judd Apatow, Clayton Townsend, Barry Mendel, producers. Craig Alpert, Brent White, editors. Universal Pictures, Sony Pictures Releasing.

Galaxies Are Colliding. 1992. USA. John Ryman, director, screenplay. John Ryman, Stanley Wilson, producers. Ivan Ladizinsky, editor. Film Horizon, SC Entertainment International, Cinemavault, Paramount Home Video.

Gangs of New York. 2002. USA. Martin Scorsese, director. Jay Cocks, Steven Zaillian, Kenneth Lonergan, screenplay. Alberto Grimaldi, Harvey Weinstein, producers. Thelma Schoonmaker, editor. Miramax.

Get Out. 2017. USA. Jordan Peele, director, screenplay. Jason Blum, Edward H. Hamm Jr., Sean McKittrick, Jordan Peele, producers. Gregory Plotkin, editor. Blumhouse Productions, Universal Pictures.

Ghost Busters. 1984. USA. Ivan Reitman, director, producer. Dan Aykroyd, Harold Ramis, screenplay. David E. Blewitt, Sheldon Kahn, editors. Columbia Pictures.

Girl with the Dragon Tattoo, The. 2011. USA/Sweden. David Fincher, director. Steven Zaillian, screenplay. Cean Chaffin, Scott Rudin, Ole Søndberg, Søren Stærmose, producers. Kirk Baxter, Angus Wall, editors. Columbia Pictures, Metro Goldwyn Mayer.

Gone in 60 Seconds. 1974. USA. H. B. Halicki, director, screenplay, producer. Warner E. Leighton, editor. H. B. Halicki Mercantile Company, H. B. Halicki International.

Good Morning, Vietnam. 1987. USA. Barry Levinson, director. Mitch Markowitz, screenplay. Larry Brezner, Mark Johnson, producers. Stu Linder, editor. Buena Vista Pictures.

Gran Torino. 2008. USA. Clint Eastwood, director. Nick Schenk, screenplay. Clint Eastwood, Bill Gerber, Robert Lorenz, producers. Joel Cox, Gary D. Roach, editors. Warner Bros.

Gravity. 2013. USA/UK. Alfonso Cuarón, director. Alfonso Cuarón, Jonás Cuarón, screenplay. Alfonso Cuarón, David Heyman, producers. Alfonso Cuarón, Mark Sanger, editors. Warner Bros.

Great McGinty, The. 1940. USA. Preston Sturges, director, screenplay. Paul Jones, producer. Hugh Bennett, editor. Paramount Pictures.

Great Train Robbery, The. 1903. USA. Edwin S. Porter, director, screenplay, producer, editor. Edison Manufacturing Company.

Guess Who's Coming to Dinner. 1967. USA. Stanley Kramer, director, producer. William Rose, screenplay. Robert C. Jones, editor. Columbia Pictures.

Gunfight at Red Sands. 1963. Italy/Spain. Ricardo Blasco, director. Albert Band, Ricardo Blasco, James Donald Prindle, screenplay. Albert Band, Jose Gutierrez Maesso, producers. Rosa G. Salgado, editor. Unidis, Jolly Film.

Hail the Conquering Hero. 1944. USA. Preston Sturges, director, screenplay, producer. Stuart Gilmore, editor. Paramount Pictures.

Harry Potter and the Sorcerer's Stone. 2001. UK/USA. Chris Columbus, director. Steve Kloves, screenplay. David Heyman, producer. Richard Francis-Bruce, editor. Warner Bros.

Hereditary. 2018. USA. Ari Aster, director, screenplay. Kevin Scott Frakes, Lars Knudsen, Buddy Patrick, producers. Jennifer Lame, Lucian Johnston, editors. A24.

Hidden Fortress, The. 1958. Japan. Akira Kurosawa, director, editor. Ryuzo Kikushima, Hideo Oguni, Shinobu Hashimoto, Akira Kurosawa, screenplay. Sanezumi Fujimoto, Akira Kurosawa, producers. Toho Co.

High Strung. 1991. USA. Roger Nygard, director. Robert Kuhn, Steve Oedekerk, screenplay. Rubin M. Mendoza, Roger Nygard, producers. Tom Siiter, editor. Film Brigade Productions.

His Girl Friday. 1940. USA. Howard Hawks, director, producer. Charles Lederer, Ben Hecht, screenplay. Gene Havlick, editor. Columbia Pictures.

Hoffmeyer's Legacy. 1912. USA. Mack Sennet, director, producer. Keystone Film Company, Mutual Film.

How the Grinch Stole Christmas. 2000. USA/Germany. Ron Howard, director. Jeffrey Price, Peter S. Seaman, screenplay. Brian Grazer, Ron Howard, producers. Dan Hanley, Mike Hill, editors. Universal Pictures.

Hunger, The. 1983. UK. Tony Scott, director. Ivan Davis, Michael Thomas, screenplay. Richard Shepherd, producer. Pamela Power, editor. MGM/UA Entertainment Company.

Idiot's Delight. 1939. USA. Clarence Brown, director. Robert E. Sherwood, screenplay. Clarence Brown, Hunt Stromberg, producers. Robert Kern, editor. Metro Goldwyn Mayer.

Incredible Shrinking Man, The. 1957. USA. Jack Arnold, director. Richard Matheson, Richard Alan Simmons, screenplay. Albert Zugsmith, producer. Al Joseph, editor. Universal Pictures.

In Search of the Castaways. 1962. USA. Robert Stevenson, director. Lowell S. Hawley, screenplay. Hugh Attwooll, producer. Gordon Stone, editor. Walt Disney Productions, Buena Vista Distribution.

In the Heat of the Night. 1967. USA. Norman Jewison, director. Stirling Silliphant, screenplay. Walter Mirisch, producer. Hal Ashby, editor. United Artists.

Into the Wild. 2007. USA. Sean Penn, director, screenplay. Art Linson, Sean Penn, Bill Pohlad, producers. Jay Cassidy, editor. Paramount Pictures.

Iron Giant, The. 1999. USA. Brad Bird, director. Tim McCanlies, Brad Bird, screenplay. Allison Abbate, Des McAnuff, producers. Darren T. Holmes, editor. Warner Bros.

It's a Mad, Mad, Mad, Mad World. 1963. USA. Stanley Kramer, director, producer. William Rose, Tania Rose, screenplay. Gene Fowler Jr., Robert C. Jones, Frederic Knudtson, editors. United Artists.

It's a Wonderful Life. 1946. USA. Frank Capra, director, producer. Frances Goodrich, Albert Hackett, Frank Capra, screenplay. William Hornbeck, editor. RKO Radio Pictures.

Jabberwocky. 1977. UK. Terry Gilliam, director. Charles Alverson, Terry Gilliam, screenplay. Sandy Lieberson, producer. Michael Bradsell, editor. Python Films, Columbia-Warner Distributors, Cinema 5.

Jaws. 1975. USA. Steven Spielberg, director. Peter Benchley, Carl Gottlieb, screenplay. David Brown, Richard D. Zanuck, producers. Verna Fields, editor. Universal Pictures.

Jeremiah Johnson. 1972. USA. Sydney Pollack, director. Edward Anhalt, John Milius, screenplay. Joe Wizan, producer. Thomas Stanford, editor. Warner Bros.

Jerk, The. 1979. USA. Carl Reiner, director. Steve Martin, Carl Gottlieb, Michael Elias, screenplay. William E. McEuen, David V. Picker, producers. Bud Molin, Ron Spang, editors. Universal Pictures.

Journey to the Center of the Earth. 1959. USA. Henry Levin, director. Charles Brackett, Walter Reisch, screenplay. Charles Brackett, producer. Stuart Gilmore, Jack W. Holmes, editors. 20th Century Fox.

Jurassic Park. 1993. USA. Steven Spielberg, director. Michael Crichton, David Koepp, screenplay. Kathleen Kennedy, Gerald R. Molen, producers. Michael Kahn, editor. Universal Pictures.

Killer, The. 1989. Hong Kong. John Woo, director, screenplay. Tsui Hark, producer. Fan Kung-Ming, editor. Golden Princess Film Production Limited, Media Asia Entertainment Group, Circle Films.

Killing, The. 1956. USA. Stanley Kubrick, director. Stanley Kubrick, Jim Thompson, screenplay. James B. Harris, producer. Betty Steinberg, editor. United Artists.

King Kong vs. Godzilla. 1963. Japan. Ishiro Honda, director. Shinichi Sekizawa, screenplay. Tomoyuki Tanaka, producer. Reiko Kaneko, editor. Toho Company, Universal Pictures.

King of Staten Island, The. 2020. USA. Judd Apatow, director. Judd Apatow, Pete Davidson, Dave Sirus, screenplay. Judd Apatow, Barry Mandel, producers. Jay Cassidy, William Kerr, Brian Scott Olds, editors. Universal Pictures.

Knocked Up. 2007. USA. Judd Apatow, director, screenplay. Judd Apatow, Shauna Robertson, Clayton Townsend, producers. Craig Alpert, Brent White, editors. Universal Pictures.

Kramer vs. Kramer. 1979. USA. Robert Benton, director, screenplay. Stanley R. Jaffe, producer. Gerald B. Greenberg, editor. Columbia Pictures.

La Cage aux Folles. 1978. France. Édouard Molinaro, director. Marcello Danon, Édouard Molinaro, Jean Poiret, Francis Veber, screenplay. Marcello Danon, producer. Monique Isnardon, Robert Isnardon, editors. United Artists.

Lady Eve, The. 1941. USA. Preston Sturges, director, screenplay. Paul Jones, producer. Stuart Gilmore, editor. Paramount Pictures.

La La Land. 2016. USA. Damien Chazelle, director, screenplay. Fred Berger, Gary Gilbert, Jordan Horowitz, Marc Platt, producers. Tom Cross, editor. Summit Entertainment, Lionsgate.

Lifeboat. 1944. USA. Alfred Hitchcock, director. John Steinbeck, Jo Swerling, screenplay. Kenneth Macgowan, producer. Dorothy Spencer, editor. 20th Century Fox.

Lion King, The. 1994. USA. Roger Allers, Rob Minkoff, directors. Irene Mecchi, Jonathan Roberts, Linda Woolverton, screenplay. Don Hahn, producer. Ivan Bilancio, editor. Walt Disney Pictures, Buena Vista Pictures.

Lion King, The. 2019. USA. Jon Favreau, director. Jeff Nathanson, screenplay. Jon Favreau, Jeffrey Silver, Karen Gilchrist, producers. Mark Livolsi, Adam Gerstel, editors. Walt Disney Studios Motion Pictures.

Little Rascals, The (Our Gang Comedies). 1922–1944. USA. Gordon Douglas, James W. Horne, Ray McCarey, Robert A. McGowan, Robert F. McGowan, Gus Meins, Fred C. Newmeyer, James Parrott, Nate Watt, directors. Art Lloyd, Robert A. McGowan, Robert F. McGowan, Hal Roach, H. M. Walker, writers. Robert F. McGowan, producer. Richard C. Currier, Bert Jordan, William H. Ziegler, editors. Hal Roach Studios, Metro-Goldwyn-Mayer.

Live and Let Die. 1973. UK. Guy Hamilton, director. Tom Mankiewicz, screenplay. Albert R. Broccoli, Harry Saltzman, producers. Bert Bates, Raymond Poulton, John Shirley, editors. United Artists.

Major Dundee. 1965. USA. Sam Peckinpah, director. Harry Julian Fink, Oscar Saul, Sam Peckinpah, screenplay. Jerry Bresler, producer. Howard Kunin, William A. Lyon, Donald W. Starling, editors. Columbia Pictures.

Man Who Knew Too Much, The. 1956. USA. Alfred Hitchcock, director, producer. John Michael Hayes, screenplay. George Tomasini, editor. Paramount Pictures.

Midnight Express. 1978. UK/USA. Alan Parker, director. Oliver Stone, screenplay. Alan Marshall, David Puttnam, producers. Gerry Hambling, editor. Columbia Pictures.

Miracle of Morgan's Creek, The. 1944. USA. Preston Sturges, director, screenplay. Stuart Gilmore, editor. Paramount Pictures.

Monolith Monsters, The. 1957. USA. John Sherwood, director. Norman Jolley, Robert M. Fresco, screenplay. Howard Christie, producer. Patrick McCormack, editor. Universal Pictures.

Monty Python and the Holy Grail. 1975. UK. Terry Gilliam, Terry Jones, directors. Graham Chapman, John Cleese, Eric Idle, Terry Gilliam, Terry Jones, Michael Palin, screenplay. Mark Forstater, Michael White, producers. John Hackney, editor. Python (Monty) Pictures, National Film Trustee Company, Cinema 5 Distributing, EMI Films.

Monty Python Live at the Hollywood Bowl. 1982. UK. Terry Hughes, Ian MacNaughton, directors. Monty Python, screenplay. Terry Hughes, producer. Julian Doyle, Jimmy B. Frazier, editors. HandMade Films, Columbia Pictures.

Monty Python's Life of Brian. 1979. UK. Terry Jones, director. Graham Chapman, John Cleese, Eric Idle, Terry Gilliam, Terry Jones, Michael Palin, screenplay. John Goldstone, producer. Julian Doyle, editor. Python (Monty) Pictures, HandMade Films, Orion Pictures.

Monty Python's The Meaning of Life. 1983. UK. Terry Jones, Terry Gilliam, directors. Graham Chapman, John Cleese, Eric Idle, Terry Gilliam, Terry Jones, Michael Palin, screenplay. John Goldstone, producer. Julian Doyle, editor. Celandine Films, The Monty Python Partnership, Universal Pictures.

My Fair Lady. 1694. USA. George Cukor, director. Alan Jay Lerner, screenplay. Jack L. Warner, producer. William H. Ziegler, editor. Warner Bros.

Mysterious Island. 1961. UK/USA. Cy Endfield, director. John Prebble, Daniel B. Ullman, Crane Wilbur, screenplay. Charles H. Schneer, producer. Frederick Wilson, editor. Columbia Pictures.

National Lampoon's Animal House. 1978. USA. John Landis, director. Harold Ramis, Douglas Kenney, Chris Miller, screenplay. Ivan Reitman, Matty Simmons, producers. George Folsey Jr., editor. Universal Pictures.

Nature of Existence, The. 2010. USA. Roger Nygard, director. Roger Nygard, Paul Tarantino, producers, editors. Blink, Inc.

North by Northwest. 1959. USA. Alfred Hitchcock, director, producer. Ernest Lehman, screenplay. George Tomasini, editor. Metro Goldwyn Mayer.

Odd Couple, The. 1968. USA. Gene Saks, director. Neil Simon, screenplay. Howard W. Koch, producer. Frank Bracht, editor. Paramount Pictures.

Once Upon a Time in the West. 1968. Italy/USA. Sergio Leone, director. Sergio Donati, Sergio Leone, screenplay. Fulvio Morsella, producer. Nino Baragli, editor. Euro International Film, Paramount Pictures.

One Flew Over the Cuckoo's Nest. 1975. USA. Milos Forman, director. Lawrence Hauben, Bo Goldman, screenplay. Michael Douglas, Saul Zaentz, producers. Sheldon Kahn, Lynzee Klingman, editors. United Artists.

One, Two, Three. 1961. USA. Billy Wilder, director, producer. I. A. L. Diamond, Billy Wilder, screenplay. Daniel Mandell, editor. United Artists.

Palm Beach Story, The. 1942. USA. Preston Sturges, director, screenplay. Stuart Gilmore, editor. Paramount Pictures.

Pass the Light. 2015. USA. Malcolm Goodwin, director. Victor Hawks, screenplay. Angie Canuel, Malcolm Goodwin, Victor Hawks, Nikki Love, producers. Rosanne Tan, editor. Diginext Films.

Phantasm. 1979. USA. Don Coscarelli, director, screenplay, producer, editor. AVCO Embassy Pictures.

Philadelphia Story, The. 1940. USA. George Cukor, director. Donald Ogden Stewart, screenplay. Joseph L. Mankiewicz, producer. Frank Sullivan, editor. Metro Goldwyn Mayer.

Pink Panther, The. 1963. USA. Blake Edwards, director. Maurice Richlin, Blake Edwards, screenplay. Martin Jurow, producer. Ralph E. Winters, editor. United Artists.

Pink Panther Strikes Again, The. 1976. USA. Blake Edwards, director. Frank Waldman, Blake Edwards, screenplay. Blake Edwards, producer. Alan Jones, editor. United Artists.

Pinocchio. 1940. USA. Ben Sharpsteen, Hamilton Luske, Bill Roberts, Norman Ferguson, Jack Kinney, Wilfred Jackson, T. Hee, directors. Ted Sears, Otto Englander, Webb Smith, William Cottrell, Joseph Sabo, Erdman Penner, Aurelius Battaglia, screenplay. Walt Disney, producer. Uncredited, editor. Walt Disney Productions, RKO Radio Pictures.

Police Story. 1985. Hong Kong. Jackie Chan, Chi-Hwa Chen, directors. Jackie Chan, Edward Tang, screenplay. Leonard Ho, producer. Peter Cheung, editor. Golden Harvest, Media Asia Group, Fortune Star Media Ltd.

Poltergeist. 1982. USA. Tobe Hooper, director. Steven Spielberg, Michael Grais, Mark Victor, screenplay. Frank Marshall, Steven Spielberg, producers. Michael Kahn, editor. MGM/UA Entertainment Co.

Pretty Woman. 1990. USA. Garry Marshall, director. J. F. Lawton, screenplay. Arnon Milchan, Steven Reuther, producers. Raja Gosnell, Priscilla Nedd, editors. Touchstone Pictures, Buena Vista Pictures.

Project A. 1983. Hong Kong. Jackie Chan, Sammo Hung, directors. Jackie Chan, Edward Tang, screenplay. Leonard Ho, producer. Peter Cheung, editor. Golden Harvest, Media Asia Group.

Project A: Part II. 1987. Hong Kong. Jackie Chan, director. Jackie Chan, Edward Tang, screenplay. Leonard Ho, David Lam, Edward Tang, producers. Peter Cheung, editor. Golden Harvest, Media Asia Group.

Purge, The. 2013. USA. James DeMonaco, director, screenplay. Jason Blum, Michael Bay, Andrew Form, Brad Fuller, Sebastien K. Lemercier, producers. Peter Gvozdas, editor. Universal Pictures.

Raising Arizona. 1987. USA. Joel Coen, director. Joel Coen, Ethan Coen, screenplay. Ethan Coen, producer. Michael R. Miller, editor. Circle Films, 20th Century Fox.

Rashomon. 1950. Japan. Akira Kurosawa, director, editor. Ryûnosuke Akutagawa, Akira Kurosawa, Shinobu Hashimoto, screenplay. Minoru Jingo, producer. RKO Radio Pictures.

Reservoir Dogs. 1992. USA. Quentin Tarantino, director, screenplay. Lawrence Bender, producer. Sally Menke, editor. Miramax Films.

Return of the Pink Panther, The. 1975. UK. Blake Edwards, director, producer. Blake Edwards, Frank Waldman, screenplay. Tom Priestly, editor. United Artists.

Robocop. 1987. USA. Paul Verhoeven, director. Edward Neumeier, Michael Miner, screenplay. Arne Schmidt, producer. Frank J. Urioste, editor. Orion Pictures.

"Rock-a-Bye Bear." 1952. USA. Tex Avery, director. Tex Avery, Fred Quimby, producers. Heck Allen, Rich Hogan, screenplay. Jim Faris, editor. Metro Goldwin Mayer.

Rocky. 1976. USA. John G. Avildsen, director. Sylvester Stallone, screenplay. Robert Chartoff, Irwin Winkler, producers. Richard Halsey, Scott Conrad, editors. United Artists.

Roger and Me. 1989. USA. Michael Moore, director, screenplay, producer. Jennifer Beman, Wendey Stanzler, editors. Warner Bros.

Rushmore. 1998. USA. Wes Anderson, director. Wes Anderson, Owen Wilson, screenplay. Barry Mendel, Paul Schiff, producers. David Moritz, editor. Touchstone Pictures, Buena Vista Pictures.

Scarface. 1932. USA. Howard Hawks, director. W. R. Burnett, Ben Hecht, John Lee Mahin, Seton I. Miller, screenplay. Howard Hawks, Howard Hughes, producers. Edward Curtiss, editor. United Artists.

Scent of a Woman. 1992. USA. Martin Brest, director. Bo Goldman, screenplay. Martin Brest, producer. William Steinkamp, Michael Tronick, Harvey Rosenstock, editors. Universal Pictures.

Separation, A. 2011. Iran. Asghar Farhadi, director, screenplay, producer. Hayedeh Safiyari, editor. Filmiran, Sony Pictures Classics.

Sergeant York. 1941. USA. Howard Hawks, director. Harry Chandlee, Abem Finkel, John Huston, Howard E. Koch, Sam Cowan, screenplay. Jesse L. Lasky, Hal B. Wallis, producers. William Holmes, editor. Warner Bros.

Seven Samurai. 1954. Japan. Akira Kurosawa, director. Akira Kurosawa, Shinobu Hashimoto, Hideo Oguni, screenplay. Sōjirō Motoki, producer. Akira Kurosawa, editor. Toho Company.

Shawshank Redemption, The. 1994. USA. Frank Darabont, director, screenplay. Niki Marvin, producer. Richard Francis-Bruce, editor. Castle Rock Entertainment, Columbia Pictures.

Shining, The. 1980. USA/UK. Stanley Kubrick, director, producer. Stanley Kubrick, Diane Johnson, screenplay. Ray Lovejoy, editor. Warner Bros.

Silent Movie. 1976. USA. Mel Brooks, director. Mel Brooks, Ron Clark, Rudy De Luca, Barry Levinson, screenplay. Michael Hertzberg, producer. Stanford C. Allen, John C. Howard, editors. 20th Century Fox.

Singin' in the Rain. 1952. USA. Stanley Donnen, Gene Kelly, directors. Betty Comden, Adolph Green, screenplay. Arthur Freed, producer. Adrienne Fazan, editor. Metro-Goldwyn-Mayer.

Six Days in Roswell. 1999. USA. Timothy B. Johnson, director. Roger Nygard, producer, editor. Blink, Inc., Synapse Films.

Slumdog Millionaire. 2008. UK. Danny Boyle, director. Simon Beaufoy, screenplay. Christian Colson, producer. Chris Dickens, editor. Fox Searchlight Pictures.

Snoopy Come Home. 1972. USA. Bill Melendez, director. Charles M. Schulz, screenplay. Bill Melendez, Lee Mendelson, producers. Robert T Gillis, Charles McCann, Rudy Zamora Jr., editors. National General Pictures.

Spirited Away. 2001. Japan. Hayao Miyazaki, director, screenplay. Toshio Suzuki, producer. Takeshi Seyama, editor. Tokuma Shoten, Toho Company.

Stand by Me. 1986. USA. Rob Reiner, director. Bruce A. Evans, Raynold Gideon, screenplay. Bruce A. Evans, Raynold Gideon, Andrew Sheinman, producers. Robert Leighton, editor. Columbia Pictures.

Starship Troopers. 1997. USA. Paul Verhoeven, director. Edward Neumeier, screenplay. Jon Davison, Alan Marshall, producers. Mark Goldblatt, Caroline Ross, editors. TriStar Pictures, Touchstone Pictures, Sony Pictures Releasing, Buena Vista International.

Star Trek II: The Wrath of Kahn. 1982. USA. Nicholas Meyer, director. Jack B. Sowards, screenplay. Robert Sallin, producer. William Paul Dornisch, editor. Paramount Pictures.

Star Wars: Episode IV—A New Hope. 1977. USA. George Lucas, director, screenplay. Gary Kurtz, producer. Richard Chew, Paul Hirsch, Marcia Lucas, editors. 20th Century Fox.

Star Wars: Episode V—The Empire Strikes Back. 1980. USA. Irvin Kershner, director. Leigh Brackett, Lawrence Kasdan, screenplay. Gary Kurtz, producer. Paul Hirsch, editor. 20th Century Fox.

Steamboat Bill, Jr. 1928. USA. Charles Reisner, Buster Keaton, directors. Carl Harbaugh, screenplay. Joseph M. Schenck, producer. Sherman Kell, editor. United Artists.

Stepford Wives, The. 1975. USA. Bryan Forbes, director. William Goldman, screenplay. Edgar J. Scherick, producer. Timothy Gee, editor. Columbia Pictures.

Straw Dogs. 1971. UK. Sam Peckinpah, director. David Zelag Goodman, Sam Peckinpah, screenplay. Daniel Melnick, producer. Paul Davies, Tony Lawson, Roger Spottiswoode, editors. Cinerama Releasing Corporation, 20th Century Fox.

Strictly Ballroom. 1992. Australia. Baz Luhrmann, director. Baz Luhrmann, Craig Pearce, Andrew Bovell, screenplay. Tristam Miall, producer. Jill Bilcock, editor. Miramax Films.

Suckers. 2001. USA. Roger Nygard, director, editor. Roger Nygard, Joe Yannetty, screenplay. W. K. Border, producer. HBO, Genius Squad, Neo Art & Logic, Blink, Inc.

Sullivan's Travels. 1941. USA. Preston Sturges, director, producer, screenplay. Stuart Gilmore, editor. Paramount Pictures.

Superman. 1978. USA. Richard Donner, director. Robert Benton, David Newman, Leslie Newman, Mario Puzo, screenplay. Pierre Spengler, producer. Stuart Baird, Michael Ellis, editors. Warner Bros.

Take the Money and Run. 1969. USA. Woody Allen, director. Woody Allen, Mickey Rose, screenplay. Charles H. Joffe, producer. Paul Jordan, Ron Kalish, editors. Cinerama Releasing Corporation.

Talladega Nights: The Ballad of Ricky Bobby. 2006. USA. Adam McKay, director. Will Ferrell, Adam McKay, screenplay. Judd Apatow, Jimmy Miller, producers. Brent White, editor. Columbia Pictures.

Tarantula. 1955. USA. Jack Arnold, director. Robert M. Fresco, Martin Berkeley, screenplay. William Alland, producer. William Morgan, editor. Universal Pictures.

Terminator, The. 1984. USA. James Cameron, director. James Cameron, Gale Anne Hurd, William Wisher, screenplay. Gale Anne Hurd, producer. Mark Goldblatt, editor. Orion Pictures, Metro Goldwyn Mayer.

Terms of Endearment. 1983. USA. James L. Brooks, director, screenplay, producer. Richard Marks, editor. Paramount Pictures.

There's Something About Mary. 1998. USA. Bobby Farrelly, Peter Farrelly, directors. Ed Decter, John J. Strauss, Peter Farelly, Bobby Farrelly, screenplay. Michael Steinberg, Bradley Thomas, Charles B. Wessler, Frank Beddor, producers. Christopher Greenbury, editor. 20th Century Fox.

They Call Me Trinity. 1970. Italy. Enzo Barboni (E. B. Clutcher), director, screenplay. Italo Zingarelli, producer. Gianpiero Giunti, editor. AVCO Embassy Pictures.

Thief Catcher, A. 1914. USA. Ford Sterling, director. Mack Sennett, producer. Keystones Film Company, Mutual Film.

This Is Spinal Tap. 1984. USA. Rob Reiner, director. Christopher Guest, Michael McKean, Harry Shearer, Rob Reiner, screenplay. Karen Murphy, producer. Kent Beyda, Kim Secrist, editors. Embassy Pictures.

Throw Momma from the Train. 1987. USA. Danny DeVito, director. Stu Silver, screenplay. Larry Brezner, producer. Michael Jablow, editor. Orion Pictures.

Titanic. 1997. USA. James Cameron, director, screenplay. James Cameron, Jon Landau, producers. Conrad Buff, James Cameron, Richard A. Harris, editors. Paramount Pictures, 20th Century Fox.

Trekkies. 1997. USA. Roger Nygard, director, editor. W. K. Border, producer. NEO Motion Pictures, Paramount Classics.

Trekkies 2. 2004. USA. Roger Nygard, director, editor. Michael Leahy, producer. Neo Art and Logic, Paramount Pictures.

Truth About Marriage, The. 2020. USA. Roger Nygard, director, screenplay, producer, editor. Gravitas Ventures, Blink, Inc.

12 Monkeys. 1995. USA. Terry Gilliam, director. David Peoples, Janet Peoples, screenplay. Charles Roven, producer. Mick Audsley, editor. Universal Pictures.

Uncut Gems. 2019. USA. Benny Safdie, Josh Safdie, directors. Ronald Bronstein, Benny Safdie, Josh Safdie, screenplay. Sebastian Bear McClard, Oscar Boyson, Eli Bush, Scott Rudin, producers. Ronald Bronstein, Benny Safdie, editors. A24, Netflix.

Unfaithfully Yours. 1948. USA. Preston Sturges, director, screenplay, producer. Robert Fritch, editor. 20th Century Fox.

V for Vendetta. 2005. UK/USA/Germany. James McTeigue, director. The Wachowski Brothers, screenplay. Joe Silver, Grant Hill, The Wachowskis, producers. Martin Walsh, editor. Warner Bros.

Walk Hard: The Dewey Cox Story. 2007. USA. Jake Kasdan, director. Judd Apatow, Jake Kasdan, screenplay. Judd Apatow, Jake Kasdan, Clayton Townsend, producers. Tara Timpone, Steve Welch, editors. Columbia Pictures.

Warped. 1990. USA. Roger Nygard, director, producer, editor. Jeff Copeland, Roger Nygard, screenplay. Action International Pictures (AIP), released as part of *Tales of the Unknown*.

Waterboy, The. 1998. USA. Frank Coraci, director. Tim Herlihy, Adam Sandler, screenplay. Jack Giarraputo, Robert Simonds, producers. Tom Lewis, editor. Buena Vista Pictures.

Westworld. 1973. USA. Michael Crichton, director, screenplay. Paul N. Lazarus III, producer. David Bretherton, editor. Metro Goodwin Mayer.

What's Up, Doc? 1972. USA. Peter Bogdanovich, director, producer. Buck Henry, David Newman, Robert Benton, screenplay. Verna Fields, editor. Warner Bros.

When Worlds Collide. 1951. USA. Rudolph Maté, director. Sydney Boehm, screenplay. George Pal, producer. Arthur P. Schmidt, editor. Paramount Pictures.

Where Eagles Dare. 1968. UK. Brian G. Hutton, director. Alistair MacLean, screenplay. Elliott Kastner, producer. John Jympson, editor. Metro Goldwin Mayer.

Who's Minding the Store? 1963. USA. Frank Tashlin, director. Frank Tashlin, Harry Tugend, screenplay. Paul Jones, producer. John Woodcock, editor. Paramount Pictures.

Wild Bunch, The. 1969. USA. Sam Peckinpah, director. Walon Green, Sam Peckinpah, screenplay. Phil Fieldman, producer. Louis Lombardo, editor. Warner Bros., Seven Arts.

Withnail and I. 1987. UK. Bruce Robinson, director, screenplay. Paul Heller, producer. Alan Strachan, editor. HandMade Films, Cineplex Odeon Films.

Y Tu Mamá También. 2001. Mexico. Alfonso Cuarón, director. Carlos Cuarón, Alfonso Cuarón, screenplay. Alfonso Cuarón, Jorge Vergara, producers. Alfonso Cuarón, Alex Rodriguez, editors. 20th Century Fox, IFC Films.

You Don't Mess with the Zohan. 2008. USA. Dennis Dugan, director. Judd Apatow, Adam Sandler, Robert Smigel, screenplay. Adam Sandler, Jack Giarraputo, producers. Tom Costain, editor. Columbia Pictures.

Young Frankenstein. 1974. USA. Mel Brooks, director. Mel Brooks, Gene Wilder, screenplay. Michael Gruskoff, producer. John C. Howard, editor. 20th Century Fox.

Television

All in the Family. 1971–1979. USA. Norman Lear, creator. CBS.
Barry. 2018–TBD. USA. Alec Berg, Bill Hader, creators. HBO.

Batman. 1966–1968. USA. Lorenzo Semple Jr., William Dozier, creators. 20th Century Fox. ABC.

Ben Stiller Show, The. 1992–1995. USA. Judd Apatow, Jeff Kahn, Ben Stiller, creators. HBO, FOX.

Benny Hill Show, The. 1955–1989. UK. Benny Hill, creator. BBC.

Bernie Mac Show, The. 2001–2006. USA. Larry Wilmore, creator. FOX.

Billy Crystal: Don't Get Me Started. 1986. USA. Billy Crystal, Paul Flaherty, writers. HBO.

Bob Newhart Show, The. 1972–1978. USA. David Davis, Lorenzo Music, creators. CBS.

Breaking Bad. 2008–2013. USA. Vince Gilligan, creator. AMC.

Chris Rock: Bigger & Blacker. 1999. USA. Chris Rock, writer. HBO.

Comedy Store, The. 2020. USA. Mike Binder, writer. Showtime.

Commish, The. 1991–1996. USA. Stephen J. Cannell, Stephen Kronish, creators. ABC.

Crashing. 2017–2019. USA. Pete Holmes, creator. HBO.

Curb Your Enthusiasm. 2000–TBD. USA. Larry David, creator. HBO.

Dave. 2020–TBD. USA. David Burd, Jeff Schaffer, creators. FXX.

Dexter. 2006–2013. USA. James Manos Jr., creator. Showtime.

Dick Van Dyke Show, The. 1961–1966. USA. Carl Reiner, creator. CBS.

Ernie Kovacs Show, The. 1952–1962. USA. Ernie Kovacs, creator. CBS, DuMont, NBC, ABC.

Family Matters. 1989–1998. USA. William Bickley, Michael Warren, creators. ABC, CBS.

Fawlty Towers. 1975–1979. UK. John Cleese, Connie Booth, creators. BBC.

Fernwood Tonight. 1977. USA. Norman Lear, creator. Columbia TriStar Television.

Full House. 1987–1995. USA. Jeff Franklin, creator. ABC.

Get Smart. 1965–1970. USA. Mel Brooks, Buck Henry, creators. CBS.

Gilligan's Island. 1964–1967. USA. Sherwood Schwartz, creator. CBS.

Girls. 2012–2017. USA. Lena Dunham, creator. HBO.

Grey's Anatomy. 2005–TBD. USA. Shonda Rimes, creator. ABC.

Grounded for Life. 2001–2005. USA. Bill Martin, Mike Schiff, creators. FOX.

Haywire. 1990–1991. USA. FOX.

Herman's Head. 1991–1994. USA. Andy Guerdat, Steve Kreinberg, creators. FOX.

Hogan Family, The. 1986–1991. USA. Charlie Hauck, creator. NBC, CBS.

In Living Color. 1990–1994. USA. Keenen Ivory Wayans, creator. FOX.

Jungle Emperor (a.k.a. Kimba the White Lion). 1965–1967. Japan. Osamu Tezuka, creator. Fuji Television.

Larry Sanders Show, The. 1992–1998. USA. Dennis Klein, Garry Shandling, creators. HBO.

Late Night with Conan O'Brien. 1993–2009. USA. NBC.

Late Night with David Letterman. 1982–1993. USA. David Letterman, creator. NBC.

League, The. 2009–2015. USA. Jeff Schaffer, Jackie Marcus Schaffer, creators. FX.

Lost. 2004–2010. USA. Jeffrey Lieber, J. J. Abrams, Damon Lindelof, creators. ABC.

Mad TV. 1995–2016. USA. Fax Bahr, Adam Small, creators. FOX.

Mind of the Married Man, The. 2001–2002. USA. Mike Binder, creator. HBO.

Monkeys, The. 1966–1968. USA. Paul Mazursky, Larry Tucker, creators. NBC.

Monsters. 1988–1990. USA. Richard P. Rubinstein, creator. Laurel Entertainment.

Monty Python's Flying Circus. 1969–1974. UK. Graham Chapman, John Cleese, Eric Idle, Terry Jones, Michael Palin, Terry Gilliam, creators. BBC.

Mork & Mindy. 1978–1982. USA. Garry Marshall, Dale McRaven, Joe Glauberg, creators. ABC.

MTV, Give Me Back My Life: A Harvard Lampoon Parody. 1991. USA. Alec Berg, David Mandel, Jeff Schaffer, writers. Comedy Central.

M*A*S*H. 1972–1983. USA. Larry Gelbart, creator. CBS.

Office, The. 2005–2013. USA. Greg Daniels, creator. NBC.

Outer Limits, The. 1963–1965. USA. Leslie Stevens, creator. ABC.

Parks and Recreation. 2009–2015. USA. Greg Daniels, Michael Schur, creators. NBC.

Saturday Night Live. 1975–TBD. USA. Lorne Michaels, creator. NBC.

SCTV. 1976–1984. Canada. Andrew Alexander, creator. CBC, NBC.

Seinfeld. 1989–1998. USA. Larry David, Jerry Seinfeld, creators. NBC.

Sergeant Bilko (a.k.a. The Phil Silvers Show). 1955–1959. USA. Nat Hiken, creator. CBS.

Silicon Valley. 2014–2019. USA. Mike Judge, John Altschuler, Dave Krinsky, creators. HBO.

Singles Table, The. 2006. USA. Bill Martin, Mike Schiff, creators. NBC.

Star Trek. 1966–1969. USA. Gene Roddenberry, creator. NBC.

Survivor. 2000–TBD. USA. Charlie Parsons, creator. CBS.

That's My Mama. 1974–1975. USA. Dan T. Bradley, Allan L. Rice, Stanley Ralph Ross, creators. ABC.

Tonight Show, The. 1954–TBD. USA. Steve Allen, Dwight Hemion, William O. Harbach, Sylvester "Pat" Weaver, creators. NBC.

Twilight Zone, The. 1959–1964. USA. Rod Serling, creator. CBS.

Unicorn, The. 2019–TBD. USA. Bill Martin, Mike Schiff, Grady Cooper, creators. CBS.

Veep. 2012–2019. USA. Armando Iannucci, creator. HBO.

Who Is America? 2018. USA. Sacha Baron Cohen, creator. Showtime.

Zeke and Luther. 2009–2012. USA. Matt Dearborn, Tom Burkhard, creators. Disney XD.

Index

Page references for figures are italicized.

About the Author

Photo by Daniel Lightfoot. Location courtesy of the Orlando Film Festival.

Roger Nygard is well known for his acclaimed documentary *Trekkies*, about the most obsessive fans in the universe. Nygard's other award-winning films include the car-salesman cult-film *Suckers*, a profile of UFO fanatics called *Six Days in Roswell*, and *The Nature of Existence*, which investigates the world's philosophies, religions, and belief systems. His next documentary and companion book covered an even more challenging subject than existence itself, *The Truth About Marriage*. Nygard has also directed television series such as *The Office* and *The Bernie Mac Show*. His work as a film editor includes *Grey's Anatomy*, *The League*, *The Comedy Store*, *The White House Plumbers*, and Emmy-nominated episodes of *Who Is America?* and *Veep*, and *Curb Your Enthusiasm*.